AGING AND DEMENTIA

AGING AND DEMENTIA

Edited by

W. Lynn Smith, Ph.D.

Director Cortical Function Laboratory
Porter Memorial Hospital
Denver, Colorado

and

Department of Biological Sciences
University of Denver

and

Marcel Kinsbourne, B.M., B.CH., D.M.

Senior Staff Physician and
Director, Learning Clinic
The Hospital for Sick Children
Toronto, Ontario, Canada

and

Departments Pediatrics and Psychology
University of Toronto

S P Books Division of
SPECTRUM PUBLICATIONS, INC.
New York

In Memory of

David Kinsbrunner

Charles and Clara Smith

Arthur Harvey

Copyright © 1977 Spectrum Publications, Inc.

SPECTRUM PUBLICATIONS, Inc.
175-20 Wexford Terrace, Jamaica, N.Y. 11432

Library of Congress Cataloging in Publication Data
Main entry under title:

Aging and dementia.

    Bibliography: p.
    Includes indexes.
    1. Senile psychosis. 2. Aging. 3. Aged–Psychology.
I. Smith, Wallace Lynn, 1922-   II. Kinsbourne,
Marcel. [DNLM: 1. Psychoses, Senile. WT150 A264]
RC524.A34   616.8'983   77-418
  ISBN 0-89335-013-3

Contributors

D. C. GAJDUSEK, M.D.
National Institute of Neurological
and Communicative Disorders and
Stroke
National Institutes of Health
Bethesda, Maryland

C. J. GIBBS, JR., M.D.
National Institute of Neurological
and Communicative Disorders and
Stroke
National Institutes of Health
Bethesda, Maryland

L. R. C. HAWARD, Dr. Psy.
Reader in Clinical Psychology
University of Surrey
Guildford, England

MARCEL KINSBOURNE, D.M.,
M.R.C.P.
Senior Staff Physician
The Hospital for Sick Children
Toronto, Ontario
Professor of Pediatrics
University of Toronto
School of Medicine
Professor of Psychology
University of Toronto
Toronto, Ontario
Professor of Psychology
University of Waterloo
Waterloo, Ontario

LESTON B. NAY, M.D.
Neurologist
Porter Memorial Hospital/
Swedish Medical Center
Denver, Colorado
Assistant Clinical Professor of
Neurology
University of Colorado
School of Medicine
Denver, Colorado

MICHAEL D. O'BRIEN, M.B.,
M.R.C.P
Senior Lecturer
Department of Neurology
Guys Hospital
London, England

BERT LINCOLN PEAR, M.D.,
F.A.C.R.
Radiology Department
Porter Memorial Hospital/
St. Joseph Hospital
Denver, Colorado
Associate Clinical Professor of
Radiology
University of Colorado
School of Medicine
Denver, Colorado

CONTRIBUTORS

R. D. SAVAGE, D. Sc., Ph. D.
Senior Lecturer in
Applied Psychology
University of Newcastle Upon Tyne
Newcastle Upon Tyne, England

W. LYNN SMITH, Ph. D.
Director
Cortical Function Laboratories
Porter Memorial Hospital
Denver, Colorado
White Memorial Medical Center
Los Angeles, California
Glendale Adventist Medical Center
Glendale, California
Professor of Neurobiology
University of Denver
Denver, Colorado

B. E. TOMLINSON, M.B.
Consultant Neuropathologist
Newcastle General Hospital
Newcastle Upon Tyne, England
Honorary Professor of Pathology
University of Newcastle Upon Tyne
Newcastle Upon Tyne, England

ROGER TRAUB, M.D.
National Institute of Neurological
and Communicative Disorders and
Stroke
National Institutes of Health
Bethesda, Maryland

H. S. WANG, M.B., F.A.P.A.
Professor of Psychiatry and
Senior Fellow
Center for the Study of Aging and
Human Development
Duke University Medical Center
Durham, North Carolina

Contents

CONTENTS

Introduction

Whatever poet, orator or sage
May say of it, old age is still old age.
. . . Longfellow

Oscar Wilde commented on old age in two distinctly different ways. For the healthy, "The tragedy of old age is not that one is old, but that one is young." But for the less fortunate, "My experience is that as soon as people are old enough to know better, they don't know anything at all." Richter, in his comment, "It is not the end of joy that makes old age sad, but the end of hope," clearly emphasizes the existential despair in the aging process.

The above quotations reflect different perspectives on aging. However, the quotation which seems to best focus on the age-related cognitive decline studies in this volume is by William Hazlitt, "The worst old age is that of the mind."

Until quite recently, the study of aging has been a relatively unappealing subject in our American society. What has appeared on the subject of aging has been largely physiological, sociological, and economic in focus, with little attention given to psychological factors correlated with the aging process. Studies involving neuro-anatomical/behavioral interactions have been sorely needed to delineate behavioral decline in terms of brain change and emotional contributing factors. In surveying the English language literature, one notes almost immediately that much of the good neuro-anatomical/behavioral correlative research comes from the United Kingdom; hence the predominance of British contributions in this volume.

Aging and Dementia is an attempt to fill the gap in studies involving neuroanatomical/behavioral correlates. Although the original idea was initiated by me in the fourth meeting of the Cerebral Function Symposium in late 1972, only two of the presented papers appearing then have been included in the present volume. These nuclear chapters, it should be added, have been brought up to date for this publication. The remaining papers have been solicited and are of the most recent vintage, so it would be in error to refer to this present volume as published proceedings of that particular meeting, although it fits in with the thinking behind the symposium series. Grateful acknowledgment is made to the following who made the meeting possible: Abbott Laboratories, American Medical International, Inc., Hoffman-LaRoche, Inc., Ives Laboratories, Inc., Marion Laboratories, Inc., McNeil Laboratories, Inc., and Riker Laboratories.

The increase of well over one hundred percent in the elderly population in the United States over the past thirty-five years is a staggering increase—and there is every indication that this increase in elderly population will continue. With the increase in life span, especially after the seventh decade, comes an increase in the occurrence of a disorder commonly referred to as dementia. The prevalence of dementia is probably one of the most widespread and disabling disorders of the aged. A sufficient number of the elderly population in this country may have dementia severe enough to require long-term institutional care, care which entails intensive personal and medical care for a prolonged period of time, a burden to families, to health care professionals, and to society itself.

Our understanding of dementia, in spite of the research done through almost a half century and our resulting clinical abilities to treat this disorder, is not much better now than when this remarkable increase in elderly population started. To complicate matters further, we do not fully understand the aging process itself, let alone the development of dementia within the final stage of life. We do know, however, that with the poor prognosis associated with aging, the health professionals have developed a fatalistic, if not almost nihilistic, attitude toward the demented patient. This attitude is seen in the small number of qualified persons in the professions showing any great interest in the area.

The problem of dementia is not easy to define. The term has been variously used at different times, and usage has changed from the original Latin "demons," meaning "out of one's mind," to senile psychosis to chronic brain syndrome, a rubric within the nomenclature of the *Diagnostic and Statistical Manual of Mental Disorders* of the American Psychiatric Association. Aspects of this descriptive syndrome are emphasized differently, given the same symptom description. Elderly in Britain are likely to be diagnosed as depressed, while Americans tend to diagnose in the direction of organic brain syndrome.

Other areas unresolved, besides the previously mentioned lack of understanding of normal aging process, involve the correlation between severity of cognitive impairments and severity of brain changes. Depression has been referred to as the most human of all psychological states, yet is often overlooked in the aged as an entity per se because of accompanying somatic symptoms or even its contribution to somatic symptomology in depressive equivalents. Depression leads to social inactivity and social deprivation, and depression often masquerades itself as psuedo-organicity. Perhaps long periods of untreated depression can lead to a fixed pathological state in which further delineation in terms of conflicting influences is no longer even relevant. Depression and accompanying cognitive deficit may be superimposed on organic conditions, making clinical differentiation very difficult if not sometimes impossible.

The descriptive phrase, "fixed pathological state," is attributed to a Russian researcher; it describes a patient attitude which precludes change. As the placebo reactor has wrought havoc with results in otherwise well-designed studies of effects of anti-anxiety compounds on suggestible patients, those elderly subjects fitting the fixed pathological state nullify drug/placebo comparisons. In a recent study by this writer, for example, involving double-blind crossover of elderly patients on a cerebrovasodilator and placebo, the internist referring his patients for the study was asked to predict, on the basis of his clinical judgment, the likelihood of movement or improvement, including placebo reactions, versus those patients who would not show improvement and, in fact, wouldn't even get worse under each condition. His predictions, when matched to the outcome of the study, were over 75% accurate, as he correctly predicted non-change in eleven out of fourteen patients.

The fixed pathological state is one of many important intervening variables which must be considered if we are to arrive at definitive findings in an effective study of the elderly. Problems of the aging process affect us directly or indirectly sometimes during our lives. Perhaps we should conclude with Emerson: "It is time to be old, to take in sail."

W. Lynn Smith, Ph.D

$$\boxed{1}$$

Dementia of Old Age

H. S. WANG

In 1970, elderly persons (65 years and over) totaled 20.16 million and accounted for 9.8 percent of the population in the United States (Siegel, 1975). This is an increase of 123 percent over the elderly population in 1940. Such a great increase can be attributed to many factors, one of which is clearly the progress in medicine and health service that has led to a reduction of mortality in early and middle life and the longer survival of many individuals.

The elderly population will definitely continue to increase in the future. The increase will be augmented by the extensive efforts devoted to the search for and development of more effective measures for the prevention, early diagnosis and treatment of the three leading causes of death, heart disease, malignant neoplasms and cerebrovascular disease. Together these currently account for three out of every four deaths in the United States (Siegel, 1975). The increase of the elderly population in the next three decades

Table I. Estimated and Projected Elderly Population in the United States*

Year	Elderly Population (Number in Thousands)			Percent Increase of Elderly Population in Preceding Three Decades		
	64-74 years	75+ years	Total 65+ years	65-74 years	75+ years	Total 65+ years
1910	2,816	1,170	3,986	–	–	–
1940	6,367	2,664	9,031	+126%	+127.7%	+126.6%
1970	12,465	7,691	20,156	+95.8%	+188.7%	+123.2%
2000	16,363	12,476	28,839	+31.3%	+62.2%	+43.1%

*Abstracted and calculated from Siegel 1975.

(after 1970) is expected to be slower than that in the past three decades (see Table I). It is projected that the elderly population will increase another 43 percent and will reach 28.84 million by the year 2000. Of great significance, however, is the increasing proportion of elderly persons who will survive beyond the age of 75. The 75+ group will account for 43.3 percent of the total elderly population in 2000. The corresponding figures are 38.2 percent for 1970 and 29.5 percent for 1940.

One serious but expected consequence arising from the prolongation of life span and the significant increase of the elderly population, especially those 75 years old and over, is the increase of a disorder commonly referred to as dementia. The increase of dementia, in turn, leads to an increase of the elderly patient population in mental hospitals. This was reported by Malzberg (1963) who has studied the number of elderly first admissions to all civil mental hospitals in New York. He found that the rate of elderly first admissions and psychoses due to cerebral arteriosclerosis increased at a remarkable rate from 4.7 (per 100,000 population) in 1919–1921 to 22.3 in 1949–1951. The number of first admissions with senile psychosis has also risen drastically from 6.4 to 16.2 (per 100,000 population) during the same period.

The findings from New York State are also observed in nearly all other states. Based on the 1966 statistical data published by the National Institute of Mental Health, it was estimated that in 1966,

29.5 percent of resident patients and 16.8 percent of first admission patients (those with no prior psychiatric hospitalization) in all psychiatric inpatient facilities in the United States were 65 years old and over (Wang, 1969). About 47 percent of these resident patients and 78 percent of the elderly first admissions were given the diagnosis "organic brain syndrome," in which dementia is usually a very prominent component. When the data from psychiatric hospitals are combined with those from a survey of nursing and personal-care homes published by the U. S. National Center for Health Statistics (1967), it appears that approximately 3,700 out of every 100,000 old persons in the population require institutional care. Of these geriatric patients, 62.2 percent most likely had dementia. In other words, 2.3 percent of the elderly population in the United States may have dementia of such severity that institutional care becomes necessary (Wang, 1969).

Dementia has long been recognized as an important disorder because it is so prevalent and because patients with such a disorder usually require intensive personal care as well as medical care for a long period of time. The care of these patients has always been a burden to families, to health professionals, and to society as a whole. Although some research work has been done through the years, our understanding of dementia and our clinical ability to treat this disorder are not much more advanced than they were 20 or 30 years ago.

This lack of progress in the understanding and treatment of dementia is the result of multiple factors which interact with each other causing a vicious cycle that becomes a formidable obstacle to advancement. First, our stereotyped view of dementia assumes that it is due to brain impairment, and since brain damage is not reversible, dementia therefore has a very poor prognosis. In our industrialized society productivity and growth are highly valued and the aged are therefore often neglected. Dementia is usually associated with aging, the final stage of life. And since it has a poor prognosis, it is not surprising that most health professionals and scientists develop a rather fatalistic attitude toward elderly psychiatric patients, especially those with dementia. Consequently, very few physicians and scientists have the strong interest needed to devote their efforts to the problem of dementia. This can be illustrated by a survey done in 1970 (Arnhoff and Kumbar, 1973) which revealed that out of 11,081 psychiatrists who responded, only 0.5 percent considered geriatric psychiatry their area of specialization. In contrast, 9.3 percent of the respondents considered child psychiatry and 10.5 percent psychoanalysis their area of specialization. The 0.5 percent actually represents a tremendous increase in the interest in dementia, considering other reports. A previous survey done in 1965 (U.S. National Institute of Mental Health, 1969) did not find a single psychiatrist, among more than 16,000 surveyed, who considered geriatric psychiatry the primary subfield of specialization. The lack of qualified professionals working in the field of geriatric psychiatry, whether in clinical service, research or training, has been an important factor contributing to the problem of support. Little support has been given by the federal government or private foundations to work related to dementia compared to the support given to drug abuse, alcoholism and many other mental disorders (Eisdorfer, 1968). The lack of support, in turn, has probably turned many young psychiatrists and scientists away from pursuing a career in the field of dementia or geriatric psychiatry.

The many problems dementia has imposed upon the society with an increasing elderly population have been better acknowledged in recent years. This is clearly reflected by the many publications that are devoted to the various aspects of dementing disorders in the last five years (Wolstenholme and O'Connor, 1970; Wells, 1971; Gaitz, 1972; Van Praag and Kalverboer, 1972; Pearce and Miller, 1973; Maletta, 1974; Slaby and Wyatt, 1974; Brody et al., 1975). In view of the complexity of these problems, the present paper will limit itself to review several important conceptual and practical issues that remain to be clarified and resolved.

PREVALENCE OF DEMENTIA IN OLD AGE

The prevalence of dementia in old age is almost universally acknowledged. This disorder is probably one of the several most common and serious disabling disorders afflicting the aged. Nevertheless, the exact magnitude of its prevalence has never been clearly established, especially in the United States. A search of the litera-

Table II. Prevalence of Dementia in the Aged

Investigator, year reported (location of study)	Number of Subjects	Age	Rate of Dementia Severe	Mild	Total
Sheldon[a] 1948 (England)	369	65+	3.9	11.7	15.6
Bremer[a] 1951 (Norway)	119	60+	–	–	2.5
Lin 1953 (China)	1113	60+	–	–	0.5
Essen-Moller[a] 1956 (Sweden)	443	60+	5.0	10.8	15.8
Primrose[a,b] 1962 (Scotland)	222	65+	–	–	4.5
Nielson[a,b] 1962	978	65+	3.1	15.4	18.5
Kay[a, b] 1964 (England)	297	65+	5.6	5.7	11.3
Parsons[b] 1965 (England)	228	65+	4.4	10.0	14.0
Hagnell[b] 1966 (Sweden)	441	60+	9.1	7.0	16.1
Kaneko[b] 1967 (Japan)	531	65+	–	–	7.2
Akesson[b] 1969 (Sweden)	4198	65+	–	–	1.0
Wang 1969 (U.S.A.)	e	65+	2.3	–	–
Kay[b] 1970 (England)	758	65+	6.2	2.6	8.8
Bentson[c] 1970 (Norway)	942	60+	–	–	5.3
Halgason[c] 1973 (Iceland)	2642	74-76	–	–	5.0
Bollerup[c] 1975 (Denmark)	626	70+	1.6	3.4	5.0
Pfeiffer[d] 1975 (U.S.A.)	925	65+	7.1	24.7	31.8
Mean			4.8	10.14	
Median			5.3	10.0	

a. obtained from Pearce and Miller 1973.
b. obtained from Kay 1972.
c. obtained from Bollerup 1975
d. calculated from Table 4 and 5 from Pfeiffer 1975.
e. total elderly population in the United States of comparable period when the data was accumulated.

ture uncovers about seventeen reports concerning the prevalence of dementia which have been reviewed and discussed in several recent articles (Pearce and Miller, 1973; Kay, 1972; Bollerup, 1975). Table II summarizes the data obtained from these three articles as well as three other publications (Lin, 1953; Wang, 1969; Pfeiffer, 1975). It is obvious that the majority of investigations were done outside the United States, primarily in England and northern European countries. Two studies were carried out in Asia, one in

Japan and the other in Taiwan—an island province in China. Only two concern the United States. According to these reports, the rate of dementia ranged from 0.5 percent to 31.8 percent. Two-thirds of these reports differentiate among cases of dementia based on severity. The rate of "severe" dementia ranged from 1.6 percent (Bollerup) to 9.1 percent (Hagnell) and "mild dementia" from 2.6 percent (Kay) to 24.7 percent (Pfeiffer).

The great variation in prevalence rates of dementia in these studies can be attributed to many methodological differences. First, there is an obvious difference in the age limit of the samples which varies from 60, 65, 70 to 74–76 years of age. Second, the source and the size of the samples are also quite different. The U.K. studies deal primarily with urban areas, while the Scandinavian studies deal with rural communities which, in some cases, were located in remote areas or on an isolated island. The subjects used for study or calculation may be a representative sample of a community, city or county, or they may represent the entire population of a village, an island or a country. Frequently, the characteristics of the sample are not described in detail. The results from any two studies cannot be readily compared. A high prevalence rate can be expected from a sample which includes a comparatively large number of subjects who are over 75 years old (Kay, 1972) and male (Bollerup, 1975). Educational background and intelligence level of the subjects may also be of some importance, especially when the procedure or instrument of measurement used to define dementia is dependent on these two factors (Pfeiffer, 1975).

The relationship of the elderly population to the total population may be another important factor. For example, the lowest prevalence rate (0.5 percent) was observed by Lin (1953) in a Chinese province. Such a low rate may be related to the criterion (psychosis only) used by the investigator. Or it may be related to the Chinese society, which consists primarily of three-generation families or to the Chinese culture which tends to respect the elderly and to accept the many aberrant behaviors commonly observed in demented elderly persons. On the other hand, Lin's study was carried out in a society in which only 5 percent of the population survived beyond the age of 65, while many other studies involved a population in which 10 or more percent were beyond 65 years of age.

Malzberg (1963) has hypothesized that those surviving to middle age a generation ago probably constituted a better physical selection. The control of many fatal diseases in recent decades has extended the life expectancy and consequently more people have reached that period of life at which circulatory and other degenerative disease become manifest. The increasing rates of both senile and arteriosclerotic mental disorders may be due to the fact that individuals composing the susceptible age groups today are probably not selected as rigorously as were the corresponding age groups of earlier generations. This hypothesis sounds reasonable and may be applicable to the difference between a highly developed and a less developed society, or between a population of large numbers and one of small numbers of older people. Nevertheless, this hypothesis, though logical and interesting, clearly requires further confirmation. If this hypothesis is true, we can then expect the prevalence rate of old age dementia to increase faster than the increase of elderly population in the future. Using the mean prevalence rate calculated from the reports in Table II (about 5 percent for "severe" dementia and 10 percent for "mild" dementia), it is estimated that there were at least one million elderly patients with severe dementia and another two million elderly persons suffering from mild dementia in 1970 in the United States. By 2000, the elderly population is expected to increase by 43 percent, while the number of elderly patients with dementing disorders may increase 50 percent or more.

Probably the most important factor accounting for the great variation in the prevalence rate is the criteria used to define dementia. For example, it has been shown in a cross-national study of diagnosis that the U. S. psychiatrists are inclined to diagnose mental disorders in the aged as organic, while U. K. psychiatrists tend to diagnose them as affective (Copeland et al. 1975). In the seventeen epidemiological studies reviewed, some used the clinical diagnosis of senile psychosis or organic brain syndrome based on direct clinical examination, survey questionnaire or hospital records. Others used the performance on certain psychological scales or on mental status questionnaires. There has been considerable confusion and inconsistency in the definition and usage of the term "dementia" which makes the interpretation of any epidemiological finding very difficult, especially in comparison with other studies.

DEFINITION AND USAGE OF DEMENTIA—PAST AND PRESENT

Dementia, which derives from the Latin word *demens,* meaning out of one's mind, was probably first used in neuropsychiatry by Pinel. It was translated and adopted into English in the mid-nineteenth century (Skinner, 1970). Since then the meaning and usage of dementia has gone through at least three identifiable stages. In the first stage during the late nineteenth century "dementia" was synonymous with insanity, madness, lunacy, and was used to include all mental disease (Skinner, 1970). At the end of the nineteenth century there was considerable progress in the field of neuropathology. For example, in 1898 Redlich reported miliary plaques in the brain in two cases of senile cerebral atrophy which was associated with the clinical phenomena of memory defect, mental confusion, amnesic aphasic and a symbolic apraxia (Zilboorg, 1941). This was soon followed by the report on senile plaques by Blocq and Marinesco in 1892 and the classical papers by Pick in 1892 and Alzheimer in 1907 (Pearce and Miller, 1973). These have clearly contributed to the many attempts, during the next 30 to 40 years of the study of dementia, to relate the detailed morphology of the brain to its clinical correlates. During this second stage "dementia" was often used more specifically as a diagnostic term for a given form of mental disease. "Senile dementia" had become a common term either used interchangeably with "senile psychosis" or else considered one of several diseases categorized under senile psychosis. For example, Kraepelin (1907) listed senile dementia, along with melancholia and presenile delusional insanity, as one of the three forms of involutional psychoses. According to Kraepelin, senile dementia was characterized by a gradual progressive mental deterioration, occurring during the period of involution and accompanied by a series of lesions in the central nervous system. It comprised several groups of cases, including simple senile deterioration, presbyophrenia, senile delirium and senile delusional insanity. Bleuler (1924), however, retained the terms "senile" and "presenile insanity" which were grouped under senile psychosis. During the second stage Alzheimer's and Pick's disease were initially included in "senile psychosis" because they were considered only a form of senile dementia or senile psychosis that had an exceptionally early onset (Kraepelin, 1907; Bleuler, 1924; Noyes, 1939). It was in the forties that Alzheimer's and Pick's disease were gradually recognized to be separate from senile dementia or psychosis (Henderson and Gillespie, 1956; Mayer-Gross, Slater and Roth, 1960). From 1940 on, "dementia," too, gradually came to be a descriptive term for a syndrome while the diagnostic use of this term continued. As a syndrome, dementia was defined by Noyes (1939) as a reduction of mental stock and capacity resulting from any structural disturbance or degeneration of the higher cortical neurones. The clinical manifestations varied from an impairment in the capacity for fine discrimination, in the ability to make decisions involving delicate moral issues, and in the ability to employ abstract ideas, to a reduction of aptitude and learning capacity, defective memory, disorientation, confusion and an inability to assimilate impressions. This definition has remained almost unchanged, although the textbook was revised many times (Kolb, 1968).

The 1950's signified the beginning of the third stage. The diagnostic use of the term "dementia" was almost completely discarded. In the first edition of the *Diagnostic and Statistical Manual of Mental Disorders* published by the American Psychiatric Association (1952), mental disorders that used to be called "senile dementia" were classified as "chronic brain syndrome (CBS)" associated with senile brain disease; Alzheimer's disease was classified as CBS associated with other disturbances of metabolism, growth or nutrition; Pick's disease was classified as CBS associated with disease of unknown or uncertain cause. Meanwhile, our European colleagues continued to prefer the term "senile psychosis." It was defined by Roth (1955) as "a condition with a history of gradual and continually progressive failure in the common activities of everyday life and a clinical picture dominated by failure of memory and intellect and disorganization of a personality, where these were not attributable to specific causes such as infections, neoplasms, etc." Such definition was highly regarded and popularly used in Europe.

As the years went by, the term "dementia" gradually began to reappear more often in the medical literature and has been used more commonly as a descriptive term for a syndrome (Alpers and Mancall, 1971). Now and then it was used as a diagnostic term by some authors. For example, both "senile" and "presenile dementia" are employed again as official diagnostic terms under the category of psychoses associated with organic brain syndrome in the second edition of the *Diagnostic and Statistical Manual of Mental Disorders,* published by the American Psychiatric Association (1968).

In using dementia as a term to describe a syndrome, various aspects of the syndrome are emphasized by different authors or publications. Some equate dementia with intellectual deficit or impairment. For example, Webster's Third New International Dictionary (1961) defines dementia as a condition of deteriorated mentality that is characterized by marked decline from the individual's former intellectual level and often by emotional apathy without any reference to its etiological factors. Other authors, however, place more emphasis on the role of brain disorder. Wells (1971) stated that dementia comprises the spectrum of mental states resulting from disease of man's cerebral hemispheres in adult life. An identical definition was adopted by Barrett (1972). In the fourth edition of *A Psychiatric Glossary,* published by the American Psychiatric Association (1975), dementia is defined as an *irreversible* mental state characterized by decreased intellectual function, personality change, impairment of judgment, and often change in affect, and is due to *permanently* altered cerebral metabolism. It thus introduces new elements in the definition, namely, the irreversibility and permanence of this syndrome and the implication of its hopeless prognosis.

The three stages in the evolution of the term "dementia" were not distinctly separated. Frequently all three usages of dementia were employed by different authors in the same period. This has clearly led to considerable confusion in the literature and in the field of neuropsychiatry. This confusion is magnified by the inconsistent use of the term within one publication or one system of classification. For example, in the second edition of the *American Psychiatric Association Diagnostic Manual* (1968), dementing disorders due to neuropathological changes of the Alzheimer's type in the presence of psychotic manifestation are classified as "senile" or "presenile dementia." The same disorders in the absence of psychotic manifestation are called "organic brain syndrome" with "senile or presenile *brain disease*" (instead of dementia). Another example of inconsistency can be illustrated by the medical subject headings (MeSH) used in the *Index Medicus* published by the National Library of Medicine (1960–1975). The introduction given in the *Index Medicus* states that in selecting terms as subject headings, the most commonly used form of English expressions are generally preferred. The criteria for the selection of subject headings are based on the frequency of term usage in the medical literature, the recognition of need for the term by the various users of MeSH, the recommendation by an advisory panel on terminology, and the ability to assign a relatively clear and precise definition to the term. The MeSH, therefore, can be considered an authoritative view of a topic or subject in a given period of our scientific development. In 1960, there was a heading for "psychosis, senile" which has remained unchanged through the years. Presenile dementia was referred to as "senile psychosis" in 1960 and 1961 and then a new heading of "psychosis, presenile" began to appear in 1963. It remained that way until 1967 when "dementia, presenile" and "psychosis, presenile" both appeared as headings in addition to the term "psychosis, senile." In 1973, the heading "psychosis, presenile" was dropped and "dementia, presenile" was retained. It has not been changed since.

The chaos caused by inconsistency in the use of the term "dementia" reflects the problem we have been facing in psychiatry in general. It is certain that considerable progress has been made in understanding many mental disorders. The understanding we have today, however, is not sufficient. Consequently, we are struggling between the adoption of an etiological classification and a symptomatic classification of mental disorders. The result of such uncertainty is the combination of these two systems of classifications. "Dementia" is therefore used as a descriptive term for a syndrome as well as a diagnostic term for a particular mental disorder, depending on the orientation of the author or investigator and the circumstance under which the term is used.

In reviewing the literature concerning dementia, or organic brain syndrome, it appears that as a disorder dementia (be it a syndrome or a disease) consists of three basic components: (1) cognitive impairments including memory deficit, (2) neuropathological changes underlying these cognitive impairments, and (3) the clinical manifestations and the outcome resulting from these cognitive impairments.

COGNITIVE CHANGES IN OLD AGE

In early studies of the aged, a steady decline of cognitive function with advancing age was consistently observed. For this reason, most measures for the assessment of cognitive function such as the Wechsler Adult Intelligence Scale and Wechsler Memory Scale are constructed with a correction factor for age. Younger persons are given an age debit; older ones, an age credit (Botwinick, 1967). It is only recently that the validity of such an age trend in intellectual deterioration is being challenged as more and more data have been generated by several longitudinal investigations. The age trend observed in early studies is probably exaggerated by their cross-sectional design in which the age difference can be contaminated by cohort or generation difference. The findings from several longitudinal studies indicated that many elderly persons may maintain their overall intellectual function for some time during senescence (Jarvik et al., 1962; Eisdorfer, 1963; Pierce and Berkman, 1967; Birren, 1968).

There is no consensus yet concerning the test or battery of tests most reliable, valid and sensitive in detecting the cognitive changes in the aged. Cognitive function is usually evaluated either by clinical neuropsychiatric examination or by psychometric testting. As a rule, the psychometric measures are better structured and standardized than the clinical measures. Nonetheless, both have the same limitations because they evaluate the individual's behavioral responses which are known to be vulnerable to the influence of many factors such as motivation, attention, concomitant emotional disorder, psychological reaction to the testing itself or the deficits revealed through testing, and the circumstance under which the testing is done. The many tests currently available for the evaluation of cognitive function are, in most cases, designed primarily for young adults and involve time limits. These tests may accentuate the cautiousness that tends to develop in many elderly persons and exaggerate the degree of impairment in certain kinds of performance, particularly those involving speed. The test results are therefore biased against the elderly.

Intellectual impairments are greater and more conspicuous in elderly persons with dementia or senile psychosis. It is unclear, however, whether the difference in cognitive changes between the demented and non-demented elderly is quantitative or qualitative. The tests or subtests which were found sensitive in distinguishing normal elderly persons from normal young adults were not necessarily the same ones which distinguished old dementeds from old normals (Botwinick, 1967).

Cognitive function is not a simple unitary function. It is a mosaic composed of many diversive but sometimes interrelated abilities. Not all abilities are equally affected by aging or by a given dementing disorder. It is generally accepted that verbal abilities, particularly those involving vocabulary and information, may show no decline at all in many elderly persons. In some, they may even show some improvement through repeated measurements. Remote memory and recognition ability are usually better preserved than recent memory, perceptual-integrative ability and psychomotor skills, especially those involving speed (Botwinick, 1967; Jarvik et al., 1973). The characteristic pattern of cognitive deficit in the elderly may reflect a differential rate of change in different parts of the brain. As an alternative hypothesis, it may reflect the protective effects of overlearning (Piercy, 1964). In other words, the unimpaired skills are those that tend to be used more frequently. The rapid decline in cognitive function in some elderly may also be related to declining health or impending death. The latter phenomenon has been frequently referred to as "terminal drop" which, however, needs further clarification and confirmation (Siegler, 1975).

BRAIN CHANGES IN OLD AGE

It is unquestionable that the brain of old persons, particularly those with significant cognitive impairment, undergoes many changes, which have been reviewed and discussed by several recent articles (Tomlinson et al., 1970; Torack, 1971; Malamud, 1972; Pearce and Miller, 1973; Terry and Wisniewski, 1974; Berry, 1975; Shelanski, 1975). There are two common types of change. One is characterized by neuronal loss, senile plaques, neurofibrillary tangles, granulovacuolar degeneration and is considered the manifestation of cellular degeneration. The cause of cellular degeneration is still unknown, although many theories are proposed. The other type of change is characterized by focal cerebral softening or multiple lacunar infarcts in addition to a loss of neurons. This is considered to be the manifestation of vascular disorder and is most likely the result of cerebral arteriosclerosis or hypertension.

From clinical and conceptual points of view, one very important issue regarding dementia is the relationship between brain changes and cognitive decline. It is well known that certain localized lesions of the brain are associated with rather specific neurological or mental manifestations such as aphasia, visual defects, dyspraxia, etc. Pathological changes in the cortex and those in the subcortex may lead to different types of memory difficulty designated cortical and axial amnesia (Barbizet, 1970).

In the majority of elderly patients with significant cognitive impairment, either senile or presenile, the brain changes are diffuse and of the degenerative type. In about one-fifth of these patients changes of the vascular type may be superimposed upon the degenerative changes (Corsellis, 1962; Tomlinson et al., 1970; Malamud, 1972). These degenerative changes are not limited to demented elderly as well as in younger patients with other neurological diseases such as Down's syndrome. It is still unresolved whether the difference among normal aging, senile dementia and presenile dementia (Alzheimer's disease) is an intensity, extensity, locational, or subtle qualitative ultrastructural difference. Another controversial issue is whether the severity of cognitive impairments is correlated with the severity of brain changes. This controversy can be attributed, to a great extent, to the measures or procedures currently available for the evaluation of the cognitive function and the brain, particularly in vivo. The limitations in evaluating cognitive function have already been discussed. For evaluating the brain, biopsy of brain tissue, pneumoencephalography, arteriography, ultrasonic encephalography and the most recently developed computerized transverse axial tomography are procedures that may provide information regarding the structural status of the brain (histopathological changes, cortical atrophy or ventricular dilation). Electroencephalography, the measurement of cerebral oxygen or glucose consumption and cerebral blood flow, on the other hand, may reflect the functional or metabolic status of the brain. All these procedures have their inherent limitations in sensitivity, validity and practicality for routine uses.

A review of the literature reveals that the severity of cognitive deficits is more often than not correlated with the severity of brain changes (Wang et al., 1970; Wang, 1973). However, the correlation between these two variables is rather gross with many discrepancies between them (Wang and Busse, 1971). The most convincing findings that support a quantitative relationship between cognitive deterioration and brain changes come from the work by the Newcastle group recently summarized and reviewed by Roth (1972). This group quantified the patient's ability to deal with practical tasks of everyday life and the patient's performance in a number of simple psychological tests of orientation, remote memory, recent memory and concentration. These tests were used to indicate the degree of personality and intellectual deterioration. They found that these two cognitive measurements are closely correlated with several quantitative measurements of brain changes, including mean plaque count, gradations of neurofibrillary changes, frequency of granulovacuolar degeneration and the total volume of cerebral softening. Nevertheless, the relationship between cognitive and brain variables is not exactly a linear one. The correlation is highly significant only in patients with mild to moderate deterioration, but not in those with severe cognitive impairment. The variance of the cognitive variable is rather large and cannot be accounted for solely by the brain variable.

The discrepancy observed between cognitive impairment and brain changes can be attributed to many factors. In addition to the

methodological limitations, depression, inactivity, social deprivation and functional disorders of the brain are probably the most
important. Depression is very common among the aged. It is frequently overlooked because depression in many elderly persons is
often overshadowed by somatic symptoms. Because of our social
system, our attitude toward aging, and many other psychological
and social factors, social isolation and inactivity (particularly of
intellectual function) are also very common among the aged. Some
elderly who are depressed, intellectually inactive, or out of contact
with the outside world for long periods of time show cognitive
defects which may not be distinguishable from those observed in
people with brain changes. This "psychological" type of cognitive
defect may be superimposed upon the "organic" type of deficits in
some individuals. The clinical differentiation of these two types
is at times very difficult and becomes possible only after a trial
with various treatments. The "psychological" type of cognitive
defect usually responds to such treatment and has often been
referred to as "pseudo-dementia" (Kiloh, 1961; Post, 1975) or
"pseudo-senility" (Libow, 1973).

Functional disorder of the brain tissue is another common
disorder in the aged because aged persons commonly have many
physical illnesses. It is estimated that about three of every four
persons aged 65 or older have at least one disabling chronic condition (Confrey and Goldstein, 1960). Many diseases commonly
associated with senescence may affect the brain adversely (Harris,
1972; Karp, 1972). The brain that is already afflicted with significant
degenerative changes is particularly vulnerable to the adverse
effects from many systemic diseases and to many medications that
act on the central nervous system. The functional disorder of brain
tissue either accentuates the impairment of cognitive function or
the reduction of brain metabolic activity which is reflected in the
electroencephalogram, cerebral oxygen consumption or cerebral
blood flow. This type of functional disorder is usually considered
reversible and is designated "acute," in contrast to the term
"chronic" meaning irreversible. Once again, the clinical differentiation between "acute" and "chronic" brain disorders, especially when
they occur in the same individual, is often possible only after a
trial treatment. Functional disorders of the brain if untreated may
ultimately lead to structural changes of the brain.

CLINICAL MANIFESTATIONS AND
PROGNOSIS OF COGNITIVE IMPAIRMENT

The deficits in cognitive function, particularly when they are
very pronounced, will affect the individual's ability to take care
of himself, to relate to other people, to cope with the many life
situations arising from his environment. Nevertheless, the cognitive
deficits play a relatively small role in the clinical and behavioral
manifestations, especially when the dementing disorder develops
over a period of many years. Cognitive decline is a relative matter.
A decline of 30 to 40 percent will result in little difficulty in the
overall adjustment of an individual who originally had Wechsler
Intelligence Quotient or Memory Quotient of 130 or above. On the
other hand, considerable problems may result from such a decline
in some individuals who initially had average or below average
intelligence or memory ability. In other words, the absolute level
of functioning capacity is frequently but not always an important
determinant in the clinical picture. It is well known that many
patients, young or old, with an I.Q. of 50 or 60 manifest few behavioral disturbances in certain environments. It was found, as stated
previously, that the psychological tests and subtests sensitive in
distinguishing normal old adults from young adults were not
necessarily the same tests that distinguished old psychotics from
old normals.

The basic factors underlying the severity and other characteristics of the clinical picture in demented patients are similar to
those involved in many other mental disorders, such as schizophrenia and depression. In the demented patients, cognitive deficit
is the primary determinant while in schizophrenics and depressives
"psychological deficit or inadequacy" of the individual is of primary
importance. Nevertheless, in both types of disorder, the clinical
picture is influenced by a great number of other factors which can
be grouped into three general categories.

The first group consists of intrapsychic factors. To a great
extent, these are determined by the patient's preexisting personality. They would include his basic needs and expectations, the
defense mechanisms routinely used in coping with anxiety-pro-
voking situations and his prevailing emotional status and attitude.
The second group consists of interpersonal factors. These would

include the type, number and stability of the patient's ongoing relationship with members of his immediate family, relatives. friends, neighbors, etc. It may also include the patient's potential for developing new satisfying relationships with others. Societal or environmental factors comprise the third category. These factors would include the prevailing attitude toward aging and aged persons in the patient's immediate environment, and the resources of support and service (be it material, emotional, physical or medical) available to him.

It is undeniable that patients with cognitive impairment, particularly those of great severity, generally have a poor prognosis (Wang and Whanger, 1971). Many studies in the past have revealed that these patients have a tendency to be admitted for institutional care, requiring long periods of institutionalization, and having a high mortality rate. The findings from these studies have often been misinterpreted and unjustifiably taken to indicate that *all* patients with severe cognitive impairment have a poor, even hopeless chance for improvement. The poor prognosis is true only when a *group* of demented patients is compared with a *group* of nondemented patients. There is, however, considerable variation within the demented group. It has been shown that almost 10 percent of those having so-called organic disorders were living in the community and even a larger proportion (11 to 33 percent) were still alive in the institution two years after their admission (Roth, 1955; Trier, 1966). To predict the outcome for an *individual* patient is extremely difficult and unreliable (Kay, 1956). Predictions by psychiatrists or internists that death would occur within a specified period after admission were found to be correct for only one-third of the aged institutionalized patients (Goldfarb et al., 1966).

Dementia, with few exceptions, usually occurs in the later period of senescence (70 to 75 years old). Patients with such a disorder therefore tend to have a short survival. When the ages of subjects are controlled the difference in longevity between those with and those without dementing disorders becomes less conspicuous (Wang and Busse, 1974). Of great importance is the unknown effect of institutional care on the mortality rate in these elderly patients who are known to have many physical illnesses. For these patients in most public mental hospitals, nursing homes or personal-care homes, the quality of medical and nursing care is very likely inadequate. Our current concept of dementia as an irreversible and permanent disorder makes the diagnosis of dementia or chronic brain syndrome almost synonymous with "no-treatment." This clearly contributes to a high mortality rate. This is supported by the findings from the cross-national study between the United States and the United Kingdom (Copeland et al., 1975). These findings suggest that when elderly patients with affective disorder are labeled as having organic brain syndrome they may follow a prognostic course with as high a mortality rate as those who really have organic brain syndrome.

CONCLUSION

Dementia is a common disorder in aged persons and is expected to continue to increase as a burden to many families, health professionals and society as a whole. The definition and usage of the term "dementia" has been very confusing and inconsistent. This has contributed significantly to the lack of progress in the past and to the fatalistic attitude prevailing among health workers who provide care for elderly patients with dementia. Our current knowledge and ability to identify and differentiate the various types of dementing disorders are obviously limited and inadequate. The use of dementia as a diagnostic term and the concept of dementia as an irreversible condition are unjustified and of little meaning. The terms "pseudo-dementia" and "chronic brain syndrome," though theoretically reasonable, are clinically impractical because the diagnosis cannot be accurately made and can often be confirmed only after intensive treatment. The continuing use of these terms may perpetuate or augment the ongoing pessimistic, fatalistic attitude toward patients with dementia. It may also impede future progress in the research and treatment of this disorder.

At the present time, and probably for many years in the future, the many issues and problems related to the neuropathological and cognitive aspects of dementia will remain unresolved. Our knowledge and ability to accurately differentiate various types of

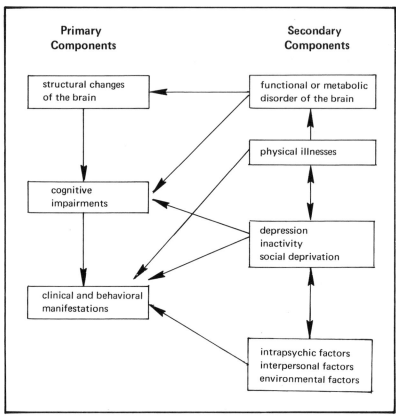

Primary Components

structural changes of the brain

cognitive impairments

clinical and behavioral manifestations

Secondary Components

functional or metabolic disorder of the brain

physical illnesses

depression inactivity social deprivation

intrapsychic factors interpersonal factors environmental factors

1 Holistic view of dementia as a syndrome: The possible interactions among primary and secondary components

dementing disorder, though improving slowly, will continue to be limited and inadequate. From the clinical point of view, it appears to be more realistic and practical to use "dementia" only as a descriptive term for a syndrome that is characterized by clinical and behavioral manifestations primarily due to or associated with cognitive impairment. The term "dementia" should be qualified by an etiological term only when it can be accurately identified. As a syndrome, dementia can be viewed as a bio-psycho-social disorder that consists of many components. The structural changes of the brain, cognitive impairments and the behavioral manifestations are the primary factors. These, in turn, will interact with or be influenced by many secondary components (Figure 1). More careful investigations are clearly needed to understand better these various elements and their interactions. It is hoped that such investigations will ultimately make it possible to accurately classify the various types of dementing disorders. More specific measures may then be developed for their prevention, early diagnosis and effective treatment. Before this is accomplished, all components, both primary and secondary, should be considered in the management of a patient with dementia. With such careful evaluation, those factors that can be corrected, alleviated or arrested should be vigorously treated.

REFERENCES

Alpers, B.J., and Mancall, E.L.: *Clinical Neurology* (6th ed.). Philadelphia, F.A. Davis Co., 1971.

American Psychiatric Association: *Diagnostic and Statistical Manual of Mental Disorder* (1st ed.). Washington, D.C., American Psychiatric Association, 1952.

American Psychiatric Association: *Diagnostic and Statistical Manual of Mental Disorders* (2nd ed.). Washington, D.C., American Psychiatric Association, 1968.

American Psychiatric Association: *A Psychiatric Glossary* (4th ed.). Washington, D.C., American Psychiatric Association, 1975.

Arnhoff, F.N., and Kumbar, A.H.: *The Nation's Psychiatrists—1970 Survey.* Washington, D.C., American Psychiatric Association, 1973.

Barbizet, J.: *Human Memory and Its Pathology.* San Francisco, W.H. Freeman and Co., 1970.

Barrett, R.E.: Dementia in adults. *Med. Clin., North Am.* 56:1405–1418, 1972.

Berry, R.G.: Pathology of dementia. In Howells, J.G. (ed.), *Modern Perspectives in the Psychiatry of Old Age.* New York, Brunner/Mazel, Publ., 1975, pp. 51–83.

Birren, J.E.: Increments and decrements in the intellectual status of the aged. In Simon, A., and Epstein, L.J. (eds.). *Aging in Modern Society: Psychiatric Research Report 23.* Washington, D.C., American Psychiatric Association, 1968, pp. 207–214.

Bleuler, E.: *Textbook of Psychiatry.* New York, Macmillan Co., 1924.

Bollerup, T.R.: Prevalence of mental illness among 70-year-olds domiciled in nine Copenhagen suburbs. *Acta Psychiat. Scand.,* 51:327–339, 1975.

Botwinick, J.: *Cognitive Processes in Maturity and Old Age.* New York, Springer Publ. Co., 1967.

Brody, H., Harman, D., and Ordy, J.M. (eds.): *Aging, Vol. 1: Clinical, Morphologic, and Neurochemical Aspects in the Aging Central Nervous System.* New York, Raven Press, 1975.

Confrey, E.A., and Goldstein, M.S.: The health status of aging people. In Tibbitts, C. (ed.), *Handbook of Social Gerontology.* Chicago, University of Chicago Press, 1960, pp. 165–207.

Copeland, J.R.M., et al.: Cross-national study of diagnosis of the mental disorders: A comparison of the diagnoses of elderly psychiatric patients admitted to mental hospitals serving Queens County, New York, and the former Borough of Camberwell, London. *Brit. J. Psychiat.*, 126:11–20, 1975.

Corsellis, J.A.N.: *Mental Illness and the Aging Brain.* London, Oxford University Press, 1962.

Eisdorfer, C.: The WAIS performance of the aged: A retest evaluation. *J. Gerontol.*, 18:169–172, 1963.

Eisdorfer, C.: Patterns of federal funding for research in aging. *Gerontologist*, 8: 3–6, 1968.

Gaitz, C.M. (ed.): *Aging and the Brain.* New York, Plenum Press, 1972.

Goldfarb, A.I., Fisch, M., and Gerber, I.E.: Predictors of mortality in the institutionalized aged. *Dis. Nerv. Syst.*, 17:21–29, 1966.

Harris, R.: The relationship between organic brain disease and physical status. In Gaitz, C.M. (ed.), *Aging and the Brain.* New York, Plenum Press, 1972. pp. 163–177.

Henderson, D., and Gillespie, R.D.: *A Textbook of Psychiatry.* New York, Oxford University Press, 1956.

Jarvik, L.F., Kallman, F.J., and Falek, A.: Intellectual changes in aged twins. *J. Gerontol.*, 17:289–294, 1962.

Jarvik, L.F., Eisdorfer, C., and Blum, J.E. (eds.), *Intellectual Functioning in Adults.* New York, Springer Publ. Co., Inc., 1973.

Karp, H.R.: Dementia in cerebrovascular disease and other systemic illness. *Current Concepts of Cerebrovascular Disease*, 7:11–16, 1972.

Kay, D.W.K., Norris, V., and Post, F.: Prognosis in psychiatric disorders of the elderly, an attempt to define indicators of early death and early recovery. *J. Ment. Sci.*, 102:129–140, 1956.

Kay, D.W.K.: Epidemiological aspects of organic brain disease in the aged. In Gaitz, C.M. (ed.) *Aging and the Brain.* New York, Plenum Press, 1972, pp. 15–27.

Kiloh, L.G.: Pseudo-dementia. *Acta Psychiat. Scand.*, 37:336–351, 1961.

Kolb, L.C.: *Noyes' Modern Clinical Psychiatry* (7th ed.). Philadelphia, W.B. Saunders Co., 1968.

Kraepelin, E.: *Clinical Psychiatry.* New York, Macmillan Co., 1907.

Libow, L.S.: Pseudo-senility: Acute and reversible organic brain syndromes. *J. Am. Geriat. Soc.*, 21:112–120, 1973.

Lin, A.Y.: A study of the incidence of mental disorder in Chinese and other cultures. *Psychiatry*, 16:313–336, 1913.

Malamud, N.: Neuropathology of organic brain syndromes associated with aging. In Gaitz, C.M. (ed.), *Aging and the Brain*. New York, Plenum Press, 1972, pp. 63–87.

Maletta, G.J. (ed.): *Survey Report on the Aging Nervous System*. Washington, D.C., U.S. Government Printing Office, 1974.

Malzberg, B.: The frequency of mental disease. *Acta Psychiat. Scand.*, 39:19–30, 1963.

Mayer-Gross, W., Slater, E., and Roth, M.: *Clinical Psychiatry* (2nd ed.). Baltimore, Williams & Wilkins Co., 1960.

National Library of Medicine: *Medical Subject Headings, Cumulated Index Medicus*. Washington, D.C., U.S. Government Printing Office, 1960–1975.

Noyes, A.P.: *Modern Clinical Psychiatry* (2nd ed.). Philadelphia, W.B. Saunders Co., 1939.

Pearce, J., and Miller, E.: *Clinical Aspects of Dementia*. Baltimore, Williams & Wilkins Co., 1973.

Pfeiffer, E.: A short portable mental status questionnaire for the assessment of organic brain deficit in elderly patients. *J. Am. Geriat. Soc.*, 23:433–441, 1975.

Pierce, R.C., and Berkman, P.L.: Change in intellectual functioning. In Lowenthal, M.F., Berkman, P.L., and Associates (eds.), *Aging and Mental Disorder in San Francisco*. San Francisco, Jossey-Bass, Inc., 1967, pp. 177–189.

Piercy, M.: The effects of cerebral lesions on intellectual function: A review of current research trends. *Brit. J. Psychiat.*, 110:310–352, 1964.

Post, F.: Dementia, depression and pseudodementia. In Benson, D.F., and Blumer, D. (eds.), *Psychiatric Aspects of Neurological Diseases*. New York, Grune & Stratton, 1975.

Roth, M.: The national history of mental disorders arising in the senium. *J. Ment. Sci.*, 101:281–301, 1955.

Roth, M.: Recent progress in the psychiatry of old age and its bearing on certain problems of psychiatry in earlier life. *Biological Psychiatry*, 5:102–125, 1972.

Shelanski, M.L.: The aging brain: Alzheimer's disease and senile dementia. In Ostefeld, A.M., and Gibson, D.C. (eds.), *Epidemiology of Aging*. Washington, D.C., U.S. Government Printing Office, 1975, pp. 113–127.

Siegel, J.S.: Some demographic aspects of aging in the United States. In Ostefeld, A.M. and Gibson, D.C. (eds.), *Epidemiology of Aging*. Washington, D.C., U.S. Government Printing Office, 1975, pp. 17–82.

Siegler, I.C.: The terminal drop hypothesis: Fact or Artifact. *Exper. Aging Res.*, 1:169–185, 1975.

Skinner, H.A.: *The Origin of Medical Term* (2nd ed.). New York, Hafner Publ. Co., 1970.

Slaby, A.E., and Wyatt, R.J.: *Dementia in the Presenium*. Springfield, Charles C. Thomas, 1974.

Terry, R.D. and Wisniewski, H.M.: Pathology of the aging nervous system.

In Maletta, G.J. (ed.), *Survey Report on the Aging Nervous System.* Washington, D.C., U.S. Government Printing Office, 1974, pp. 125–132.

Tomlinson, B.E., Blessed, G., and Roth, M.: Observations on the brains of demented old people. *J. Neurol. Sci.,* 11:205–242, 1970.

Torack, R.M.: Studies in the pathology of dementia. In Wells, C.E. (ed.), *Dementia.* Philadelphia, F.A. Davis Co., 1971, pp. 111–132.

Trier, T.R.: Characteristics of mentally ill aged: A comparison of patients with psychogenic disorders and patients with organic brain syndromes. *J. Geront.,* 21:354–364, 1966.

U.S. National Center for Health Statistics: *Prevalence of Chronic Conditions and Impairments Among Residents of Nursing and Personal Care Homes --United States, May–June, 1964.* Washington, D.C., U.S. Government Printing Office, 1967.

U.S. National Institute of Mental Health: *The Nation's Psychiatrists.* Washington, D.C., U.S. Government Printing Office, 1969.

Van Praag, H.M., and Kalverboer, A.F. (eds.): *Aging of the Central Nervous System.* Haarlem, De Erven F. Bohn N.V., 1972.

Wang, H.S.: Organic brain syndromes. In Busse, E.W., and Pfeiffer, E. (eds.), *Behavior and Adaptation in Late Life.* Boston, Little, Brown and Co., 1969, pp. 263–287.

Wang, H.S., Obrist, W.D., and Busse, E.W.: Neurophysiological correlates of the intellectual function of elderly persons living in the community. *Amer. J. Psychiat.,* 126–1205–1212. 1970.

Wang, H.S., and Busse, E.W.: Dementia in old age. In Wells, C.E. (ed.), *Dementia.* Philadelphia, F.A. Davis Co., 1971, pp. 151–162.

Wang, H.S., and Whanger, A.: Brain impairment and longevity. In Palmore, E., and Jeffers, F. (eds.), *Prediction of Life Span-Recent Findings.* Lexington, Mass., D.C. Heath Co., 1971, pp. 95–105.

Wang, H.S.: Cerebral correlates of intellectual function in senescence. In Jarvik, L.F., Eisdorfer, C., and Blum, J.E. (eds.), *Intellectual Functioning in Adults.* New York, Springer Publ. Co., 1973, pp. 95–106.

Wang, H.S., and Busse, E. W.: Brain impairment and longevity in community aged persons. In Palmore, E. (ed.), *Normal Aging II.* Duke University Press, 1974, pp. 263–268.

Webster's Third New International Dictionary. Springfield, Mass., G. & C. Merriam Co., 1961.

Wells, E.C. (ed.): *Dementia.* Philadelphia, F.A. Davis Co., 1971.

Wolstenholme, G.E.W., and O'Connor, M. (eds.): *Alzheimer's Disease and Related Conditions.* London, J. & A. Churchill, 1970.

Zilboorg, G.: *A History of Medical Psychology.* New York, W.W. Norton Co., 1941.

2

Morphological Changes and Dementia in Old Age

B. E. TOMLINSON

Numerous diseases are capable of producing dementia in old age. Among these are cerebrovascular disease, senile dementia, cerebral tumours, neurosyphilis, Korsakoff's Psychosis, Pick's disease, chronic subdural haematoma, myxoedema, low pressure hydrocephalus and Jakob-Creutzfeldt disease. A comprehensive list of causes of dementia is given by Haase (1971). In fact, all these causes, with the exception of the first two, are uncommon in Western Europe. Above the age of 60 years only cerebral softening, producing what is usually known as arteriopathic or arteriosclerotic dementia, and changes of a kind similar if not identical to those that occur in Alzheimer's disease but which in older subjects tends to be called senile dementia, are commonly associated with dementia. The frequent use of the term "senile dementia" without precise definition is unfortunate. For some it covers all the slowly progressive dementias of old age, while for many it refers to the dementing process in old people which is associated with morphological changes similar to Alzheimer's presenile dementia. The adoption of the terms "senile dementia of Alzheimer's type," "of arteriosclerotic origin," "of unknown cause," etc., would be an advantage at this time when referring to old people with chronic dementing processes who fall outside the presenile group. Further, the three histological changes of Alzheimer's presenile dementia, that is, senile plaques and Alzheimer's neurofibrillary degeneration and granulovacuolar degeneration, are commonly referred to as "senile brain changes." Delay et al. (1962), Corsellis (1962) and Post (1965) have stressed that cerebral softening and the changes of senile dementia are not uncommonly found together in demented subjects. In my own experience the changes which occur in Alzheimer's disease are the commonest accompaniment of dementia in old age; severe cerebral softening either on its own or associated with severe changes of Alzheimer type is found in many of the remaining cases and in only a small proportion is another pathology involved or no specific morphological diagnosis possible.

The problem of assigning either senile change or ischemic loss of cerebral tissue in focal or diffuse form as the explanation of the development of dementia arises from the fact that both cerebral softening, sometimes producing profound physical disability, and senile degenerative changes may be found within the brains of intellectually well preserved old subjects (Gellerstedt, 1933; Hirano and Zimmerman, 1962; and Tomlinson, Blessed, and Roth, 1968). This latter fact has so impressed a considerable number of previous observers that they have maintained that the morphological changes within the brains of old subjects are only part of the answer to the problem of dementia in old age and that a major contributory factor is the previous personality of the subject concerned. Rothschild (1939, 1942, and 1956) has expounded this view, and in more recent times Wolf (1959), Noyes and Kolb (1963) have emphasized the interrelationship of psychological and organic factors in the development of the dementia in old age. The interplay of socio-psycho-somatic factors which may influence the development of dementia in old age is summarized by Wang and Busse (1971). The work of Corsellis (1962), however, clearly indicated that dementia was associated with severe brain changes of senile or ischemic type in some 80% of old people, but as in the great majority of publications some doubt about the precision of the findings remained because the diagnosis in this series was made on retrospective study of the clinical records. Quite apart from the inherent problems of such a procedure, the difficulty of distinguishing dementia from severe depression in old age is well recognized, and the possibility of such errors in a retrospective study partly invalidating otherwise important findings seemed strong.

In an endeavor to resolve this problem a collaborative study involving a careful physical and psychiatric examination of normal and demented old subjects shortly before death was made by Professor Sir Martin Roth and Dr. Garry Blessed, and the brains of those coming to autopsy were examined without knowledge of the diagnostic categories into which the subjects had been placed on clinical grounds. Clinically the degree of intellectual and personality deterioration was quantified by questioning relatives or friends about the patient's capacity to deal with a standard series of personal, domestic and social activities, the score for which (Dementia Score) increased with deterioration of function (Blessed et al., 1968); in addition, the patient's ability to cope with a number of simple psychological tests of recent and remote memory, concentration and orientation was measured and a score produced which increased with the competence of the patient (Psychological Test Score). This latter test was based on features shown to differentiate between groups of demented and nondemented old people (Roth and Hopkins, 1953; Shapiro et al., 1956). On the pathological side of the investigation, attempts were made to quantify all those changes within the brain which were technically possible, and from this study has been built some knowledge of the quantity of cerebral softening and senile change within a group of old people who have been of well-preserved intellect and personality until their death, despite severe physical disability in some instances. In this way, a base-line has been drawn on which a comparison may be made of the findings in a group of normal old people with the changes in the brains of demented old people and to some extent an examination made of the possible correlations between the severity of the dementia and the intensity of the various changes studied within the brain. Naturally, this latter analysis of the severity of dementia

Table I

Senile Plaques in Demented and Nondemented Old Subjects		
	28 Controls	50 Dements
None	6	8
<5 per field	14	5
6-13 per field	8	11
14-17 per field	0	9
< 18 per field	0	17
Mean	3.3	14.7
	(P.< 0.001)	

and the severity of the morphological brain changes would have been totally worthless had it not been established that the brains of intellectually well preserved old people differ as a group from those old people who show evidences of dementia. In this paper no attempt will be made to cover all the aspects of the investigation, but the evidence relating to the presence of excessive quantities of senile-type change and of cerebral softening within the brains of demented old subjects when compared with those of nondemented old subjects will be briefly reviewed. Other details not mentioned in this paper can be found in previous papers on this subject by Blessed, Tomlinson, and Roth (1968), Tomlinson, Blessed, and Roth (1968 and 1970) and Tomlinson and Kitchener (1972).

"SENILE CHANGES OF ALZHEIMER TYPE"
IN NONDEMENTED AND DEMENTED OLD PEOPLE

In the 28 nondemented subjects examined whose ages ranged from 65 to 92 years (mean 75 years) senile plaques were found in some part of the cerebral cortex (in many in all areas of the cortex) in 71% (Table I). They were, however, in the majority of cases present in only small numbers, and by the system of quantification adopted the majority contained less than 5 senile plaques per low power field over the areas surveyed. Greater numbers than this, up to a maximum of 13 per field were, however, found in 29% of the cases, but in these none was found to have a greater mean plaque count per low power field than 13 and the mean plaque count per field for the whole group was 3.3. In the demented group (50 in number) some 80% contained senile plaques, but the significant difference between the groups was not in this total number showing plaque formation but in the numbers of cases in the demented group which showed senile plaques in far greater numbers than had been found in any of the nondemented patients. Thus, 26 out of 50, or some 52% of the demented cases showed a mean count of more than 14 plaques per low power field and 34% showed more than 18 plaques per low power field (Table I). The mean plaque count for the whole of the demented group was 14.7, compared with 3.3 for the normals, a difference which is statistically highly significant ($t = 4.5$ with 76% of freedom. $P<0.001$). Furthermore, the degree of plaque formation is positively correlated with the severity of intellectual deterioration (Fig. 1), the dementia score tending to increase as the mean plaque count increases. The correlation coefficient of these two features in the total group of 78 cases of demented and normal old subjects from whom only those subjects showing large quantities (in excess of 40 ml) of cerebral softening have been removed is $+0.723$ (highly significant statistically; $P<.001$). This high correlation between plaque counts and dementia scores is not due to the large cluster of cases with few or no plaques who were not regarded as demented. If the group of patients with low plaque counts and lacking in evidence of dementia is removed the positive correlation between plaques and dementia score is still highly significant ($P<.001$). However, among the subjects who are markedly demented no significant correlation exists between the degree of dementia and the numbers of senile plaques. The ability to cope with simple psychological tests (Test Score) also diminishes as the plaque count rises, correlations again being significant (Blessed, Tomlinson, and Roth, 1968).

Although the differences in total numbers of plaques differs significantly between the two groups, the mere figures involved only reveal part of the difference. When small numbers of plaques are present, as in the majority of normal old people (Fig. 2), although they may be found in any part of the cortex, they are only occa-

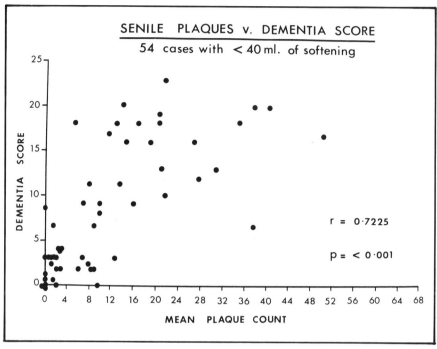

1 Relationship of dementia score to senile plaques in 54 cases with less than 40 ml of softening.

sionally found in clusters, usually at the depths of a sulcus. Probably the most consistently involved structure in normal old age is the amygdaloid complex where plaques are almost invariable if detected elsewhere in the brain. When plaques are numerous, as in about half the demented old people examined, clustering is frequent in all areas of cortex (Fig. 3). This leads to plaques lying in such close apposition that they are inseparable for counting purposes; thus when numerous plaques are present, the figures actually underestimate the involvement of the cortex. In the most severely affected cases up to one-third of the total area of cortex appears to be occupied by plaques.

A further difference is in increasing involvement of all cortical areas as the numbers of plaques increase. With small or moderate numbers (up to 10 plaques per field) the majority of plaques

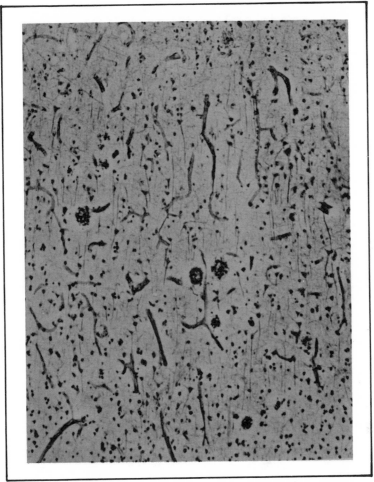

2 Appearance of senile plaques at around 8 per low-power field in the cortex of a nondemented subject. (Counts performed on circular fields) von Braunmuhl x 88

usually lie within the middle cortical layers (3 to 5) and occasional areas and a variable number of low power cortical fields (from 5 to 30% are found free of plaques. With numerous plaques, all cortical layers with the exception of the first, are heavily involved and usually no area of brain, or even a low power field can be

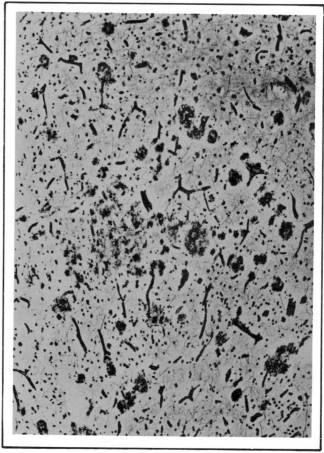

3

Appearance of senile plaques in a field containing 62 from a demented subject. In several places plaques are aggregated into large masses. von Braunmuhl x 88

found free of plaques. As a further important though less consistent difference, the intervening cortex usually appears normal in silver impregnation preparations when small or moderate numbers of plaques are present. When plaques are numerous the cortical tissue between plaques is commonly grossly abnormal, with numerous twisted, or thickened and disorderly arranged fibers. (Fig. 4) This appearance may be found in the occasional field in

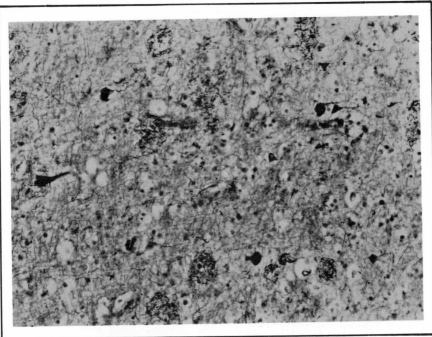

4 Neurofibrillary tangles and senile plaques in the neocortex of a demented subject. Many irregular and thickened neurofibrils are present in addition. Neurofibrillary degeneration of this severity has not been seen in a normal old subject.
Glees and Marsland x 224

cases in which the overall mean plaque count is around 10 and therefore occurs in a few sites in some nondemented subjects. Its occurrence in more than a rare field has not been seen in a non-demented case; extensive diffuse fibrillary abnormality has only been seen in demented subjects and is usually obvious and severe when the mean count is greater than 20. Indeed, two demented cases have been seen in which definable and countable plaques were few (around 5 per field) but in which all areas of cortex showed an abnormal tangle of fibers, some of which formed minute clusters which, under high-power microscopic examination, were suggestive of very small plaques. That these changes represent similar ultra-

Table II

Alzheimer's Neurofibrillary Change and G.V.D. in Old Age			
		28 Controls	50 Dements
A.N.C. in neocortex	Present	11 per cent	62 per cent
A.N.C. in neocortex	Severe	0 per cent	44 per cent
A.N.C. in hippocampus	Present	56 per cent	70 per cent
A.N.C. in hippocampus	Severe	0 per cent	36 per cent
G.V.D. in hippocampus	Present	66 per cent	83 per cent
G.V.D. in hippocampus	Severe	3 per cent	48 per cent

structural abnormalities to those found in the more readily recognized plaques seems certain. (Terry and Wisniewski, 1970)

Alzheimer's neurofibrillary change is also found to be very different in severity and distribution in the groups of normal and demented old people. (Table II) In the normal group some 50% of the cases examined showed neurofibrillary degeneration in some hippocampal neurones, and in 11% an occasional neurone affected in this way was identified in the neocortex. By comparison, in the demented subjects the hippocampus was severely involved in 36%, and neurones affected by neurofibrillary change were present within the neocortex in 62%. Furthermore, in 44% of the demented cases neurofibrillary change was present in the neocortex in an extremely severe degree, far greater than was seen in any nondemented case (Fig. 4). Thus the differences between the groups are again highly significant statistically, neurofibrillary degeneration being rare in the neocortex in normal old people or present only in a very occasional cell, but being present in more than half of demented old subjects within the neocortex and in the majority of these in very large numbers of cells.

Perhaps the most surprising finding, although it had already been stated by Woodard (1962 and 1966), was the close relationship between dementia and the presence of hippocampal pyramidal neurones showing granulovacuolar degeneration (Table II). Woodard stated that in the ventrolateral quadrant of the hippocampus 9% or more of the pyramidal cells were only involved by granulovacuolar degeneration in cases of Alzheimer's disease or senile dementia. In our observations (Tomlinson and Kitchener, 1972) the numbers of hippocampal pyramidal neurones affected in Rose's segments h_1 and h_2 were counted, these segments corresponding roughly to the better-known Sommer's sector and being only slightly different from the area examined by Woodard. In the normal group reported here, 66% of cases showed one or more cells involved in the change, but in only 10% of the nondemented subjects were approximately 9% of cells in any part of the hippocampus involved by the degeneration and in no case was 9% of cells involved throughout segments h_1 and h_2. By comparison, some cells were affected by the change in 83% of the dements, but of much greater significance is the fact that among the dements 48% of cases showed very large numbers of cells (much in excess of 9%) affected by granulovacuolor degeneration in segments h_1 and h_2.

It is apparent, therefore, that when a group of demented and normal old people are compared by the content of their so-called senile brain changes, marked and statistically significant differences exist. Fifty percent of all the demented cases were in fact sharply distinguished from any member of the nondemented group by the presence of senile plaques in large or moderate numbers throughout the cortex, and the presence of neurofibrillary tangles within the neocortex, again mostly in large numbers, but present to some degree in all cases. It was felt therefore that on the basis of pathological changes, 50% of the demented cases could be reasonably placed within the category of senile dementia of Alzheimer type, that is, cases above 65 years of age with a chronic and progressive dementing process in whom the pathological changes were closely or entirely identical with those seen in Alzheimer's presenile dementia. When the 25 cases placed in this category because of their high content of neurofibrillary degeneration and senile plaque formation are examined in relation to the degree of granulovacuolar degeneration, 80% are found to have more than 9% of cells involved by granulovacuolar degeneration in areas h_1 and h_2. In a control group (Tomlinson and Kitchener 1972) only 3% (1 out of 30 cases) of nondemented old people showed a mean of 9% of cells involved in these segments. Thus not only is the relationship of granulovacuolar degeneration in its quantitative

Table III

	28 Controls	50 Dements
Cerebral Softening in Old age		
None	29 per cent	20 per cent
< 20 mls	50 per cent	36 per cent
21- 50 mls	14 per cent	12 per cent
51-100 mos	7 per cent	14 per cent
> 100 mls	0 per cent	18 per cent
Mean softening	13.2 mls	48.9 mls
Range	0-91 mls	0-412 mls

aspect highly significant in relation to dementia in old age, but its relationship to senile dementia or Alzheimer's disease pathologically in old age is clearly established as Woodard (1962 and 1966) had previously stated.

CEREBRAL SOFTENING IN DEMENTED AND NONDEMENTED OLD SUBJECTS

The quantities of softening found in the two groups are summarized in Table III. In the nondemented group 71% showed some ischemic lesions; these were easily visible to the naked eye in 46%. In this group the total softenings ranged from 2 to 91 ml in volume with a mean of 13.2 ml. Small softenings were relatively common in the basal ganglia, thalamus, pons and cerebral hemispheres; in the latter, lesions of 1 to 5 cm across involving cortex and white matter were present in several cases. The mean volume of softening in the demented group was 48.9 ml, a quantity not statistically different from the nondemented group. Softenings of more than 20 ml volume, however, occurred in 44% of the demented group and only 21% of the controls, and in fact only 2 of 28 controls showed more than this amount. Further, the case with the largest volume of softening among the controls (and intentionally included in this group) may have shown slight evidence of a dementing process. In the whole group softening greater than 100 ml was confined to the demented cases entirely, and 9 out of the 50 showed softenings in excess of this figure. In 6 demented cases softening in excess of 100 ml was present (the range being 101 to 412 ml), unaccompanied by any evidence of a significant degree of senile change. In another 4 cases, however, softenings varying from 93 to 222 ml were present and accompanied by moderate or large numbers of senile plaques in the neocortex and neurofibrillary change.

Thus in terms of the quantity of softening found in individual brains the two groups differed in a major and significant way. Further differences which are worth noting between the two groups in relation to softening are as follows: In the dements 6 cases were present in which the whole of one or more major arterial territories was destroyed. No such case was seen among the controls. In 7 of the demented cases ischemic lesions involved the frontal lobes to a considerable degree, again a situation not encountered in the controls. Considerable softening of the hippocampus and adjacent limbic structures also occurred in 7 of the dements, and no major ischemic lesion sited in this area of the brain was found in any of the nondemented group. In addition, considerable destruction of the corpus callosum was only seen within the demented group. No demented case with lesions confined to the frontal lobe, hippocampus or corpus callosum was seen, but damage to those areas was greater in the demented group.

In those demented cases in which the only abnormality detected in the brain of any apparent morphological significance was large areas of cerebral softening, the distribution of lesions was as follows. In the first, bilateral areas of softening destroyed the lateral parieto-occipital cortex from the level of the splenium of the corpus callosum to the occipital tip and small white matter softenings were present in the frontal lobe on the left and in each temporal lobe, the total quantity of brain destroyed being 145 ml. Microscopic lesions in frontal lobes and periventricular tissues of the third ventricles were seen in addition. In the second case large parietal and temporal softenings were present on the right, and similar though smaller lesions on the left and bilateral parietal occipital softenings were also present, as well as a centimeter focus of ischemic destruction in the corpus callosum, the total destroyed brain being around 120 ml. In the third case, in which 101 ml of old softening was found, the areas destroyed were the whole of the right superior frontal convolution, much of the right basal ganglia and adjacent internal capsule and most of the left inferior occipito-temporal lobe, including the posterior two-thirds of the left hippocampus. Areas of softening 1 to 2 cm across were present in almost every coronal slice of the right parietal and occipital lobe and cerebellar and pontine softenings were also present. Microscopic lesions were found in many parts of both hemispheres. In the fourth case, in which 175 ml of softening was found, bilateral parietal ischemic lesions were present as well as areas of focal destruction from the frontal pole along almost the whole of the supero-lateral parts of both hemispheres as far as the posterior thalamic level. The greater part of the supero-lateral parieto-occipital lobe on each side was also extensively damaged and the entire corpus callosum was extremely thinned; thalamic, putamen, pontine and cerebellar softenings were also present. In the fifth case 412 ml of softening was estimated to be present. Numerous small ischemic foci of .5–1 mm across were present throughout all parts of the cortex and many in the subcortical white matter. These lesions stretched from the posterior frontal lobes to the posterior extremity of the parietal lobe, with scarcely any uninvolved tissue over this extensive territory. In this case the basal ganglia, thalamus, brain stem and hippocampus were free of ischemic lesions. In the sixth case in which 176 ml of brain was destroyed the main softening was massive and involved the entire territory supplied by the left middle cerebral artery and included destruction of the insula, the left basal ganglia and thalamus and the cerebral peduncle down to the superior colliculus. On the opposite side a small softening was found in the white matter of the posterior frontal lobe and one in the inferior parietal lobule.

One of the striking features of these 6 cases was the fact that all the softenings were readily visible to the naked eye, and in 5 of the cases large territories of the brain had been destroyed and in only one were the lesions of the multiple small cortical type, with which, in the past, so-called arteriosclerotic dementia has been frequently said to be associated.

In the 4 cases in which extensive cerebral softening and senile changes were found together, all the ischemic lesions were again macroscopically large, in 2 cases involving the entire right middle cerebral artery territory, in a third bilaterally involving the occipito-temporal lobes and in the fourth involving both parietal lobes and the left hippocampus. Thus another feature of note in the cases in which softening presumably produced or contributed greatly to the dementing syndrome is that the lesions were bilaterally large in 7 of the 10 cases, and in the cases in which softening was pre-dominantly unilateral, involved, whether by coincidence or not, the middle cerebral artery territory in all 3, though in 2 of these, extensive senile-type changes were also present.

The distribution of the massive softening in these 10 cases has been detailed not only to describe the areas of brain involved, but to emphasize the major degree of ischemic destruction which in our cases has distinguished the demented from the nondemented group. Small softenings, in the basal ganglia and elsewhere, were seen so frequently in the nondemented group as to cast grave doubt on the validity of attributing dementia to ischemia in anything but the presence of massive or very numerous, widespread lesions. On the other hand, 4 of the 10 cases with massive ischemic lesions showed significant senile changes, illustrating the inadvisability of accepting even massive ischemia as the only cause of dementia without detailed histological investigation. Further, a significant correlation exists between the degree of dementia (Dementia Score) and the quantity of softening present in the brain from a group of cases (32 in number) in which those showing moderate senile-type degeneration (more than 5 senile plaques per field) have been removed (Fig. 5).

THE PATHOLOGICAL DIAGNOSIS IN
50 DEMENTED OLD PEOPLE

Based on these findings, an attempt has been made to place into diagnostic categories the 50 demented cases analyzed in detail in relation to their morphological changes. In the first place, cases in the demented group were only placed within particular cate-gories if they showed a quantity of lesions of senile or of ischemic type which were quite outside those seen in any of the controls.

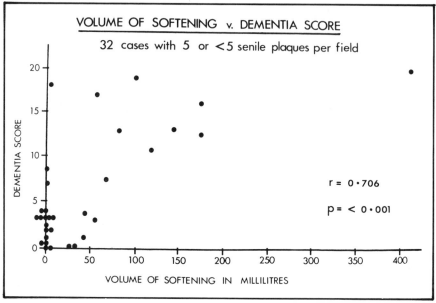

VOLUME OF SOFTENING v. DEMENTIA SCORE

32 cases with 5 or <5 senile plaques per field

r = 0·706

p = < 0·001

VOLUME OF SOFTENING IN MILLILITRES

5 Relationship of dementia score to quantity of cerebral softening in 32 cases with 5 or less than 5 plaques per field.

When this was done the 50 demented cases fall into the following groups (Tables IV and V). Fifty percent (25 of the cases) were distinguished from all controls by the presence of senile plaques in large or considerable numbers throughout the neocortex, by neurofibrillary tangles throughout the neocortex and by granulovacuolar degeneration of extreme or high degree in hippocampal pyramidal cells. These 25 cases were therefore classified as cases of senile dementia, or, in pathological terms, Alzheimer's disease in old age. Six cases showed massive cerebral softening with little senile change, and these were classifiied as cases of arteriopathic or arteriosclerotic dementia. A further 4 cases showed both extensive senile changes and massive cerebral softening, and were classified as mixed senile and arteriosclerotic dementia. Thus 35 or 70% of the total group of dements showed changes which were in excess of any seen in a single nondemented subject. A further 3 cases were thought probably to be due to arteriosclerotic dementia, since they had quantities

Table IV

	Plaques	A.N.C. in neocortex	G.V.D.	Softenings	
			Morphological Changes in 50 Demented Old People		
16	< 18 per field	Severe	Severe	Absent or as controls	
9	14 - 17 per field	Present or severe	Present or severe	Absent or as controls	
6	0 - 2 per field	None	Present (2 cases)	Severe	(101 - 412 mls)
4	9 - 18 per field	Present	Present	Severe	(92 - 222 mls)
3	0 - 2 per field	None	Present (1 case)	Considerable	(60 - 82 mls)
5	7 - 17 per field	None	Present	Considerable	(18 - 60 mls)
3	7 - 15 per field	Present (1 case)	Severe or considerable	Minimal	
2	0	None	None	None (Wernicke's encephalopathy)	
2	0 - 1 per field	None	None	None None (Trauma)	

of softening which lay within the upper limit of what has been found in the nondemented subjects but with a distribution of softening which had not been found in the nondemented group. Thus 2 of the 3 had considerable destruction of the hippocampus and all had marked ischemic destruction of the corpus callosum. A further 5 cases presented a combination of a considerable degree of ischemic and senile-type change. Again in this group bilateral hippocampal ischemia and involvement of the splenium of the corpus callosum was present in 2 cases; these cases were therefore possibly instances of mixed senile and arteriosclerotic dementia, though in terms of pure quantity of lesions the diagnosis could not be regarded as absolutely certain.

Of the remaining 7 cases one proved to be a typical example of Wernicke's encephalopathy and a second had, as the only morphological abnormality, considerable old traumatic lesions in the

Table V
Pathological Classification of Dementia in Old Age

50 Cases		Females	Males
Senile dementia (Alzheimer's disease in old age)	50 per cent	15	10
Arteriosclerotic (ischaemic) dementia	12 per cent	1	5
Mixed senile and arteriosclerotic dementia	8 per cent		4
Probably arteriosclerotic dementia	6 per cent		3
Probably mixed senile and arteriosclerotic dementia	10 per cent		5
Unclassified (possibly related to senile dementia)	6 per cent		3
Other specific causes	4 per cent		2
No morphological changes	4 per cent		2
Mean age in senile dementia (25 cases)	80 years		
Mean age in arteriosclerotic dementia (6 cases)	65 years		

frontal and temporal lobes as well as a number of small softenings. The dementia in this latter case possibly was of posttraumatic origin. Five cases were unclassified on the basis of morphological lesions, but even these presented some interesting findings; thus one case had 15.4 senile plaques throughout the neocortex and occasional neurofibrillary tangles in the neocortex with a considerable amount of granulovacuolar degeneration. It seemed likely, therefore, that this was really a case of senile dementia, but because of the similarity of the findings in this case to what had been found among the most severely affected controls, the case was not definitely classified. A further case presented a moderate number of senile plaques but no neurofibrillary tangles were found, although there was extensive bilateral hippocampal gliosis. This latter feature, which was more extreme in this case than in any other in the series, undoubtedly was a significant lesion in relation to the development of dementia or at least to severe memory defects, but in terms of a specific pathological category none was felt to be definable. Yet a third case had a moderate number of senile plaques and a considerable degree of granulovacuolar degeneration. No neurofibrillary tangles were found in the neocortex so that again this was left as an unclassified case. In 2 cases, no obvious neurological changes were detected.

To summarize the position, therefore, if one takes only quantitative findings, 70% of dements are markedly different from non-demented subjects in old age in the amount of senile change and cerebral softening present. If one takes slightly less strict quantitative criteria, a further 16% of demented subjects are classifiable as mixed senile and arteriosclerotic dementia or as arteriosclerotic dementia. In fact, on pathological grounds only 2 cases (4%) in this series showed no lesions on which a positive suggestion of etiology could not be made, and 92% of the cases are probably accounted for in terms of senile or cerebral ischemic disease on their own or in combination.

It will be observed that as in other series reported, though in which the diagnosis has not been made with relation to quantitative findings, cases of senile dementia or Alzheimer's disease form the single largest group, constituting between 50 and 80% of the total (Newton, 1948; Corsellis, 1962; Sourander and Sjögren, 1970; and Escourolle and Poirier, 1973). In our series of 50 analyzed cases senile dementia accounted for 50% on its own and was a significant factor in a further 24%. It would appear, therefore, that senile dementia of Alzheimer type is the most significant contributor to loss of intellectual function in the aged community. By contrast, only 12% of cases appeared to be demented solely as a result of massive ischemic lesions, though massive ischemia was found in another 8% and considerable ischemic lesions probably contributed to a further 16%. In Great Britain at least this pathological diagnosis of the major contribution coming from senile cerebral change is at variance with the much more frequent diagnosis of arteriosclerotic dementia on clinical grounds. The principal explanation for what appears to be the overdiagnosis of arteriosclerotic dementia is probably the fact that small strokes, a degree of hypertension or other evidences of vascular diseases are not infrequent in cases of senile dementia; even minor strokes tend to be dramatic and to be brought to the physician's notice, and often unduly influence the diagnosis; the insidious nature of the early stages of senile dementia may result in a patient in whom deterioration had been occurring over a considerable time being brought to the clinician's attention by an ischemic incident.

Analysis of this series by sex and age shows a considerable

difference in distribution of the morphological changes (Table V). Fifteen of the 16 demented female patients were, on morphological grounds, cases of Alzheimer's disease in old age, only one being of arteriosclerotic origin; by comparison not more than 13 out of 34 males were cases of Alzheimer's disease in old age uncomplicated by other changes; 8 cases showed changes of ischemic origin only, and 9 changes of senile and ischemic origin. These findings agree in general with the widely accepted view that senile dementia is more common among females (Kay et al., 1964; and Corsellis, 1969) and arteriosclerotic dementia in males (Kay 1972). The table also demonstrates that the mean age of death from senile dementia was similar in the series for males and females, but that arteriosclerotic dementia was fatal at a significantly younger age. This series of cases may well not be representative of the proportions of demented old subjects by sex and age and brain morphology in the whole community, but the finding that the majority of demented females in old age were pathologically cases of senile dementia is probably significant, as is the greater proportion of younger males with arteriosclerotic dementia.

DISCUSSION

The findings reported here were based on the detailed clinical and pathological investigation of old people dying in hospitals in which the majority of the demented group had been confined for many months or several years; most of the "controls" (the non-demented group) had been incapacitated and confined to hospital for more than several weeks. Cases were selected for pathological study only by death and autopsy permission.

It is not possible to say how the incidence of senile and arteriosclerotic dementia found in this group compares with that found among the demented population as a whole. While many demented old people occupy beds and die in psychiatric and long-stay institutions, many more, between 5 to 15% of the general population over the age of 65 years (Kay 1972), live in the community. It seems certain that the majority of these are suffering from senile or arteriosclerotic dementia alone or in combination, but the proportion of cases in these categories could differ from those found in this study. Subjects who dement from cerebral ischemia alone have large areas of cerebral softening mostly associated with severe physical disability for which hospital admission will frequently be sought and obtained in the United Kingdom. Fewer are likely to be nursed at home until death than among the senile dementia group in whom physical activity is often maintained even when the dementing process is well advanced. It seems likely, therefore, that senile dementia would be found to have an even higher incidence in the "demented" population at large than in those hospitalized, but this is not by any means certain. An attempt is being made at this time in Newcastle upon Tyne to collect quantitative clinical and pathological data on intellectually normal and demented old subjects who live in the community until shortly before death. Even this will not be a random or nonselected group and what is needed is a clinical and pathological study of *all* old people living and dying in a small town of mixed social groups, or a relatively circumscribed area of a city with a similar population structure.

At the same time quantification of cortical neurones in specified areas of brain from demented and nondemented old people using a mechanical scanning device is being attempted. Neurone loss in the cortex in senile dementia is apparently present in many cases, and the belief that such loss is the basis for dementia in these cases is widely held. Cortical neuronal loss occurs throughout life to some extent in some areas of brain (Brody, 1955), and it is important to establish whether or not the neurone counts are significantly different in normal and demented old people. The knowledge that senile plaques are essentially clusters of abnormal neuronal processes, many at synaptic level, and that neurofibrillary tangles are masses of abnormal intracytoplasmic tubules (Kidd, 1963 and 1964; Terry, 1963, Terry, Gonatas, and Weiss, 1964; and Terry and Wisniewski, 1970) raises the possibility that these structures, without neuronal loss, might induce sufficient functional abnormality to account for dementia when they are numerous and widespread. The demonstration of greatly reduced neurotransmitter activity in the brains of patients with senile dementia (Bowen et al., 1974) might well be the enzymatic counterpart of these morphological abnormalities. Of equal importance is knowledge of neurone counts in the apparently unaffected areas of brain in demented and non-demented subjects with focal ischemic lesions. The majority of cases in the series reported here as arteriosclerotic dementia showed discrete and often large cerebral softenings, and a comparison of the demented and nondemented cases suggests that the quantity of brain destroyed by focal lesions is of itself of significance in the development of dementia. In these cases, extensive microscopic examination showed ischemic lesions not detected macroscopically, but the contribution of these to the total cortical destruction appeared relatively small. Perhaps, however, large, focal, ischemic lesions are accompanied in many instances by a degree of diffuse neuronal loss of ischemic origin, only detectable by neurone counting, and the degree of the latter may be related to the quantity of brain totally destroyed by focal lesions. This attractive hypothesis requires testing. My subjective impression is that the cortex is often normal over large areas of the hemispheres in demented patients with massive focal ischemic lesions, but only the results of laborious quantitative procedures are of value in this, as in many other aspects of this difficult subject.

It should, however, be noted that if the reduction of cortical neurone population reported by Brody (1955) and Colon (1972) in normal old age is confirmed with a large group of normal people, it may not be necessary to postulate still further neurone loss to precipitate dementia if senile plaque formation is extensive, Alzheimer's neurofibrillary degeneration is severe and widespread, or infarcts have destroyed large areas of brain or smaller ischemic lesions have affected particular areas. On the present ascertained facts, the following hypothesis is advanced. Throughout adult life cortical neurones diminish in number, but only rarely are sufficient lost for dementia to occur without other changes which interfere with cerebral function. Very severe neurone loss on its own may account for those cases of dementia which show no identifiable pathological lesions. In middle and old age, however, when the neurone population has considerably declined in many people, other changes commonly occur. The most frequent of these are synaptic abnormalities (senile or dendritic plaques), intracytoplasmic abnormalties (neurofibrillary tangles), and areas of ischemic destruction. The results on intellectual functioning will depend on the summation of these various factors and on their siting. It has been shown that the severity of dementia is to some extent correlated with the number of senile plaques, the quantity of neurofibrillary tangles, and the amount of brain destroyed by ischemia. It would appear that few people remain intellectually well preserved if synaptic abnormalities (plaques) are widespread and numerous, if large numbers of neurones have abnormal cytoplasmic tubules (neurofibrillary degeneration) or if large areas of brain have been destroyed by ischemia. In a brain already considerably depleted of neurones, relatively little change of these latter types may be needed to precipitate clinical evidence of dementia; when neurone loss has been slight, much more severe changes may occur before dementia is manifest.

If this hypothesis is correct, one would expect to encounter the occasional case in which plaques, tangles or ischemic damage is present in an intellectually well preserved individual in quantities which are usually associated with dementia, and considerable variation in the degree of dementia in cases with similar quantitative change of one type. One would also expect that some evidence of the additive effect of different pathological changes might be demonstrable in an increasing degree of dementia in cases with both "senile" and ischemic lesions; Roth (1971) in an analysis of this material has produced some evidence that this is so.

It could also be that small ischemic lesions may precipitate evidence of dementia in "nondemented" old people who already have a moderate amount of "senile change," or that an individual whose intellect survives one or more ischemic attacks may become manifestly demented through the development of only moderate numbers of synaptic abnormalities or the diffuse loss of more neurones with increasing age. Thus the very considerable variation in response to similar degrees of change of any one kind may be explicable on the complexity of the morphological processes rather than on the interplay of morphological and personality factors.

The importance of the severity of synaptic abnormalities, neurofibrillary change and ischemic lesions in association with dementia in old age has been established; quantitation of cortical neurones on a large scale remains to be accomplished. Colon (1973) has produced evidence of considerable neurone loss of the inner cortical layers in 3 cases of Alzheimer's presenile dementia as compared with 2 controls. While the differences in neuronal population were marked in these cases, the need for quantitative neuronal studies in a large group of "normal" and demented old people is of importance and is likely only to be achieved by the use of automatic apparatus. An attempt to use an automated scanning and counting device is being made in Newcastle upon Tyne; preliminary results suggest the particular machine achieves considerable accuracy in total cell and large neurone counting, and that the evidence of cortical neuronal loss throughout adult life is likely to be confirmed. If a reliable and rapid method for estimating neurone populations in specified cortical areas can be devised, the effects on the numbers of cortical neurones of many different disease states may be tested.

Our studies have produced no evidence, so far, that morphological differences can be demonstrated which distinguish the brains of depressive, confused or schizophrenic patients in old age from "normal" old subjects; only that quantitative differences of the type described occur between demented and nondemented subjects across various diagnostic categories. Thus, in a group of depressive or schizophrenic old people, differences of senile and ischemic change are to be expected only if those in whom dementia supervenes are separated out from those whose intellect remains well preserved. Our present findings merely suggest that when dementia supervenes in a long-standing functional illness, the brain changes are similar to those to be found in any other group of demented old people.

Dementia is a clinical state recognized by the loss of many facets of normal cerebral functioning; many patients show evidence of marked deterioration of memory, social habits, awareness, ability to communicate and eventually almost total lack of higher cerebral function. The association of severe cerebral morphological changes with this advanced stage of cerebral function is established in the majority of cases. Many old people show evidence of decline of intellectual capacity and memory and decreasing interest and efficiency in coping with life in general, but without that degree of change to which the term "dementia" is applied. Many studies have indeed shown that memory performance declines throughout adult life. The morphological counterpart of these common and less serious accompaniments of increasing years has not, to my knowledge, been demonstrated and any attempt to do so faces enormous difficulties. Nevertheless, some clues exist to suggest that there is a connection between the normal intellectual deterioration of middle and old age and morphological change.

A series of 45 "normal" old subjects established as being free of evidence of dementia (and including the 28 discussed in this paper) have been separated into two groups. Group 1 were exceptionally well preserved (15 cases), and Group 2, though nondemented, showed minor features of intellectual decline. Senile plaque formation in the two groups differed significantly, the mean plaque count per field being 1.5 in Group 1 against 5.6 in Group 2 (p<.01 using the Mann Witney U Test). Thus the possibility exists that some of the features of "normal" aging are associated with increasing numbers of synaptic abnormalities. No significant difference was present in the quantity of ischemic change, which was almost identical in the two groups.

Also of relevance is the evidence that so-called senile changes occur in many "normal" people in the presenium (Tomlinson, 1972). This fact was elicited by the examination of the brain for plaques, tangles and granulovacuolar degeneration in 219 consecutive autopsies on cases dying suddenly outside hospital, or dying in acute medical or surgical wards or an acute geriatric assessment unit. None of these cases had been clinically assessed in life for evidence of dementia, and no attempt was made to measure ischemic destruction, which was, however, absent (on macroscopic examination) in the majority.

Senile plaques were found in the neocortex in a significant proportion of cases throughout middle age, rising from 15% in the 4th to 40% in the 6th decade (Fig. 6). In the great majority of these cases, plaque formation anywhere in the cortex was accompanied by some plaques in the hippocampus or hippocampal gyrus. By the 10th decade plaque formation was present in 75% of all subjects. Only 2 out of 71 cases below 50 years showed neurofibrillary tangles in the hippocampus, but these were present in 20% of subjects dying in the 6th decade, almost 60% in the 7th decade and 90% in the 8th. All the few cases examined in the 10th decade showed some hippocampal neurones affected by neurofibrillary tangles.

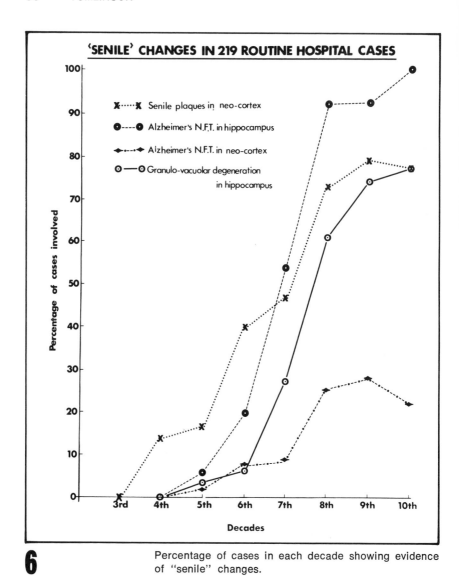

6   Percentage of cases in each decade showing evidence of "senile" changes.

Neurofibrillary tangles in the neocortex were found in very few cases by comparison with their occurrence in the hippocampus. They were seen in only 4 cases below 60 years of age out of 106 examined, and only from the 8th decade on were they present in more than 20% of subjects and in half of these, cells affected in the neocortex were few and similar in number to what may be found in proven nondemented subjects. In a total of 15 cases of the 219, many neurofibrillary tangles were present in the neocortex, accompanied by moderate or large numbers of senile plaques and, in most cases, severe granulovacuolar degeneration in hippocampal neurones. These cases, therefore, presented the morphological changes which are invariably, in our experience, accompanied by evidence of dementia of some degree. Unfortunately, the patients were not assessed for such evidence before death. The numbers found to show such changes are in themselves of interest, since the majority of these cases had been living in the community until shortly before death. Only one case, a man of 59 years, was below 65; the other 14 cases (14%) came from a total of 101 examined between 65 and 97 years of age. Fourteen percent is not greatly different from clinical estimates of subjects living in the community showing mild or severe evidences of dementia. Kay et al. (1964) found around 11% of subjects so affected in Newcastle upon Tyne. Sheldon (1948) also in England put the figure at 15%, and Essen-Moller (1966) and Neilson (1963) produced similar findings. In the general community other pathological processes probably account for a small number of cases of dementia, but it seems certain the majority of cases are of Alzheimer type. The 14% found in this group may well therefore not overestimate the proportion of such cases in the community, particularly in a hospital-based survey which included about a quarter dying in a geriatric assessment unit, for the proportion of demented patients admitted to such units in the United Kingdom is probably much in excess of this figure (Denham and Jeffreys, 1972).

Granulovacuolar degeneration, limited to hippocampal pyramidal neurones, was only found once below the age of 40 years and was present in around 5% of cases in the 6th decade; the incidence then rose steeply to 60% in the 8th decade.

Thus, in the 6th decade, 40% of people have synaptic abnormalities (plaques in the neocortex and hippocampus), 20% have neurofibrillary tangles and 5% have granulovacuolar degeneration in hippocampal neurones, all changes which, when present in the elderly in large numbers, are significantly associated with dementia. The brunt of these "senile" changes, in middle as well as late life, falls on the hippocampus, the amygdaloid complex and the hippo-

campal gyrus. Severe memory disturbances are known to follow
destructive lesions in these areas (Victor et al., 1961; Milner, 1966;
Brierley, 1966), and the question must inevitably be raised, though
without any satisfactory answer at this time, that the "senile" changes
in this area (and synaptic abnormalities elsewhere), might be the
morphological counterpart of the decline in memory which is common throughout adult life. Of course, the morphological changes
described have been found in a high proportion of cases only in
late middle age, whereas decrease in memory efficiency is demonstrable at a much earlier age in the majority. Two points, however,
should not be overlooked. Firstly, the histological studies reported
here were based (as of necessity are the great majority of brain
studies) on the examination of very minute samples of brain in
comparison with the vast territory which may be affected. The
numbers of cases affected by senile changes might well be increased
by examination of more material. Secondly, this report is based on
light microscopy. It could well be that electron microscopy will
demonstrate synaptic and intraneuronal abnormality at a much
earlier age than shown by light microscopy. Until such studies have
been performed on the human hippocampus in the 3rd and 4th
decade we shall not know the frequency of ultrastructural abnormalities at an age when memory disturbances first arise.

The possible association between minimal intellectual change
and fine morphological abnormality prompts a comment on the
crudity of the present studies. Dementia, as stated, probably only
manifests itself when severe morphological abnormalities are present, and in the majority of old people the factors which induce
the clinically demonstrable onset of dementia are multiple (diffuse
loss of cortical neurones, synaptic and intraneuronal tubular abnormalities, total destruction of one or many areas of brain by
ischemia and possibly many other factors not yet analyzed). Without decrying the importance of associations between severe clinical
and morphological states, the prime necessity for studies of the
subtler changes caused by more minor abnormalities remains. The
effects of synaptic abnormalities of the type which constitute the
important feature of the senile plaque in specific areas of brain
cannot be studied in humans. Synaptic abnormalities (plaques)
may produce no obvious changes when present in small numbers;
when present in large numbers they are found in all areas of the

cortex. Similarly large or many ischemic lesions are needed to produce dementia. Neurological abnormalities associated with discrete ischemic lesions are well documented, but studies on intellectual or psychiatric disturbances and associated ischemic lesions are not so well documented. Old age, with multiple cerebral changes almost always present, presents little possibility for assessing the intellectual effects of circumscribed ischemic lesions. Some opportunities do, however, exist for studying the effects of ischemia in people whose brains are otherwise normal, and the most promising group has not, to my knowledge, been adequately utilized.

Subarachnoid hemorrhage from rupture of an intracranial aneurysm produces death in the first several weeks in 50% of cases; of the 50% of initial survivors, many die of recurrent hemorrhage in the succeeding months or several years. Fatal subarachnoid hemorrhage is commonly accompanied by cerebral infarction (Wilson, Riggs, and Rupp, 1954; Tomlinson, 1959 and 1966; Birse and Tom, 1960; and Crompton, 1962), and there is good reason to believe that infarction has occurred in many cases who survive. The great majority of deaths occur below 60 years of age when the morphological brain changes are much less advanced than in old age. Those who survive the initial hemorrhage could well be studied intensively (as has been done by Logue et al., 1968, in a group of ruptured anterior cerebral or communicating aneurysms), and in those who die from a second hemorrhage the ischemic lesions following the initial bleed could be accurately delineated and attempts made to correlate such findings with the clinical and psychiatric assessments. Few such "experiments" can be devised on human material which are not rendered inordinately difficult by multiple factors encountered both clinically and morphologically. Only by such detailed, longitudinal studies are we likely to elucidate the more subtle aspects of the role of morphological abnormalities relating to the intellectual and personality changes which are manifest in the increasingly important (medically and socioeconomically) group of old people who suffer from dementia.

REFERENCES

Blessed, G., Tomlinson, B.E., and Roth, M.: The association between quantitative measures of dementia and of senile change in the cerebral grey matter of elderly subjects. *Brit. J. Psychiat.*, 114: 797, 1968.

Birse, S.H., and Tom, M.I.: Incidence of cerebral infarction associated with ruptured intracerebral aneurysms. *Neurology*, 10, 101, 1960.

Bowen, D.M., White, P., Flack, R.H.A., Smith, C.B., and Davison, A.N.: Brain—decarboxylase activities as indices of pathological change in senile dementia. *Lancet* (1) 1247, 1974.

Brierley, J.B.: The neuropathology of amnesic states. In Whitty, C.W.M., and Zangwill, O.L. (eds.), *Amnesia*. London, Butterworth, 1966, p. 150.

Brody, H.: Organisation of the cerebral cortex. A study of aging in the human cerebral cortex. *J. Comp. Neurol.*, 102, 511, 1955.

Colon, E.J.: The cerebral cortex in presenile dementia. A quantitative analysis. *Acta neuropath.* (Berlin), 23. 281, 1973.

Colon, E.J.: The elderly brain. A quantitative analysis in the cerebral cortex in 2 cases. *Psychiat. Neurol. Neurochir.* (Amsterdam), 75, 261, 1972.

Corsellis, J.A.N.: The pathology of dementia. *Brit. J. Hosp. Med.*, 2: 695, 1969.

Corsellis, J.A.N.: *Mental Illness and the Ageing Brain*. London, Oxford University Press, 1962.

Crompton, M.R.: The pathology of ruptured middle cerebral aneurysms with special reference to the difference between the sexes. *Lancet*, ii, 421, 1962.

Delay, J., Brion, S., Escourolle, R., and Dujarier, L.: Etude anatomique des arteres carotides et vertebrales. *Rev. neurol.*, 106: 772, 1962.

Denham, M.J., and Jefferys, P.M.: Routine Mental Testing in the Elderly. *Mod. Geriat.*, 2: 275, 1972.

Escourolle, R., and Poirier, J.: *Manual of Basic Neuropathology*. Philadelphia, W.B. Saunders Co., 1973.

Essen-Moller, E.: Individual traits and morbidity in a Swedish rural population. *Acta Psychiat. et Neurol. Scand.*, 1956. Supplement 100.

Gellerstedt, N.: Zur Kenntnis der Hirnveranderungen bei der normalena Altersinvolution. *Upsala Lak-Fören. Forh.*, 38, 193, 1933.

Hasse, G.R.: Diseases presenting as dementia. In Wells, C.E. (ed.), *Dementia*. Philadelphia, F.A. Davis Co., 1971.

Hirano, A., and Zimmerman, H.M.: Alzheimer's neurofibrillary changes; a topographic study. *Arch. Neurol.*, 7, 227. 1962.

Kay, D.W.K.: In Gaitz, C.M. (ed.), *Ageing and the Brain*. New York, Plenum Publishing Corporation, p. 15, 1972.

Kay, D.W.K., Beamish, P., and Roth, M.: Old age mental disorders in Newcastle upon Tyne, Part 1 (a study of prevalence). *Brit. J. Psychiat.*, 110: 146, 1964.

Kidd, M.: Paired helical filaments in electron microscopy in Alzheimer's disease. *Nature* (London), 197, 192, 1963.

Kidd, M.: Alzheimer's disease—an electron microscopical study. *Brain*, 87, 307, 1964.

Logue, V., Durward, M., Pratt, R.T.C., Piercy, M., and Nixon, W.L.B.: The quality of survival after rupture of an anterior cerebral aneurysm. *Brit. J. Psychiat.*, 114, 137, 1968.

Milner, B.: Amnesia following operation on the temporal lobes. In Whitty, C.W.M., and Zangwill, O.L. (eds.), *Amnesia*. London, Butterworth, 1966, p. 109.

Neilson, J.: Geronto-psychiatric period prevalence investigation in a geographically delimited population. *Acta Psychiat. Scand.*, 1963, 38, 307.

Newton, R.D.: The identity of Alzheimer's disease and senile dementia and their relationship to senility. *J. Ment. Sci.*, 94: 225, 1948.

Noyes, A.P., and Kolb, L.C.: *Modern Clinical Psychiatry*. Philadelphia, Saunders, 1963.

Post, F.: *The Clinical Psychiatry of Late Life*. Oxford, Pergamon Press, 1965.

Roth, M.: Classification and aetiology in mental disorders of old age; some recent developments. In recent developments in psychogeriatrics—An R.M.P.A. symposium, edited by Kay, D.W., and Walk, A. Special Publication No. 6. *Brit. J. Psychiat.* 1971.

Roth, M., and Hopkins, B.A.: Psychological test performance in patients over 60. Part 1: Senile psychosis and the affective disorders of old age. *J. Ment. Sci.*, 99, 439, 1953.

Rothschild, D.: The pathological changes in senile psychosis and their psychobiologic significance. *Amer. J. Psychiat.*, 93, 757, 1937.

Rothschild, D.: Neuropathologic changes in arteriosclerotic psychoses and their psychiatric significance. *Arch. Neurol. Psychiat.*, 48, 417, 1942.

Rothschild, D.: Senile psychoses and psychoses with arteriosclerosis. In Kaplan, O.J. (ed.), *Mental Disorders in Later Life*. Stanford, Calif., Stanford University Press, 1956.

Shapiro, M.B., Post, F., Lofving, B., and Inglis, J.: "Memory Function" in psychiatric patients over 60; some methodological and diagnostic implications. *J. Ment. Sci.*, 102, 233, 1956.

Sheldon, J.H.: The social medicine of old age. Published for the Trustees of the Nuffield Foundation, London, 1948.

Sourander, P., and Sjogren, H.: The concept of Alzheimer's disease and its clinical implications. In Wolstenholme, G.E.W., and O'Connor, M. (eds.), *Alzheimer's Disease and Related Conditions*. A Ciba Foundation Symposium. London, J. & A. Churchill, 11–32, 1970.

Terry, R.D.: The fine structure of neurofibrillary tangles in Alzheimer's Disease. *J. Neuropath. Exp. Neurol.*, 22, 629, 1963.

Terry, R.D., Gonatas, N.K., and Weiss, M.: Ultrastructural studies in Alzheimer's presenile dementia. *Am. J. Path.*, 44, 269, 1964.

Terry. R.D., and Wisniewski, H.: The ultrastructure of the neurofibrillary tangle and the senile plaque. In Wolstenholme, G.E.W., and O'Connor, M. (eds.), Alzheimer's disease and related conditions. A Ciba Foundation Symposium. London, J. & A. Churchill, 1970.

Tomlinson, B.E.: Brain changes in ruptured intracranial aneurysm. *J. Clin. Path.*, 12, 391, 1959.

Tomlinson, B.E.: Ischaemic lesions of the cerebral hemispheres following rupture of intracranial aneurysms. Part 1: Description of the ischaemic lesions. *Newc. Med. J.* 29, 81, 1966.

Tomlinson, B.E.: Morphological brain changes in non-demented old people. Ageing of the central nervous system. Biological and psychological aspects. Van Praag, H.M. and Kalverboer, A.F., (eds.) De Erven F. Bohn N.V., Haarlem, 1972.

Tomlinson, B.E., Blessed, G., and Roth, M.: Observations on the brains of non-demented old people. *J. Neurol. Sci.*, 7: 331, 1968.

Tomlinson, B.E., Blessed, G.. and Roth, M.: Observations on the brains of demented old people. *J. Neurol. Sci.* 11:205, 1970.

Tomlinson, B.E., and Kitchener, D.: Granulovacuolar degeneration of hippocampal pyramidal cells. *J. Path.*, 106: 165, 1972.

Victor, M., Angevine, J.B., Mancall, E.L., and Fisher, C.M.: Memory loss with lesions of the hippocampal formation. *Arch. Neurol. Psychiat.*, 5, 224, 1961.

Wang, H.S., and Busse, E.W. Dementia in old age.: In Wells, C.E. (ed.), *Dementia*. Philadelphia, F.A. Davis Co., 1971.

Wilson, G., Riggs, H.E., and Rubb, C.: The pathological anatomy of ruptured cerebral aneurysms. *J. Neurosurg*, 11, 128, 1954.

Wolf, A.: Clinical neuropathology in relation to the process of ageing. In Birren, J.E. (ed.), *The Process of Ageing in the Nervous System*. Springfield, Ill., Thomas, 1959.

Woodard, J.S.: Clinico-pathological significance of granulovacuolar degeneration in Alzheimer's disease. *J. Neuropath. Exp. Neurol.* 21: 85, 1962.

Woodard, J.S.: Alzheimer's disease in late adult life. *Amer. J. Path.* 49, 1157, 1966.

3

The Radiographic Morphology of Cerebral Atrophy

BERT LINCOLN PEAR

Senescence and senility are not synonymous. Senescence implies growing old or aging, while senility, particularly in its medical connotation, indicates a *pathological excess* of the decline which is characteristic of old age. The one is inevitable; the other, hopefully avoided.

Surprisingly little is known about the involution of the brain with senescence, since it is difficult both clinically and pathologically to distinguish between "normal" and "pathological" aging. It is stated that the weight of the human brain reaches its peak between 14 and 20 years of age and then decreases steadily by 6 to 7% of its maximum weight between ages 25 and 70, and by 8 to 9% by ages 80 to 90 years (21,22). Atrophy in excess of this is probably related to atherosclerosis or disease rather than merely to senescence. Riese studied the brain of eight patients over 90 years of age, including one centenarian, and concluded that the degree of atrophy as exemplified by decline in brain weight and extent of convolutional shrinkage was not consistently proportional to increasing age (22).

There is also debate as to whether the ventricles increase in size with age and whether involution begins after age 20, 35, 45 or even 60.

Heinrich, in 1939, found an increase in surface area of the ventricular system to be directly proportional to age. This was gradual after age 10 and more marked after ages 60 or 65 (10). Knudsen also reported an increase in average volume of the lateral ventricles in patients over 50 years of age, but significantly one-third of his patients aged 70 and 80 had the same ventricular volume as 90% of the 20 to 40 age group (14).

Burhenne and Davies noted a mean "physiological dilatation" of only 1.5 mm (4%) of the width of the lateral ventricles at the cellae mediae in patients ranging from the second to the seventh decade of life (6).

More recently Borgersen has shown a clear tendency for the third venticle to increase in width with age and his findings are similar to those of Engeset and Lönnum. In Borgersen's series of 93 patients, who ranged in age from 6 to 75, the average size of the third ventricle was 8.77 mm for the entire group, but averaged 9.88 mm in the 56 to 65 age subgroup and 10.33 mm for the 66 to 75 year age subgroup (3).

In the living these changes of senescence as well as the more drastic changes of senility are hidden by the carapace of the skull; however the morphological features can often be revealed by the varied modalities of radiological imaging.

THE IMAGING METHODS

Following its inception by Dandy in 1918, pneumoencephalography (PEG) has until recently been the principal method of visualization of the dilated ventricles, deepened sulci and widened fissures of cerebral atrophy. The advent of cerebral angiography provided opacification of the macro and micro circulation of the brain as well as delineation of the cortical substance and outline of the ventricular system by demonstration of the subependymal vessels which course within its walls.

Ultrasonic scanning has also been increasingly utilized as another method of ventricular mapping. Further sophistication in design of sonic equipment will bring additional dimension to this new modality. Pathological changes in histological structure are potentially discernible by alteration in the velocity of passage of the sound waves through brain when tumor is present or when gliosis has replaced neurons or demyelination has occurred.

Radionuclides are another form of brain imaging and also allow for physiological evaluation of cerebral blood flow and of cerebrospinal fluid dynamics.

The most recent single major quantum advance in the radiographic examination of the brain has been the development of the computerized tomogram (CT). This has been variously termed CT, CTT, CAT, and is still referred to as the "EMI" after its first prototype introduced by EMI, Ltd., in 1973.* CT provides a noninvasive, nonhazardous technic, free of the artifacts, morbidity and even mortality of pneumoencephalography. It is rapidly replacing other modalities for screening senile dementing patients for the detection of cortical and ventricular atrophy and for the presence of other organic disease.

Simply stated a narrow rotating x-ray beam passes through a succession of axial "slices" of the cranium. The variation in attenuation of the x-rays by differences in absorptive capacity of the intervening tissues is amplified and presented as a computer-printed digital display and/or as a pattern of varying light intensities on an oscilloscope which is then photographed. The manner of presentation is that of transverse rather than of coronal or sagittal anatomy as in conventional radiography. Progress is already being made to manipulate the computerized data to provide other dimensional displays.

Computerized enhancement of the varied spectrum of absorption of the CT x-ray beam allows differentiation between bone, calcium, extravasated blood, circulating blood, gray matter, white matter, cerebrospinal fluid, edema fluid and fat. The ventricular system, the fissures and sulci, and the varying densities of gray

---

*CT for computed tomography, a term recently adopted at a users' conference held at the Montreal Neurological Institute; CTT, computerized transverse tomography; CAT, computerized axial tomography; and EMI, Electronic Musical Instruments, Ltd.

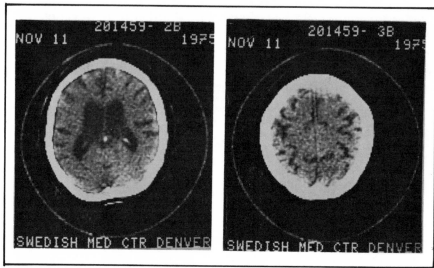

1 Two CT axial slices clearly delineate lateral ventricular dilatation (left) and gyral atrophy with sulcal deepening (right). The higher slice demonstrates the "walnut" appearance of cerebral atrophy. Some individuals may show predominantly central and others predominantly cortical atrophy, but this case illustrates both. (Through the kindness of Drs. Seibert & Swanson, Neuroradiology Section of Radiology: Drs. Freed, Gaylord, Jobe, Seibert & Associates, Swedish Medical Center, Denver, Colorado.)

and white matter can be visualized without the addition of air (Fig. 1). Distinction between vascular and avascular masses is achieved by intravenous perfusion of iodinated contrast media. By this method alone, or in combination with other radiographic imaging modalities, the diagnosis of atrophy—or of those entities which are masked by or mimic it—can be established.

CEREBRAL ATROPHY

The radiographic appearance of cerebral atrophy is unrelated to its cause. Occasionally accompanying roentgen findings, such as a depressed skull fracture or an arteriovenous malformation, reveals the underlying etiology.

Cerebral atrophy is usually rather simplistically classified as either central or cortical. The two may be combined and can be either generalized or focal (17).

Central or ventricular atrophy results in dilatation of the lateral and third ventricles.

The size and the capacity of the normal ventricles of the brain has been reasonably established by a variety of methods, possibly the most reliable being the ventricular casts of Last and Tompsett. Utilizing the brains of 24 adult cadavers, they found the combined volume of the lateral ventricles of the smallest cast to be 7.4 ml and that of the largest 56.6 ml, with an average of 22.4 ml. The additional volume of the third ventricle, aqueduct and fourth ventricle was subsequently estimated as varying between 0.8 to 1.7 ml (5,15).

Knudsen determined the ventricular volume of 183 grossly normal brains by measuring the air escaping from the ventricles when immersed in water (14). He found the average volume of the two lateral ventricles to be 14 ml, the third and fourth ventricles together 1.5 ml, with an average combined capacity of 15.5 ml for the system. Rarely did the volume of the two lateral ventricles exceed 30 ml.

When Bull disregarded the four casts of Last and Tompsett which exceeded 30 ml, the average total capacity of the remaining 20 "normal" ventricular casts was 16.8 ml (5). This corresponds closely to the 15.5 ml recorded by Knudsen.

Norms of ventricular dimensions have been proposed based upon PEG, angiographic and sonic studies (Tables I and II). These are useful, although they suffer from dissimilarities in technic, differences in roentgen image magnification related to target-film distance and to variations in patient selection. In general, "normal" patients rarely come to pneumoencephalography or cerebral angiography.

Ultrasonic measurements are related directly to a scale shown on the cathode screen. In CT scanning the true dimensions can be obtained by multiplying the photographic image by a factor of about 3 depending upon machine calibration. These methods give unmagnified images which are comparable to actual ventricular size.

In their article confirming the validity of CT critera for the evaluation of cerebral atrophy, Huckman, Fox and Topel used both subjective and objective standards for determining ventricular and cortical atrophy. In measuring ventricular size they added the width

Table I.
PEG Criteria of Ventricular Size

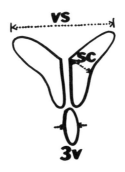

VS - Ventricular breadth at the cellae mediae

40 mm	upper limit of normal	Davidoff & Dyke, 1946
40 mm	upper limit of normal	Bruijn, 1969
44 mm	upper limit of normal	Robertson, 1957
45 mm	upper limit of normal	Burhenne & Davis, 1963
40 mm	normal	
40-44 mm	slight atrophy	Willanger et al, 1958
45-49 mm	moderate atrophy	
50 mm	severe atrophy	

SC - Septum-caudate line

15 mm	upper limit of normal	Schatski & Troland, 1947
15 mm	upper limit of normal	Engeset & Lonnum, 1958
>15 mm	normal	
15-16 mm	slight atrophy	Willanger et al, 1958
17-18 mm	moderate atrophy	
>19	severe atrophy	

Transverse diameter of third ventricle

6-8 mm	normal	Davidoff & Dyke, 1946
5-10 mm	normal	Borgersen, 1966
<6 mm	normal	
6-8 mm	slight atrophy	Willanger et al, 1958
9-11 mm	moderate atrophy	
<12 mm	severe atrophy	

Sulcal width

< 3 mm	normal	
> 3 <5 mm	slightly widened	Willanger et al, 1958
> 5 mm	greatly widened	

Rounding of ventricular corners

Table II.
Some Angiographic Criteria of Ventricular Enlargement

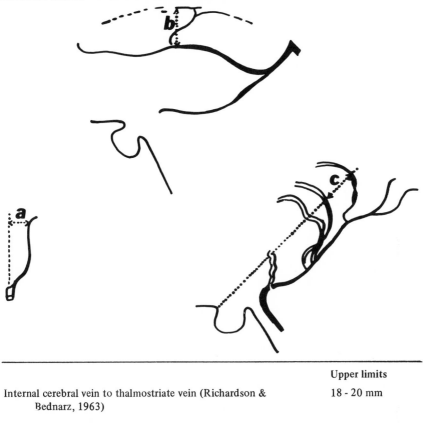

	Upper limits
Internal cerebral vein to thalmostriate vein (Richardson & Bednarz, 1963)	18 - 20 mm
Peripheral ramifications of caudate & thalmostriate veins to internal cerebral vein at or just behind venous angle (Stears & Sanders, 1970)	18 - 20 mm
Lateral posterior choroidal to posterior pericallosal (splenial) arteries (Galloway, Greitz & Sjogren, 1964)	21 mm

of a line "A" drawn between the most lateral portion of each frontal horn and a line "B" representing the width of the lateral ventricles in the region of the caudate nuclei. The resultant sum determined in mm on the photograph was then utilized as an index of ventricular size (12).

Bull had previously expressed the opinion that the single most satisfactory linear measurement relating to ventricular volume is the minimum thickness of the body of the lateral ventricle which he found to be the width of the ventricular floor. He also showed that measurement of the span of the frontal horns is of little value (5). This he illustrated by the almost identical spread of the anterior horns of Last and Tompset's third largest cast and their smallest cast, although the one had a ventricular volume of 55.3 ml and the other a volume of only 7.4 ml. The single measurement of line "B" may become an important linear determinant of ventricular volume by CT.

The PEG measurement of maximal breadth of both lateral ventricles at the plane of the cellae mediae also correlates with ventricular volume (4,6). Burhenne and Davies refer to this as ventricular span (VS). The upper limits of normality for VS varies with investigator and ranges from 40 to 45 mm (Table I). This gives a better insight into ventricular capacity than the ventricular index, which is maximum internal cranial breadth divided by maxmum ventricular span at the cellae mediae.

A comparable linear dimension is obtained in the venous phase of the AP cerebral angiogram by measuring the horizontal distance from the center of one internal cerebral vein to the ipsolateral thalmostriate vein where it curves laterally or fades (23). The normal value for each ventricle does not exceed 20 mm. As a corollary to this, Sears, Miller and Kilgore have noted that in cases of atrophy the curve of the thalmostriate vein is greatly widened and becomes convex rather than concave laterally due to loss of brain substance (25). This they liken to "short horns" when both sides are visualized. They, among others, have noted the manner in which the lateral ventricles become visualized as negative shadows against the opacified brain substance during the "cerebrogram" (i.e., capillary) phase of angiography.

Ventricular height is measured directly during PEG, but is also discernible during the venous phase of the lateral cerebral angiogram by the method of Stears and Sanders (28).

Mensuration is made of the vertical distance from the superior edge of the internal cerebral vein, at or just behind the venous angle, to the smallest peripheral ramifications of the caudate and thalmostriate veins where they are seen as dots on end or lines in the subependymal layer of the superior surface of the lateral ventricle. Normal ventricular height by this method is 18 mm or less, and should not exceed 20 mm (value uncorrected for a magnification of 1.13).

Ventricular dilatation is also recognized on the lateral vertebral angiogram as an increase in the distance between the lateral posterior choroidal arteries within the choroid fissure and the posterior pericallosal (splenial) arteries within the cistern of the corpus callosum. This is calculated along a line connecting the tuberculum sellae to the most posterior radius of these vessels as they arch forward. The measurement represents an estimate of the height of the body of the lateral ventricle situated between the thalamus and the corpus callosum (8). Ventricular dilatation is present when this exceeds 21 mm.

Ventricular measurements are of definite value in neuroradiology particularly as a guide to the inexperienced and uncertain. They are of less value to the experienced observer who recognizes the gestalt of brain atrophy and considers not only size but configuration of the ventricles in conjunction with the appearance of the sulci, fissures and cisterns.

CORTICAL ATROPHY

Cortical atrophy results in deepening and widening of the sulci and fissures and the appearance of the brain resembles a shrunken walnut. The atrophy may be focal or globar.

Normal sulcal width is less than 3mm. Moderate atrophy is considered present when the width is between 3 and 5 mm, and the atrophy is severe when the width exceeds 5 mm.

Evaluation of fissural widening is much more subjective but nonetheless real. The cisterns are of lesser value in the determination of atrophy, since there is a marked variation in cisternal configuration.

Delineation of sulcal width requires meticulous pneumoencephalographic technic as has been described by both Lindgren and Robertson (17, 24). Occasionally incomplete or complete air block occurs over the atrophic brain possibly because of leptomeningeal changes. CT scanning more easily reveals sulcal and fissural enlargement, and the higher tomographic cuts graphically display the deepened sulci and narrowed gyri of atrophy.

As the mantle of the brain diminishes in size, there is an increased subarachnoid space between the inner table of the skull and the atrophic brain. This can be seen by PEG and by CT, but is also visualized as an avascular zone at cerebral angiography where it must be distinguished from acute subdural hematoma. Since no pressure changes are present in atrophy, when the avascular zone is unilateral there will be no displacement of the pericallosal artery or it will be shifted to the atrophic side. This differentiation cannot be made if the zones are bilateral and equal, but can again be made if they are unequal and the artery remains in the midline (1).

ATROPHY AND DEMENTIA

The question as to whether there is a statutory age of senility is a legal as well as a medical one. Older workers are challenging employers on the issue of forced retirement and the Supreme Court has agreed to hear the case of a police lieutenant made to retire at the mandatory age of 50 (32).

The *Wall Street Journal* quotes Cyril Brickfield, legal counsel for the American Association of Retired Persons: "A person is constitutionally entitled to work, and the test of whether he is able to do so shouldn't be that he happened to turn 65."

To this Bernard Hirsh, general counsel of the American Medical Association, added: "We don't believe there is any statutory age of senility. A man may be in fine health at age 70 or poor health at 35. People don't age uniformly."

Nonetheless there is an unescapable, even if limited, correlation between atrophy—particularly cortical atrophy—and age (34).

In 1954, Engeset and Lönnum reported, in Swedish, on the clinical and PEG findings in 50 cases of cerebral atrophy. They noted that 13 of 14 patients with a third ventricle over 9 mm in width were unable to work. This was also true of 12 of 15 patients with a lateral ventricle more than 20 mm in width and of all of 8 patients with a lateral ventricle measuring more than 25 mm. In 1958, they extended their study to 100 patients with a third ventricle measuring 12 mm or more in width by PEG. When the degree of incapacity for work was used as an indicator of the patient's condition, they found that 88 percent of patients with that extent of third ventricular dilatation had completely lost their working capacity (7).

Within the context of their study, they found a definite correlation between the transverse diameter of the third ventricle and the septum-caudate measurement also seen on the brow-up of PEG.

In 1955, Gosling investigated the value of PEG in the dementias of middle life (9). The dementia was judged clinically from a perusal of the patients' records and was rated as slight, moderate or marked depending upon the history. Gosling's PEG criteria for cerebral atrophy were cortical sulci greater than 5 mm, air trapped in the insular cortex, enlargement of one or both lateral ventricles particularly marked in the region of the trigone whether or not they were enlarged elsewhere. He found that 85% of 68 cases of unexplained senile dementia showed cerebral atrophy by those standards. In an additional 213 cases where PEG was performed in the absence of dementia, 11% showed an unexpected atrophy.

These initial studies have been followed by those of Kiev and his associates, by Burhenne and Davies, and by the three papers in which Nielsen, Willanger, Peterson and Thygesen have participated (6, 13, 19, 20, 34).

Disregarding damage to brain tissue in such well-defined sites causing impairment of so-called lower-level functions such as motor and sensory losses and the various aphasias, Kiev and his colleagues found that the degree of impairment of what they have termed the "highest integrative functions"* was related approximately to the amount of enlargement of the ventricles of the brain. In accordance with a unitary or holistic concept, they concluded that the degree of impairment of these higher functions is directly related to the total number of damaged cortical neurons whether they be aggregated in one area or diffusely distributed throughout the hemispheres.

*Highest integrative functions, i.e., capacity for the expression of needs, appetites, and drives; the mechanisms for goal achievement; the capacity to initiate, organize and maintain appropriate adaptive reactions; and the capacity to maintain organization during stress and to recover promptly from its effects. (13).

Burhenne and Davies related dementia with ventricular span (VS)—the maximal breadth of the lateral ventricles at the plane of the cellae mediae (6). They reviewed a series of 500 cerebral air studies interpreted as being radiographically normal and found the VS to range from 29 mm to 45 mm with an ideal curve of normal frequency distribution on the histogram. In another series of 500 air studies with ventricles considered dilated and with a radiological diagnosis of brain atrophy, 93.5% had a VS of 45 mm or more. Four and a half percent of the radiographically normal group and 57% of the abnormal group were demented. They concluded that a patient with a VS larger than 45 mm has a 2.5% chance of being normal and a patient with a VS smaller than 45 mm has a 6.5% chance of having generalized brain atrophy.

A most comprehensive study of the relationship between ventricular and cortical atrophy and of both to intellectual impairment has been conducted by Nielson, Petersen, Thygesen and Willanger (19, 20). This was finalized in a lengthy correlative article by the same four with Willanger as the principal author (34). They embarked upon their work, despite misgivings, because they were convinced of a correlation between linear ventricular measurements and ventricular volume.

Three ventricular measurements were chosen: 1) the width of the third ventricle, 2) the width of the two lateral ventricles (VS), and 3) the height of the lateral ventricles (septum-caudate line). These were categorized as showing no, slight, moderate and severe atrophy on the basis of size (Table I). Cortical atrophy was also graded by the width of the individual sulci and the extent of the atrophy whether local or globar. The degree of atrophy was correlated with tests for intellectual impairment graded in multiple levels from none to severe.

They found the relationship between ventricular atrophy to cortical atrophy to be too capricious to suggest that one form of atrophy definitely indicated atrophy of the other. The ventricular system was either normal or only slightly dilated in about half of patients with the three most severe degrees of cortical atrophy. Cortical atrophy, to a greater extent than ventricular atrophy, was a function of age or of the disorders leading to the hospital admission of aged patients. They concede that possibly this relates to the fact that the normal elderly are not patients but remain productively at home.

Both atrophy and intellectual deficit did relate to age. It appears that the older patient does not escape intellectual impairment even though his atrophy is only moderate, while the younger patient may escape similar impairment even when his atrophy is considerable.

As in the other studies, they encountered a few patients in whom intellect was well preserved despite the presence of considerable atrophy but no patient with severe intellectual impairment where PEG did not reveal some atrophy.

The authors concluded that "as a whole the group showed a high level of correlation between the degree of intellectual impairment and cerebral atrophy; this was closer for cortical than for ventricular atrophy, and closest for the index of combined cerebral atrophy (34).

Nonetheless, despite the relevance of these close correlations, even in these studies 4% of those patients in the most atrophic half had no intellectual impairment and a further 18% had doubtful impairment.

COMPUTERIZED TOMOGRAPHY

Following the introduction of computerized tomography (CT), Huckman, a radiologist, collaborated with Fox and Topel, neurologists, in an evaluative study of the comparison of CT with the results of pathologic and PEG finding in the examination of the brains of demented and nondemented patients over 60 years of age (12). Two groups were used. The first group consisted of 35 patients with a clinical diagnosis of senile dementia as determined by the two neurologists. The second group consisted of 48 patients also over age 60 from 300 consecutive patients of all ages undergoing CT but not personally examined by the authors. Twenty of the latter had no major neurological problem; twelve had confusion or dementia by history, and 26 had other major neurological problems.

Sixty-nine percent of the demented patients over the age of 60 years in the first group had either dilated ventricles or moderate to severe atrophy by CT criteria; but, significantly, 20% had either no or questionable atrophy and an additional 11% only mild atrophy. Of the 12 patients in the second group with confusion or dementia by chart review, 50% had enlarged ventricles or moderate to severe atrophy, and of the patients with no major neurological problem by history, 15% had moderate to severe atrophy (12).

The authors contrasted their findings with two pathological studies of Tomlinson, Blessed and Roth in which there was moderate to severe increase in ventricular size in 70% of pathologically examined brains of demented old people, but similar increase in ventricular size in 40% of brains of normal old people (29, 30).

It is apparent that there is indeed a correlation between dementia and the presence and degree of atrophy as determined by CT and PEG, particularly in the aged. The correlation, however, does not apply without exception to the individual patient and there are significant numbers of nondemented patients with atrophy, and all patients with atrophy are not demented.

DIFFERENTIAL DIAGNOSIS

Radiological imaging becomes most important when it promotes a search for potentially treatable causes of dementia when there is absence of brain atrophy in a senile patient.

Numerous organic afflictions of the aged can result in dementia. These include subdural hematoma, brain tumor, occlusive, thrombotic and embolic cerebrovascular disease among others. The technics and criteria for their radiological diagnosis are clearly beyond the scope of this chapter.

More pertinent is the often confusing differential diagnosis between the atrophic brain (hydrocephalus ex vacuo) and pressure hydrocephalus; and between cerebral atrophy and normal-pressure hydrocephalus.

PRESSURE HYDROCEPHALUS

The distinction between hydrocephalus ex vacuo due to atrophy and pressure hydrocephalus due to obstruction may become difficult if the atrophy is central or ventricular and resembles hydrocephalus secondary to obstruction in the posterior fossa.

An everted anterior medullary velum has been described as one PEG sign of obstruction located distal to the fourth ventricle.

Also in pressure hydrocephalus the width of the temporal horns have been found to increase relatively more than the width of the cellae mediae of the lateral ventricles (27). Sjaastad and colleagues found a mean cella media/temporal horn ratio of 2:27 in pressure hydrocephalus as contrasted to 4:56 in hydrocephalus ex vacuo. They felt that a ratio of 3:0 best separated the two disorders with approximately 15% of pressure cases and 84% of atrophy exceeding this.

The third ventricle/temporal horn width ratio was also meaningful, and the figure 1:7 best separated the two disorders. The mean ratio for atrophy in their series was 2:97 and for pressure hydrocephalus 1:17, with approximately 8% of each group on the inappropriate side.

Atrophy can be recognized angiographically by an increased distance between the thalmostriate vein to the ipsilateral middle cerebral vein on the anteroposterior phlebogram when the anterior cerebral arterial branches are not stretched on either the anteroposterior or lateral arterial films. The anterior cerebral branches and middle cerebral sylvian branches show a normal or even increased number of curves. The sylvian point and the internal cerebral vein and vein of Galen remain in normal position (2).

This contrasts with hydrostatic or pressure hydrocephalus where the normal curvature of the anterior cerebral arteries is straightened and the sylvian group of the middle cerebral vessels show less tortuosity and even curve outward. The posterior portion of the sylvian fissure is usually elevated as the bodies of the lateral ventricles expand. The insula to vault distance relates to the degree of hydrocephalus and as the lateral ventricles increasingly dilate it decreases to less than one-third of the distance from the vault to the midline.

NORMAL-PRESSURE HYDROCEPHALUS

Normal-pressure hydrocephalus (NPH) is now included among the causes of presenile and senile dementia. Its clinical features characteristically but not exclusively consist of dementia, ataxia and urinary incontinence associated with normal cerebrospinal fluid pressure.

NPH appears to be a syndrome probably due to arachnoid thickening secondary to trauma, surgery, subarachnoid hemorrhage, meningitis or even tumor. Frequently no apparent etiology is discovered but any process capable of blocking the flow of cerebrospinal fluid to the sites of its reabsorption can result in this syndrome which basically is a form of obstructive hydrocephalus—so-called communicating hydrocephalus.

Differentiation between cerebral atrophy and NPH is essential, since the latter may benefit from shunting if irreversible changes have not occurred.

Radiographic diagnostic criteria have been proposed and these are fundamentally those of obstructive hydrocephalus as described above.

The angiographic manifestations are that of an "active" hydrocephalus and include stretching of the pericallosal artery over the corpus callosum. Because of concentric bulging of the lateral ventricular walls the thalmostriate veins resemble "parentheses" rather than the "short-horns" of atrophy (11).

Generalized ventricular dilatation is found at PEG and the aqueduct and fourth ventricle are more distended than in patients with atrophy. An occasional patient may clearly show dilatation of their basilar cisterns with an abrupt block and absence of air over the cerebral hemispheres.

Statistically significant further dilatation of the frontal horns of the lateral ventricles has been observed on a 24-hour PEG in patients with both cerebral atrophy and NPH and is therefore of no differential diagnostic significance in distinguishng between the two; however, when cortical atrophy is present it is more clearly demonstrated on the 24-hour films than on the initial filling films (18).

LeMay and New have emphasized that in normal subjects the roofs of the anterior horns of the lateral ventricles normally lie below the falx and the angle formed by their roofs on the brow-up anteroposterior PEG is usually between 130° and 140°. With increased hydrostatic pressure of NPH, the ventricles distend until the corpus callosum reaches the lower edge of the falx cerebri while the lateral ventricles continue to rise resulting in a smaller corpus callosum angle of 120° or less (16). All of their patients who responded well to surgical shunting had a corpus callosum angle of 120° or less.

Further differentiation can be achieved by isotope cisternography. Normally when an appropriate nuclide, usually now chelated Ytterbium 169, is injected into the lumbar subarachnoid space it consistently sequentially fills the cisterna magna, medullary and ambient cisterns and then proceeds to the suprasellar and quadrigeminal plate cisterns by three and four hours. The isotope passes over the cerebrum and outlines the convexity of the brain by twelve to twenty-four hours. Concentration occurs along the superior sagittal sinus and most of the isotope clears by forty-eight hours.

Patients with NPH generally demonstrate ventricular filling and little radioactivity over the surface of the cerebral convexity. In patients in whom cerebral atrophy was predominant, the isotope does not reflux into the ventricles.

Heinz, Davis and Karp correlated the PEG with isotope cisternography and found the cisternogram to usually be normal if the air study is normal or if there is a large amount of air within widened sulci. When the air study demonstrates an extraventricular block, the cisternogram will also be positive and ventricular reflux present (11). They suggest that cisternography is most useful when the other studies are borderline.

CT plays an extremely important role in the differential diagnosis of dementia, since it readily discerns deformations, displacements and obstructions of the ventricular system as well as those disease processes which alter tissue density.

Cerebral atrophy is suggested when there is dilatation of the lateral and third ventricles with accompanying enlargement of the sulci, fissures and cisterns. As with PEG, central atrophy or cortical atrophy may predominate in the individual case, but the atrophic nature of the process is evident by a decrease in parenchymal volume.

SUMMARY

Cerebral atrophy is the result of a varied group of diseases as well as of the involution of aging. There is a general correlation between senescence and increase in ventricular and sulcal size. Particularly, cortical atrophy appears more related to age than does ventricular enlargement. Increasing age also seems to accelerate the intellectual decline due to brain atrophy, but at all ages there are considerable numbers of individuals to whom this does not apply.

There is also a close correlation between cerebral atrophy as demonstrated by radiological technics and intellectual impairment, but again there are numbers of aged patients with dementia and no atrophy and others with atrophy and no dementia.

Others, as well as I, have quoted the late Robert Wartenberg: "There is no strict parallelism between the volume of the brain and the mental capacity of the individual. The encephalographic method, valuable as it is, is too crude to serve as a gauge for the possible impairment of the mental state" (33).

The same seems true of angiography, ultrasonography and CT.

(Interestingly, it was also Wartenberg who quoted Pope Julius III, who supposedly said: "It is unbelievable with how little wisdom the world is governed.")

The role of radiological imaging is to determine if the appearance of the brain of the demented, aged patient is consonant with cerebral atrophy, and if not, to exclude other radiographically recognizable causes of dementia, particularly when these are treatable.

Computerized tomography (CT) appears to be the simplest single radiological screening modality for accomplishment of these goals.

REFERENCES

1. Bergstrom, K., Lodin H.: Angiography in senile cerebral atrophy. *Acta Radiol Diagnosis*, 4: 187–192, 1966.
2. Boller, F., LeMay, M., Wright, R.L.: Diagnosis and differentiation of various types of hydrocephalus in adults by angiography. *Br. J. Radiol.*, 43: 384–390, 1970.
3. Borgersen, A.: Width of third ventricle: Encephalographic and morbid anatomical study. *Acta Radiol Diagnosis*, 4: 645–661, 1966.
4. Bruijn, G.W.: *Pneumoencephalography in the Diagnosis of Cerebral Atrophy: A quantitive study.* Utrecht, H.J. Smits, 1959.
5. Bull, J.W.D.: The Robert Wartenberg Memorial Lecture: The volume of the cerebral ventricles. *Neurol.* 11: 1–9.

6. Burhenne, H.J., Davies, H.: The ventricular span in cerebral pneumography. *Am. J. Roentgenol,* 92: 1176–1164, 1963.
7. Engeset, A., Lönnum, A.: Third ventricles of 12 mm width or more. *Acta radiol.* 50: 5–11, 1958.
8. Galloway, J.R., Greitz, T., and Sjögren, S.E.: Vertebral angiography in the diagnosis of ventricular dilatation. *Acta Radiol. Diagnosis,* 2: 321–333, 1964.
9. Gosling, R.H.: The association of dementia with radiologically demonstrated cerebral atrophy. *J. Neurol. Neurosurg. Psychiat.* 18: 129–133, 1955.
10. Heinrich, A., quoted by Borgersen (3) and Gosling (9).
11. Heinz, E.R., Davis, D.O., Karp, H.R.: Abnormal isotope cisternography in symptomatic occult hydrocephalus. *Radiol.* 95: 109–120, 1970.
12. Huckman, M.S., Fox, J., and Topel, J.: The validity of criteria for the evaluation of cerebral atrophy by computed tomography. *Radiol.* 116: 85–92, 1975.
13. Kiev, A., Chapman. L.F., Guthrie, T.C., and Wolff, H.G.: The highest integrative functions and diffuse cerebral atrophy. *Neurol.* 12: 385–393, 1962.
14. Knudsen, P.A.: Ventriklernes strorrelsesforhold i anatomisk normale hjerner fra voksne mennesker. Thesis, Copenhagen. Andelsbogtrykkeriet, Odense, 1958.
15. Last, R.J., Tompsett, D.H.: Casts of cerebral ventricles. *Brit. J. Surg.* 40: 525–543, 1953.
16. LeMay, M., New, P.F.: Radiological diagnosis of occult normal-pressure hydrocephalus. *Radiol.* 96: 347–358, 1970.
17. Lindgren, E.: Encephalography in cerebral atrophy. *Acta Radiol.* 35: 277–291, 1951.
18. Moseley, I.F., Sondheimer, F.K.: The twenty-four hour pneumoencephalogram: with particular reference to ventricular size. A series of 150 patients and a review of the literature. *Clin. Radiol.* 26: 389–405, 1975.
19. Nielsen, R., Petersen, O. Thygesen, P., and Willanger R.: Encephalographic ventricular atrophy. Relationships between size of ventricular system and intellectual impairment. *Acta Radiologica Diagnosis,* 4: 240–256, 1966.
20. Nielsen, R., Petersn, O., Thygesen, P., and Willanger R.: Encephalographic cortical atrophy. Relationships to ventricular atrophy and intellectual impairment. *Acta Radiologica Diagnosis,* 4: 437–448, 1966.
21. Pakkenberg, H.L., and Voigt, J.: *Acta Anat.* 56: 297–307, 1964.
22. Riese, W.: Weight, atrophy and repair in the very old human brain. Findings in the brain of eight patients over 90 years of age. In van Bogaert, L., Radermecker, J. (ed.), *First International Congress of Neurological Sciences* (Vol. IV). London, Pergamon Press, 1959.
23. Richardson, H.D., Bednarz, W.W.: The depiction of ventricular size by the striothalmic vein in the anteroposterior phlebogram. *Radiol.,* 81: 604–609, 1963.

24. Robertson, E.G.: *Pneumoencephalography*. Springfield, Illinois, Charles C. Thomas, 1957.

25. Sears, A.D., Miller, J.E., and Kilgore, B.B.: Diagnosis of cerebral atrophy from the anteroposterior carotid phlebogram. *Am. J. Roentgenol.* 85: 1128–1133, 1961.

26. Shah, S.H., and Kendall, B.: Elucidation of the cause of raised intracranial pressure by angiography with special reference to the deep venous system. *Brit. J. Radiol.*, 44: 245–257, 1971.

27. Sjaastad, O., Skalpe, I.O., and Engeset, A.: The width of the temporal horn in the differential diagnosis between pressure hydrocephalus and hydrocephalus ex vacuo. *Neurol.*, 19: 1087–1093, 1969.

28. Stears, J.C., and Sanders, B.B.: Angiographic evaluation of lateral ventricular size. Presented at Ninth Symposium Neuroradiologicum, Gothenberg, Sweden, August 1970 (not published).

29. Tomlinson, B.E., Blessed, G., Roth, M.: Observations on the brains of non-demented old people. *J. Neurol. Sci.* 7: 331–356, 1968.

30. Tomlinson, B.E., Blessed, G., and Roth, M.: Observations on the brains of demented old people. *J. Neurol. Sci.*, 11: 205–242, 1970.

31. Vinken, P.J., and Strackee, J.: The relation between ventricular breadth and cranial breadth in the pneumoencephalogram. *Psychiat. Neurol. Neurochir.*, 63: 17–22, 1960.

32. *Wall Street Journal*, Monday, October 13, 1975, p. 1.

33. Wartenberg, R.: Experiences in use of encephalography. *J. Nerv. Ment. Dis.* 89: 640–645, 1939.

34. Willanger, R., Thygesen, P., Nielsen, R., and Petersen, O.: Intellectual impairment and cerebral atrophy. A psychological, neurological and radiological investigation. *Danish Medical Bulletin*, 15: 65–93, 1968.

4

Vascular Disease and Dementia in the Elderly

MICHAEL D. O'BRIEN

Dementia is not a diagnosis, it is a sign or symptom with many identifiable causes. It is, therefore, absolutely essential to consider dementia on an etiological basis. The old classification into senile or presenile dementia is meaningless and should be abandoned, since it is based on age alone and has no pathological connotation. Certainly, this classification cannot be used as a basis for studies of cerebral blood flow and metabolism.

Alzheimer's disease is a pathological diagnosis and it may occur at any age. Similarly, dementia of known etiology, as may occur in some deficiency states (myxoedema, B12, B6) infections (syphilis, Jacob-Creutzfeldt disease) due to mechanical factors (low pressure hydrocephalus) or due to a genetic abnormality (Huntington's chorea) may also present at any age and these patients should be recognized and treated accordingly when they occur in the elderly; patients should never be abandoned with the label "senile dementia." When all the definable causes of dementia have been eliminated, there remain the primary cellular degenerations commonly found in old age. Most of these are Alzheimer's disease, but there is almost inevitably some degree of degenerative vascular disease.

There has been much debate in recent years about the role of vascular disease in the development of dementia. At one time most patients were diagnosed as having "arteriosclerotic dementia" even though the pathological evidence has not supported this for more than half a century. Recently it has been suggested that vascular disease plays only a very small role and then only by the production of multiple infarcts (Hachinski et al., 1974). It is probably as much a mistake to label all dementia as due to a primary cellular degeneration as to ascribe all cases to vascular disease. Vascular disease may not be the most important etiological factor numerically, but there is clear evidence that it is the cause of dementia in at least one-fifth of cases and contributes to the development of the condition in at least a further one-fifth; it is likely that these percentages increase with age.

It is important to define the role of vascular disease even when it is not the sole cause of dementia, because of the possibility of appropriate treatment, and it is also important to define the way in which vascular disease causes dementia, since this, too, will affect management. There are two possible mechanisms, by multiple infarcts with either sufficient destruction of brain tissue to cause dementia or by their critical location within the brain, or secondly, by a more generalized ischemia. These possibilities are not mutually exclusive and both mechanisms may apply in the same patient. Corsellis (1962) found that 50% of demented patients had moderate to severe large or small vessel degeneration. Is this an important factor or it is merely coincidental?

The differentiation of dementia due to primary cellular degeneration from those secondary to vascular disease may be considered from three aspects: clinical features, pathological evidence and cerebral blood flow changes with studies of cerebral metabolism.

1. *Clinical.* It may be possible to differentiate between a primary cellular degeneration and dementia secondary to vascular disease

on purely clinical grounds, but it is only the extremes which can be readily identified and this differentiation is much easier in younger patients. The typical patients with dementia of vascular origin present in their late 60's and are usually male. The dementia is rather patchy and this may show on psychometric analysis. Insight and personality are often relatively preserved, despite gross intellectual deterioration. The course of the condition is one of fluctuation with the development of focal signs and often with a pseudobulbar palsy. It is usually associated with a raised blood pressure and it is unusual under the age of 60 without severe hypertension. The condition runs an episodically progressive course over about five years and in half the patients death is due to ischemic heart disease (Corsellis, 1962).

Conversely, the primary cellular degenerations are much commoner in women and there may be an inherited tendency. The age of onset varies from the fourth decade to extreme old age. The blood pressure is usually normal. Generalized wasting is common, not only of the brain but also of muscle and the viscera. However, these factors do not help in determining the role of vascular disease in the development of dementia in the great majority of elderly patients who fall between these two extremes. A greater incidence of intellectual impairment has been found in patients with heart disease, hypertension, reduced pulmonary function and peripheral atherosclerosis, but without obvious evidence of cerebrovascular disease, this suggests a vascular component to the intellectual impairment of these patients (reviewed by Obrist, 1972).

Hachinski et al. (1975) have used an "ischemic score" which quantifies the factors suggesting a vascular cause, and they found no overlap in 24 patients between the vascular group and the primary cellular degeneration group. However, the average age of their patients was only 62 and it is doubtful if this differentiation would be as effective in an older population. The scoring method probably best identifies patients with infarcts and would tend to put the mixed cases and patients with ischemia but no infarction into the primary group. (Todorov et al. 1975)

2. *Pathological differentiation.* Pathological studies have clearly demonstrated the increasing incidence of both vascular disease and

Alzheimer changes with age in both demented and "normal" subjects. Gellerstedt (1933) showed that over 80% of 50 brains (aged between 65 and 97) examined at autopsy showed Alzheimer changes and concluded that the difference between the changes in normal old brains and in patients with dementia was a matter of degree. Malmaud (1972) reported the autopsy findings in 1,225 patients with the "chronic brain syndrome," and found Alzheimer changes in 42.4% (age range 40–98), vascular disease in 29% (age range 42–100) and mixed Alzheimer and vascular disease in a further 23% (age range 62–94), so that 52% had evidence of significant vascular disease. Malamud described two types of vascular involvement; atherosclerosis of major and medium-sized vessels associated with infarcts in which there was complete tissue breakdown and, secondly, the hyalinization of small blood vessels with perivascular gliosis and areas of incomplete destruction. Tomlinson (1972) also found evidence of small vessel disease in areas of brain which had not undergone softening. The significance of these small vessel changes is not known for certain (Fisher, 1968), but the deposition of amyloid-like material has led to the suggestion that cerebral amyloidosis is the cause of intellectual impairment. This view is not widely supported; but it is possible that these changes reduce the oxygen tension at mitrochondrial level.

Flora et al. (1968), in a study of over 5,000 circles of Willis, found a 0.5% frequency of atherosclerotic lesions in the first three decades of life and this increased to 98% in the ninth decade. It appears therefore that both Alzheimer changes and vascular degeneration are normal, or more correctly, the usual accompaniment of aging.

Sourander and Sjögren (1970) in a clinico-pathological review of 258 demented females, found 51% with Alzheimer's disease and 28% with vascular disease; since vascular disease is much less common in women, this proportion of vascular cases is almost certainly an underestimate of the overall proportion. The only completely controlled study with a proper comparison to the findings in "normal" aged brains has been reported by Tomlinson et al. (1970). The pathological findings in 50 brains from patients with proven dementia in old age were compared to the findings in an aged matched population of 28 nondemented subjects (Tomlinson et al., 1968).

The normal subjects were found to have up to 50 ml. of cerebral softening due to vascular disease (range 0–91 ml., mean 13.2 ml., two patients only with more than 50 ml.) and up to 14 Alzheimer plaques (mean 3.3) per low-powered field of 1.3 mm diameter (mean of 60 fields). Marked neurofibrillary change and granulo-vacuolar degeneration were only found in the demented subjects. The parameters for the control group were taken as "normal" and provided the basis for assessment of the brains from demented patients. In 90% of the demented patients changes were found which were sufficient to allocate the cases to a specific diagnostic category. Fifty percent showed the histological features of Alzheimer's disease alone with no evidence of significant vascular disease; 17% had evidence of vascular disease alone and mixed cases with pathological features of both Alzheimer's disease and atherosclerotic disease were found in a further 18%, so that 35% had evidence of significant vascular disease. The sex incidence is of interest in this series because 15 of the 16 females, but only 10 of the 34 males, had Alzheimer's disease. In half the men, vascular disease was thought to contribute to the dementia.

The pathological evidence therefore suggests that about 50% of all demented elderly patients have Alzheimer's disease alone, and about 40% have either vascular disease alone or mixed vascular disease and Alzheimer's disease. The incidence of vascular disease at different ages can only be determined by the pathological examination of the whole brain in a large series of subjects from the appropriate age group. It cannot be inferred from small series selected for special examination or where the differentiation is made on clinical grounds alone. (Todorov et al., 1975)

3. *Cerebral blood flow and metabolism.* Dementia was one of the first conditions to be investigated when methods of cerebral blood flow measurement became available with the introduction of the Kety-Schmidt method nearly 30 years ago. It was soon established that all patients with dementia show some reduction in cerebral blood flow and cerebral metabolism when compared to asymptomatic elderly patients and normal young subjects. Kety (1956) summarized the results of the published data between 1948 and 1955 (16 papers from 7 laboratories, 179 subjects aged 5 to 93) using

the Kety-Schmidt technique on cerebral blood flow, cerebrovascular resistance and cerebral metabolism in relation to age. There was a tendency for the cerebral blood flow to fall, the cerebrovascular resistance to rise, the delivery of oxygen to fall, and the arteriovenous oxygen differences showed a slight increase in all but two studies. However, it is not possible from these mixed series of normal and undifferentiated demented patients to know whether the changes were due to reduced supply or reduced demand.

Most supposedly normal elderly subjects show some reduction in cerebral blood flow with age; however, Sokoloff (1966) has clearly demonstrated that, provided the selection of patients is sufficiently rigorous, old age alone is not associated with a reduction in cerebral blood flow or the cerebral metabolism of oxygen. This study (Dastur et al., 1963) is the only one reported specifically to have investigated this point. Fifty-four normal elderly subjects passed the initial screening tests and were then admitted for a two-week inpatient evaluation (Lane and Vates, 1963); 27 were finally passed as entirely normal and 26 of these were studied; 20 subjects had minimal asymptomatic disease and of these 17 were studied. At the time of the examination five subjects were relegated from the first to the second group because the blood pressure was found to be raised. The results (Table I) in these elderly subjects were compared to 15 normal young subjects and 10 patients with the chronic brain syndrome. There was no difference between the normal young subjects and the normal elderly subjects in cerebral blood flow and cerebral metabolic rate for oxygen. There was a slight difference in blood pressure, and this accounts for the change in cerebrovascular resistance. The reduction in cerebral blood flow commonly found in old people therefore reflects the widespread incidence of degenerative disease of the nervous system and of the vascular system. The relative contribution of these two degenerative disorders is unclear in many patients with dementia, and to some extent both factors probably coexist, particularly in the elderly.

In normal subjects, cerebral blood flow is closely related to metabolic demand. It has often been said that the low blood flow found in patients with dementia merely reflects the low metabolic demand; certainly a low cerebral blood flow in isolation cannot differentiate between reduced demand and reduced supply. Despite these

Table I

From Dastur et al (1963)	No.	Age	MABP	CBF	(A-V)O$_2$	CMRO$_2$
1. Normal Young	15	21	84	62	5.7	3.5
2. Normal elderly	26	71	93	58	5.9	3.3
3. 'Normal' elderly hypertensive	5	71	128	55	6.8	3.6
4. Normotensive* arteriosclerotic	5	73	95	51	6.1	3.2
5. Hypertensive arteriosclerotic	4	75	118	48	6.6	3.1
6. Chronic brain syndrome	10	72	102	48	5.7	2.7

*omitting one patient who hyperventilated to a pCO$_2$ of 28.

MABP	- mean arterial blood pressure	(mmHg)
CBF	- cerebral blood flow	(ml/100g/min.)
(A-V)O$_2$	- arteriovenous oxygen difference	(vol.%)
CMRO$_2$	- cerebral metabolic rate for oxygen	(ml/100g/min.)

difficulties in the interpretation of single measurements of blood flow, O'Brien and Mallett (1970), using the 133-Xenon inhalation method, reported a study based on the hypothesis that it might be possible to distinguish between patients with a primary cellular degeneration from patients with dementia secondary to vascular disease in the very early stages, since at that time patients with a primary cellular degeneration might retain a near normal blood flow per unit mass of tissue, that is, a normal perfusion rate, although the total cerebral blood flow would be reduced in parallel with the loss of brain bulk. A slight reduction in the perfusion rate might occur because of loss of the metabolically more active cells and their replacement per unit mass of tissue with metabolically less active cells; but the degree of reduction in perfusion rate would be small and certainly less than the degree of dementia might suggest.

In patients with dementia associated with ischemia, healthy neurones are imperiled by an inadequate blood supply. In these circumstances, before cell death occurs, there would be an initial increase in the arteriovenous oxygen and glucose difference to compensate for the reduced flow. The cortex perfusion rates are therefore likely to be reduced early in the course of the disease and the reduction would be out of proportion to the degree of dementia. This distinction would only apply in the early stages of the disease because eventually a reduced supply will lead to a reduced demand and patients with advanced disease of either type are likely to show both reduced blood flow and reduced metabolism. O'Brien and Mallett (1970) found a statistically significant reduction (23%) in cortex perfusion rates in the vascular group with relative preservation of the perfusion rates and normal cerebrovascular resistance in patients in the primary group, so that within the limitations of the study this data supported the hypothesis. A similar study has recently been reported by Hachinski et al. (1975), who studied 24 patients (10 vascular and 14 primary) using the 133-Xenon injection method and they were able to confirm the report of O'Brien and Mallett, finding a 26% reduction in mean flow in the vascular group and relative preservation of flow in the primary group. They ascribe the reduction in flow in the vascular group to the global reduction in blood flow that occurs after focal infarction; this is presumably due to reduced metabolic demand and should therefore be associated with a normal or reduced arteriovenous oxygen difference.

However, if the dementia was due to multiple infarcts alone this pattern of flow change could not be predicted, since local perfusion rates following infarction usually show a low uptake of tracer due to the reduction in the volume of perfused brain and a rapid clearance rate due to the surrounding hyperemia. Although this hyperemia may only last a week or so, it may be followed by a similar flow pattern in the established infarct because of tissue shunting (Symon et al., 1975). This is, of course, also associated with a reduced arteriovenous oxygen difference because of the low metabolism of the infarcted tissue.

Simard et al. (1971) and others have disputed the concept that ischemia may contribute to the development of dementia other than by a series of large discrete infarcts, because normal cerebrovascular autoregulation and normal responses to change in arterial pCO_2 have been demonstrated in these patients. However, this was based on a study of 20 patients with advanced disease, only three of whom were thought to have a vascular etiology. Furthermore the CO_2 response is extremely difficult to abolish, it may be normal in patients with quite severe cerebrovascular disease (McHenry and Goldberg, 1970), and it may even be present, although reduced, in the region of both recent (McHenry et al., 1970) and old infarcts (Symon et al., 1975). It is evident therefore that a single cerebral blood flow or perfusion rate measurement provides very little useful information, but when blood flow studies are combined with measurements of arteriovenous oxygen and glucose differences, so that the cerebral metabolism of oxygen and glucose can be calculated, more useful information is obtained.

If the cerebral blood flow is altered in normal subjects, for example by hyperventilation or hypoventilation, the rate of oxygen and glucose extraction changes to compensate and these changes in arteriovenous oxygen difference have been widely used as measure of change in blood flow, since alterations in pCO_2 over a wide range does not seem to alter cerebral metabolism. The finding therefore of an increased arteriovenous oxygen difference in elderly patients with dementia would be clear evidence in favor of vascular insufficiency and might differentiate between the reduced blood flow due to a reduced metabolic demand from that due to a reduced supply. If the reduced flow in vascular dementia is due to the widespread reduction in metabolic demand which follows focal infarction, then the arteriovenous oxygen difference should be normal or reduced, but if it is due to a reduced blood supply it should be increased, at least in the early stages. Dastur et al. (1963), as part of a very comprehensive study carried out at the National Institute of Health, showed no significant difference between normal young subjects (Group I), normal elderly subjects (Group II), and normal elderly subjects with an elevated blood pressure alone (Group III) in either cerebral blood flow, arteriovenous oxygen differences or cerebral metabolic rate for oxygen (Table I); but the nondemented and entirely asymptomatic patients with evidence of vascular disease (Groups IV and V) showed a reduced cerebral blood flow with increased arteriovenous oxygen differences, thus maintaining the cerebral metabolic rate for oxygen at normal levels. Those patients with clinical evidence of the organic brain syndrome

Table II

From Geraud et al. (1969)			
	CBF	$(A-V)O_2$	$CMRO_2$
1. Normal	53	6.43	3.34
2. Peripheral vascular disease no cerebrovascular disease	45	6.64	3.13
3. Cerebrovascular disease no dementia	33	6.95	2.53
4. Dementia	30	5.53	1.55

(Group VI) showed a reduced cerebral blood flow with a normal arteriovenous oxygen difference and therefore a reduced cerebral metabolic rate for oxygen, indicating that the flow was now compatible with metabolic demand. If Groups IV and V are amalgamated, it can be seen that as the blood flow falls the arteriovenous oxygen difference increases to compensate, until eventually the inadequate supply results in a reduced demand and in the patients with the chronic brain syndrome there is a fall in both blood flow and the cerebral metabolic rate for oxygen.

Geraud et al. (1969) reported a series of experiments on cerebral blood flow, arteriovenous oxygen differences and cerebral metabolic rate for oxygen in four groups of patients; normal subjects, patients with peripheral vascular disease but no evidence of cerebrovascular disease, patients with cerebrovascular disease but no evidence of intellectual impairment and, finally, patients with cerebrovascular disease and evidence of dementia (Table II). They found a reduction in all three parameters in those patients with dementia, but there was an increase in the arteriovenous oxygen differences in both the second and third groups. This widening of arteriovenous oxygen differences is presumably a compensatory mechanism by viable cells in an ischemic environment, though in Group III, despite a considerable increase in the arteriovenous oxygen difference, there is an overall fall in the cerebral metabolic rate for oxygen, implying that the compensatory mechanism is in part inadequate. In a separate study, the same authors (Geraud et al., 1969) measured arteriovenous oxygen differences in 50 patients with cerebrovascular disease and intellectual impairment. The degree of dementia was graded on a three-point scale; mild, moderate and severe. The blood flow fell parallel to the degree of dementia (42, 34, 28 ml/100g/min. approximate values, normal 53) the arteriovenous oxygen differences were increased in the middle group (6.31, 7.36 and 5.78 volumes % respectively, normal 6.43).

The evidence therefore indicated the presence of a significant population of anoxic but viable cells capable of extracting more oxygen from the blood than is normally necessary in many patients with dementia, whether or not there is clinical evidence of infarction. It appears that this state of affairs exists for long enough to be measured as an increased arteriovenous oxygen difference, implying that there is a fairly large proportion of affected cells and that the cells can remain viable with a reduced cellular oxygen availability, though this leads eventually to dementia with cerebral atrophy. A recent report has shown a high incidence of generalized brain atrophy, as shown by computerized axial tomography, in patients with frequent severe migraine but who did not necessarily develop focal neurological signs or evidence of focal damage on the EMI scan (Hungerford et al., 1975); this is presumably vascular in origin, although it has not been described before (O'Brien, 1973). For many years it has been thought that brain cells, particularly neurones, could only survive about five minutes of ischemia before cell death occurs. However, there is now evidence that there is a level of ischemia at which cells cease to function but are still capable of recovering. Cell death occurs at perfusion rates below about 10 ml/100g/min. but function ceases at about 15 to 18 ml/100g/min. (Heiss et al., 1975, Branston et al., 1975), though, of course, the amount of damage depends on the duration of the ischemia. In an ischemic area there will be the full range from neurones in an adequate oxygen environment to those which are irretrievably damaged, and this would account for the findings of a widened arteriovenous oxygen difference with a reduced metabolic rate for oxygen in some patients and suggests that neurones between these extremes are present in significant numbers in many patients with intellectual impairment. These metabolic studies of course only reflect the changes in perfused brain, so that changes suggestive of ischemia do not exclude the presence of infarcts.

CONCLUSION

There is evidence that in many demented patients there are significant populations of ischemic brain cells, some functioning and others, while no longer active, remain viable and this offers some hope for treatment, since relatively small changes in perfusion may make a considerable difference to the patient's social acceptability and ability to look after himself, perhaps thereby avoiding or delaying the necessity for institutional care. It seems likely that ischemia can contribute to the development of dementia, particularly in the elderly, and this concept includes a series of small subclinical ischemic events producing a population of anoxic cells and some cell death without a pathologically identifiable infarct or clinically detectable stroke, as well as the more obvious multi-infarct dementia, where there may also be areas of ischemia without infarction. Although most patients who die of dementia associated with vascular disease have large widespread infarcts, this is an end stage and may not reflect the situation at an earlier and potentially treatable stage. Sokolof (1966) suggested that "even if the brain ages independently of the circulation, when vascular disease develops, it becomes the pacemaker of the aging process within the brain."

REFERENCES

Branston, N.M., Symon, L., Crockard, H.A., and Juhasz, J.: Dependence of the cortical evoked response on the local tissue blood flow in baboons and its sensitivity to arterial pO_2. A.M. Harper, W.B. Jennett, J.D. Miller, and J.O. Rowan (eds.), *Blood Flow and Metabolism in the Brain,* Sect: 14.22. Edinburgh, Churchill-Livingstone, 1975.

Corsellis, J.A.N.: *Mental Illness and the Ageing Brain.* London, Oxford University Press, 1962.

Dastur, D.K., Lane, M.H., Hansen, D.B., Kety, S.S., Butler, R.N., Perlin, S., and Sokoloff, L.: Effects of ageing on the cerebral circulation and metabolism in man. In J.E. Birren, R.N. Butler, S.W. Greenhouse, L. Sokoloff, and M.R. Yarrow (eds.), *Human Ageing—A Biological and Behavioral Study.* PHS Pub. No. 986, pp. 59–76. Washington, D.C., 1963.

Flora, G.C., Baker, A.B., Klassen, A.: Age and cerebral atherosclerosis. *J. Neurol. Sci.* 6:357–372, 1968.

Fisher, C.M.: Dementia in cerebral vascular disease. In J.F. Toole, R.G.

Siekert, and J.P. Whisnant (eds.), *Cerebral Vascular Diseases*, pp. 232–236. New York, Grune & Stratton, 1968.

Gellerstedt, N.: Zur Kenntnis der Hirnveranderungen bei der Normalen Altersinvolution. Uppsala: Almquist and Wiksells Boktryckeri–A.B., 1933.

Geraud, J., Bes, A., Delpla, M., and Marc-Vergnes, J.P.: Cerebral arterio-venous oxygen differences. J.S. Meyer and O. Eichhorn (eds.), In *Research on the Cerebral Circulation*, p. 209. Springfield, Ill., Thomas, 1969.

Hachinski, V.C., Iliff, L.D., Zilkha, E., du Boulay, G.H., Macallister, V.L., Marshall, J., Ross Russell, R.W., and Symon, L.: Cerebral blood flow in dementia. *Arch. Neurol.* 32: 632–637, 1975.

Heiss, W.D., Waltz, A.G., and Hayakawa, T.: Neuronal function and local blood flow during experimental cerebral ischaemia. In A.M. Harper, W.B. Jennett, J.D. Miller, and J.O. Rowan (eds.), *Blood Flow and Metabolism in the Brain*, Sect: 14.27. Edinburgh, Churchill-Livingstone, 1975.

Hungerford, G.D., Zilkha, K., and du Boulay, G.: EMI Scan findings in patients with chronic severe migraine. The Migraine Symposium, London, Sept. 19, 1975.

Jaffe, M.E., and McHenry, L.C.: New methods for regional blood flow measurement and their significance. In W. Lynn Smith (ed.), *Drugs, Development and Cerebral Function*, pp 91–107. Springfield, Ill., Chas. C. Thomas, 1972.

Kety, S.S.: Human cerebral blood flow and oxygen consumption as related to ageing. *Proc. A.R.N.M.D.* 35: 31–45, 1956.

Lane, M.H., and Vates, T.S.: Medical selection, evaluation and classification of subjects. In J.E. Birren, R.N. Butler, S.W. Greenhouse, L. Sokoloff, and M.R. Yarrow (eds.), *Human Ageing–A Biological and Behavioral Study;* PHS Pub. No. 986, pp. 13–25. Washington, D.C., 1963.

McHenry, L.C., Jaffe, M.E., Kenton, J.E., Cooper, E.S., West, J.W., Kawamura, J., Oshiro, T., and Goldberg, H.I.: Vasodilater responsiveness–Implications in cerebrovascular disease. In R.W. Ross-Russell (ed.), *Brain and Blood Flow*, pp. 258–264, 1970.

McHenry, L.C., and Goldberg, H.I.: Regional CO_2 responsiveness in stroke. *Panminerva Medica*, 13: 182, 1971.

Malamud, N.: Neuropathology of organic brain syndromes associated with ageing. In C.M., Gaitz, (ed.), *Ageing and the Brain*, pp. 63–87. New York, Plenum, 1972.

O'Brien, M.D., and Mallett, B.L.: Cerebral cortex perfusion rates in dementia. *J. Neurol. Neurosurg. Psychiat.* 33: 497–500, 1970.

O'Brien, M.D.: *Cerebral Cortex Perfusion Rates in Migraine*. M.D. Thesis, p. 64. University of London, 1973.

Obrist, W.D.: Cerebral physiology of the aged: Influence of circulatory disorders. In C.M. Gaitz (ed.), *Aging and the Brain*, pp. 117–133. New York, Plenum, 1972.

Simard, D., Olesen, J., Paulson, O.B., Lassen. N.A., and Skinhoj, E.: Regional cerebral blood flow and its regulation in dementia. *Brain.* 94: 273–288, 1970.

Sokollof, L.: Cerebral circulatory and metabolic changes associated with Ageing. *Proc. A.R.N.M.D.* 41: 237–254, 1966.

Sourander, P., and Sjogren, H.: In G. Wolstenholme and M. O'Connor (eds.), *Alzheimer Disease and Related Conditions,* p. 11. London, Churchill, 1970.

Symon, L., Dorsch, N.W.C., Crockard, H.A., Branston, N.M., and Brierley, J.B.: Clinical features, local CBF and vascular reactivity in a chronic three year stroke in baboons. In A.M. Harper, W.B. Jennett, J.D. Miller, and J.O. Rowan (eds.), *Blood Flow and Metabolism in the Brain,* Sect.: 12.10. Edinburgh, Churchill-Livingstone, 1975.

Todorov, A.B., Go, R.C.P., Constantinides, J., and Elston, R.C.: Specificity of the clinical diagnosis of dementia. *J. Neurol. Sci.* 26:81–98, 1975.

Tomlinson, B.E.: Personal Communication, 1972.

Tomlinson, B.E., Blessed, S., Roth, M.: Observations on the brains of demented old people. *J. Neurol. Sci.* 11: 205–242, 1970.

Tomlinson, B.E., Blessed, S., and Roth, M.: Observations on the brains of non-demented old people. *J. Neurol. Sci.* 7: 331, 1968.

5

Transmissible Virus Dementia: The Relation of Transmissible Spongiform Encephalopathy to Creutzfeldt-Jakob Disease

ROGER TRAUB
D. C. GAJDUSEK
C. J. GIBBS, JR.

In Memory of Dr. Joseph E. Smadel (1907–1963)

The transmission of Creutzfeldt-Jakob disease (CJD) to the chimpanzee[39] and later to monkeys[24] has made it possible to define a subgroup of CJD patients whose disease is transmissible and to determine whether some cases diagnosed as CJD may represent a distinct nontransmissible neurological illness.[71] It has further permitted an inquiry into the possibility that there are cases of transmissible virus dementias, or subacute spongiform virus encephalopathies,[23] which are being given clinical or pathological diagnoses other than CJD. These diagnoses may include such syndromes as Alzheimer's or Pick's diseases, Parkinsonism with dementia, or "cortical atrophy" or "dementia of unknown etiology." In this paper, CJD will refer to a clinico-pathologic entity. Demented patients, inoculation of whose tissues into animals has produced progressive neurologic disease, are said to have transmissible virus dementia (TVD).

To date we have transmitted the disease from 55 patients, and brain tissue from another 70 patients with CJD has been inoculated into laboratory primates which have not yet developed a neurological disease. In addition, Zlotnik et al. have transmitted the disease from a patient to 3 monkeys.[79] The illness in three of the patients from whom the disease has been transmitted was diagnosed as an entity other than CJD, from both clinical and pathological standpoints. Of the 56 transmitted patients, 7 were not of the more common sporadic type, but were CJD-like dementias with family histories of similar disease in close kinsmen.

Transmissible virus dementias of the CJD type are subacute spongiform virus encephalopathies[23,33,59] which all produce a very similar disease in inoculated primates. Other subacute spongiform virus encephalopathies are kuru in human subjects, scrapie in sheep and goats, and transmissible mink encephalopathy. All three of these diseases can similarly be transmitted to laboratory animals.[35] In our quest for further biopsy and early autopsy tissues from patients with CJD and other possibly related dementias, specimens from a large series of patients with Alzheimer's and Pick's diseases, Parkinsonism with dementia, and Huntington's chorea have been sent to us. Many of these have been inoculated into laboratory primates in an attempt to determine the possible transmissibility of these diseases. These inoculated animals also serve as controls for the animals with experimental CJD. Data on these patients with other dementias are presented in our consideration of the differential diagnosis of CJD.

CJD AS DEFINED BEFORE KNOWLEDGE OF ITS TRANSMISSIBILITY

Kirschbaum's comprehensive monograph[56] reviews the clinical and pathologic features of CJD[18,51,52] as it was understood prior to demonstration of transmissibility. Creutzfeldt-Jakob disease[56,62] is a progressive fatal central nervous system disease of middle life, affecting both sexes equally. Death usually occurs within two years. It often presents with vague symptoms, including peculiar sensations, dizziness, headache, insomnia, irritability, confusion or depression. Later, there is always progressive dementia. In addition, there may be any of a large variety of other disturbances, including psychosis, focal cortical disturbances, upper and lower motor neuron signs, visual disturbances, extrapyramidal disturbances, myoclonus, seizures, and cerebellar abnormalities. The disease progresses to a stuporous state, often with decerebrate rigidity. Frequently, there is a characteristic EEG (though not specific, since it can appear similar in subacute sclerosing panencephalitis); this consists of high voltage periodic synchronous spikes, spike and wave, or triphasic complexes on a slow background. The bursts may, or may not, coincide with visible myoclonic jerks. Routine laboratory tests are normal, with the exception that a number of patients may show evidence of liver dysfunction. Cerebrospinal fluid is usually normal, but occasionally there is an elevated protein. Pneumoencephalography is either normal or shows one or more of the following: ventricular enlargement, cerebral cortical atrophy or cerebellar cortical atrophy. Post-mortem the brain may be grossly normal or may show atrophy, possibly focal, in the cerebral cortex, basal ganglia, or cerebellum. General histopathologic features include neuronal loss and astrocytic and sometimes microglial proliferation. There is also a variable degree of spongiform change in gray matter and neuronal vacuolation. The last two features may be absent, however.

Creutzfeldt-Jakob disease has long been the subject of nosologic confusion, attested to by the number of synonyms* and subtypes applied to it. There are several reasons for this confusion:

(1) The variability of the clinical features; for example, some patients have prominent lower motor neuron signs; others have predominantly cerebellar deficits; some have marked visual disturb-

---

*Synonyms listed in Kirschbaum[56] include spastic pseudosclerosis, corticopallidospinal degeneration, corticostriatospinal degeneration, Jakob's syndrome, presenile dementia with cortical blindness, Heidenhain's syndrome, subacute vascular encephalopathy with mental disorder, focal disturbances and myoclonic epilepsy, subacute progressive encephalopathy with bulbar myoclonus, subacute presenile spongious atrophy with terminal dyskinesia, and subacute spongiform encephalopathy attributable to vascular dysfunction. Others are Nevin-Jones disease, and Brownell-Oppenheimer syndrome.

ances while others do not. This phenomenon has led several authors to define clinical subtypes of CJD. [12,56,62]

(2) The occasional nonspecific nature of pathologic changes; brains may appear atrophic or macroscopically normal. Often they show only such nonspecific features as alteration in size of neurons, or patchy neuronal loss and astrogliosis. Only about two-thirds of Kirschbaum's cases showed status spongiosus.[57] In addition, large numbers of amyloid plaques may be seen.[16,44,49,58a]

(3) The occurrence of a positive family history in some patients;[9,22,55,63] in the past this may have biased the diagnosis in a given patient away from CJD.

SUBACUTE SPONGIFORM VIRUS ENCEPHALOPATHIES

Transmission of CJD to primates [6,24,35,39] and its serial passage added a new dimension to the study of CJD. Not only was it necessary to determine the biologic properties of the new agent, but it was necessary to reexamine the spectrum of human CJD.

Gajdusek and Gibbs grouped CJD together with kuru and the two animal diseases, scrapie and transmissible mink encephalopathy (TME), under the generic name "subacute spongiform virus encephalopathies"[23,24] (Table I). These conditions have the following features in common: they are progressive, uniformaly fatal disorders of the CNS with no definite pathology elsewhere; the brains show a diffuse neuronal loss, astroglial hypertrophy and hyperplasia and neuronal vacuolation which leads to status spongiosus (sometimes lacking, however, in natural scrapie); the diseases are transmissible to overlapping ranges of experimental hosts with long incubation periods; and they are caused by unusually stable viruses, which show more resistance to heat, formaldehyde and ultraviolet irradiation than do conventional viruses. The status spongiosus in these diseases has been studied by electron microscopy, whereby it is seen to correspond to swelling and vacuolation, mainly of neurons. Focal areas of cytoplasm are filled with granular material. Plasma membranes rupture with accumulation of curled membrane fragments.[59]

Of particular interest among the spongiform encephalopathies is the human disease, kuru, the first chronic degenerative disease

Table I
Subacute Spongiform Virus Encephalopathies
Experimental Host Ranges [35, 11, 25a, 37]

Of man: Kuru	chimpanzee; gibbon; spider, squirrel, capuchin, woolly, pigtail, African green, bonnet, cynomolgus and rhesus monkeys; marmoset; mangabey; mink
Creutzfeldt-Jakob disease	chimpanzee; baboon; spider, squirrel, capuchin, cynomolgus, rhesus, stumptail, pigtail, patas, woolly and African green monkeys; marmoset; bushbaby; mangabey; domestic cat; guinea pig; mouse
Of animals: Scrapie	squirrel, spider, capuchin, cynomolgus and rhesus monkeys; sheep, goat; mink; mouse; rat; hamster; gerbil; vole
Transmissible mink encephalopathy	squirrel, rhesus and stumptail monkeys; sheep, goat; mink; ferret; racoon; skunk; hamster

of man shown to be a slow virus infection. Kuru is a progressive, uniformly fatal disease of the CNS found only among the Fore people and their close neighbors in the Eastern Highlands of Papua New Guinea. [2,36,59] Death usually occurs within one year. The disease is predominantly one of adult women and children. It begins with gait ataxia, followed by truncal and limb ataxia, a characteristic shivering-like tremor and dysarthria. Other signs include pyramidal and extrapyramidal signs and strabismus. Behavioral changes and mental slowing are prominent, but dementia is late in appearing and rarely severe. The clinical picture is remarkably uniform, allowing the Fore natives to diagnose the condition after its initial stages with perfect accuracy. There is neuronal loss, astrogliosis and status spongiosus similar to that of CJD; in addition, two-thirds of the cases (including many children) show significant numbers of argyrophilic, PAS-positive, amyloid plaques, generally more in the cerebellum than elsewhere.

Kuru is disappearing among the Fore.[23] Gajdusek has suggested that kuru is transmitted by autoinoculation with infected brain at cannibal ceremonies; the disease is known to be transmissible by peripheral routes of inoculation, but it has not been transmitted orally to primates. If this hypothesis is correct, the incubation of kuru in man can be over twenty years. Disappearance of the cannibal ritual and the associated contamination, principally of women and children with brain tissue, accounts for the decline several years later in the incidence of kuru. It also would account for the yearly rise in the age of the youngest kuru victim; persons born after cannibalism ceased will not have inoculated themselves with the agent.

Clearly, the disease patterns of kuru and CJD are different. CJD is found worldwide, with an overall incidence that, although unknown, is much lower than that of kuru among the Fore; whereas among the Fore kuru is the leading cause of death. (There does seem, however, to be a focus of CJD among Libyan Jews in Israel.[54]) Of further interest is the recent observation of CJD proved by cerebral biopsy in a native Papua New Guinean from the Central Highlands about one hundred miles from the kuru region. (Gajdusek, unpublished data) An epidemiologic study[8] within the United States revealed no apparent relationship of CJD incidence to occupation or exposure to animals or patients. The fact that one-third of patients (as well as controls) ate brains may be important, however. Furthermore, the clinical picture of CJD is highly variable. We thus have a rare, usually sporadic, sometimes familial disorder, with a variable clinical spectrum and few clues as to its natural mode of spread, contrasting with kuru, a local hyperendemic disorder clinically uniform and with a highly plausible hypothesis for its natural spread. Despite this contrast kuru is sufficiently close to CJD clinically, pathologically, and virologically that we must consider the following hypothesis: that the two diseases may represent different parts of a spectrum of one disease.

THE SPECTRUM OF TRANSMISSIBLE VIRUS DEMENTIA (TVD)

The variable clinical and pathologic expression of CJD suggests the hypothesis that only some cases of CJD are caused by a specific virus, the CJD agent. One must also entertain the possibility—now known to be true—that the CJD agent can be found in the brains of patients not considered to have CJD.

In attempts to explore these possibilities, a variety of primates and other animals have been inoculated with tissues obtained at biopsy or autopsy from a large series of demented patients referred to this laboratory. Experimental CJD has been produced from a total of 56 TVD patients to date. (This figure includes the case of Zlotnik et al.[79]) Of the other 70 CJD patients whose brain tissue has been inoculated into primates, only 25 were inoculated over two years ago, and these animals only have been observed long enough to consider them possibly negative.

The clinical characteristics of the first 12 TVD patients were analyzed by Roos et al.,[71] who compared them with 35 CJD patients who had not yet been shown to have transmissible disease. Brain from only two of these had been inoculated into chimpanzees more than 24 months prior to writing; brain from 16 of these 35 patients has since transmitted the disease to primates. The earlier summary of the 12 TVD patients included 10 males and 2 females (an unexplained sex ratio), with mean age of disease onset 57.9 ± 9.0 years and mean duration 7.2 ± 3.6 months; one had a positive family history. The 35 nontransmitted patients included 18 males and 17 females, with mean age of onset 54.5 ± 11.0 years and mean duration 13.1 ± 15.1 months; 2 had a positive family history. All of the TVD patients had myoclonus and pyramidal tract signs, while only 80% of nontransmitted CJD patients had myoclonus and 66% pyramidal tract signs. There was a higher incidence among nontransmitted patients both of disease duration greater than two years and lower motor neuron signs; the latter was not significant by χ^2, however. The frequencies of clinical characteristics taken from this earlier summary are presented in Table II. Patients having other neurological diseases were occasionally found to resemble CJD clinically. Such conditions included Alzheimer's disease, glioblastoma multiforme, and striatonigral degeneration. One patient's brain showed senile plaques, neurofibrillary tangles and microspongiosus; not only pathologically, but also clinically, he had shown features characteristic of both Alzheimer's disease and CJD.

Since the earlier summary of our transmission experience, the series of patients with known or suspected CJD brought to our

Table II

Clinical Characteristics of Transmitted and Nontransmitted CJD
Patients (from Roos et al.[71])

Characteristic	Frequency (as %)	
	Transmitted	Nontransmitted
Dementia	100	100
Myoclonus	100	80
Pyramidal tract signs	100	66
Characteristic EEG	92	71
Psychiatric symptoms	58	62
Cerebellar signs	58	54
Basal ganglia signs	50	57
Visual abnormalities	50	46
Early higher cortical dysfunction	42	49
Lower motor neuron signs	17	29
Family history	8.3	3

attention has risen considerably. The series of patients with known CJD or TVD now contains 126 cases. Transmissions have taken place from 44 additional patients (bringing the total to 56), including 3 atypical patients in whom CJD was not entertained as a diagnosis during life. In addition, transmission studies are in progress on a number of demented patients with diagnoses other than CJD or with dementia of unknown etiology.

In the following sections we shall compare clinical and pathologic features of TVD and nontransmitted CJD patients, presenting in detail the 3 atypical TVD patients and selected other cases. Data on the other demented patients and differential diagnosis of CJD will be briefly discussed. Finally, the virological properties of the CJD agent will be summarized and hypotheses offered on the natural mode of spread of TVD.

DEMENTIAS STUDIED FOR THEIR POSSIBLE TRANSMISSIBILITY TO PRIMATES

We shall review data on a series of 221 patients with dementia referred to the Laboratory of Central Nervous System Studies at

Table III
Diagnoses of Demented Patients from Whom Brain Tissue Has Been Inoculated in Primates

Diagnosis	Number	Number where biopsy only was studied
TVD*	56	9
CJD (not transmitted)**	70	23
Alzheimer's disease	35	19
Progressive supranuclear palsy	5	0
Pick's disease	2	1
Familial myoclonic epilepsy (Lafora body disease)	7	1
Parkinsonism with dementia	4	0
Huntington's chorea†	6	0
Hallervorden-Spatz disease	1	1
Striatonigral degeneration	1	0
Sudanophilic leukodystrophy	1	0
Amyotrophic lateral sclerosis with dementia	1	0
Cerebrovascular disease	2	0
Dementia of unknown etiology	33	24
Total	224 ⧣	78

* Includes 7 familial cases.
** Includes 4 familial cases.
† Includes 1 juvenile case.
⧣ Total is 3 more than the number of patients because there were 3 patients with two different diagnoses.

the National Institute of Neurological and Communicative Disorders and Stroke from whom tissues have been inoculated into primates (Table III). The largest group in this series consists of 126 patients with CJD and/or TVD. In addition, there have been specimens from 35 patients with Alzheimer's disease, 5 with progressive supranuclear palsy,[74] 7 with Lafora body myoclonic epilepsy, 4 with Parkinsonism with dementia, 2 with Pick's disease, and 6 with Huntington's chorea, and one or two each with other rare dementias. Thirty-three patients had progressive dementia of unknown etiology.

Physicians contact the laboratory about patients because of

our known interest in CJD and related degenerative diseases. Patients with CJD are more likely to be referred here than those with other diagnoses. Many of the other cases reflect our additional interests as they become known to collaborating physicians. Biopsy and/or autopsy tissue is obtained frozen and in growth medium for tissue culture. Clinical and pathological records are supplied by referring physicians. On occasion this laboratory sends fixed tissue to collaborating neuropathologists as well. Electron microscopy findings are available on some specimens. Pathology is available on all 221 (see Table III) patients from the biopsy or autopsy specimens, or from both. No autopsy information is available on 78 of the 221 patients, including 9 TVD and 23 still nontransmitted CJD patients. Biopsy reports are available in all cases where autopsy information has not been obtained.

This method of obtaining specimens from referring physicians has certain defects: (1) the patient distribution is skewed toward CJD—the data here gives no indication of the "true" incidence of CJD with respect to other cases of dementia; (2) clinical observations were made by a large number of physicians—the clinical records available to us vary widely in detail and completeness; (3) the study is a retrospective one, depending on observers with greatly varying experience with CJD, and is subject to the hazards of all such studies; (4) furthermore, none of the authors of this chapter was responsible for the care of any of the patients; (5) similarly, pathology was undertaken by a number of neuropathologists, some highly experienced in the study of CJD and others less so, and presumably having different diagnostic criteria for CJD; (6) the geographic distribution corresponds more to that of referring physicians than a "true" patient distribution; and (7) complete autopsy information is not available on all patients.

The last item, the absence of complete autopsy information for 78 of the 221 patients, raises certain problems. At autopsy some of the patients have features of two different diseases, e.g., CJD and Alzheimer's, CJD and glioma, Alzheimer's and glioma, and CJD and Pick's. A biopsy may miss an area of characteristic pathology, or in those patients having features of two diseases, it may show pathology characteristic of one, but not the other. A patient with a specific disease may end up with a biopsy relegated to the "nondiagnostic" category. With CJD the biopsy can show significantly greater or lesser degrees of status spongiosus than is found at autopsy; this kind of information is lost when only a biopsy is available. Finally, only the autopsy can provide information about the distribution of lesions.

Criteria for including patients in this series were as follows: (1) There had to be adequate clinical and pathological information to enable classification. Although pathological data were available on all patients, we have data from autopsy only on 60 patients and from biopsy only on 78. Both autopsy and biopsy information are available on 83 patients; (2) All patients had to have progressive dementia starting after the age of nine years; (3) All patients with only evidence of inflammatory, vascular, or neoplastic pathology were excluded, unless there was also pathologic evidence of one of the dementias under study. Patients with nonspecific pathology were included, however; and (4) Transmission studies need to be in progress. Generally speaking, this means only those patients from whom frozen brain tissue has been obtained; however, in a few cases tissue culture explants of brain or cornea were inoculated when frozen tissue had not been obtained.

Physicians who referred the patients are listed in Appendix 1. It cannot be emphasized too much that without the interest, effort, and cooperation of these physicians none of this work would have been possible.

Data on the patients were tabulated according to 17 features of their disease (Table VI). Case reports on all patients with TVD who have not already been reported elsewhere[22,71] are given in Appendix 2. Data for the other groups of patients are either summarized in separate tables or discussed in the text.

NOTES ON THE CLINICAL AND PATHOLOGICAL FEATURES OF THE DISEASES SELECTED FOR TABULATION

Age of onset: This was occasionally well defined when disease seemed to be precipitated by head or even emotional trauma. Usually, onset was vague. In addition, a few patients had stable Parkinsonism or schizophrenia or other psychiatric disease for a

Table IV

Clinical and Pathological Features of 11 Patients with Transmissible Virus Dementia or Nontransmitted Creutzfeldt-Jakob Disease Having a Positive Family History for Dementia

Name	Sex	Age at onset (years)	Duration (months)	Behavioral disturbance	Higher cortical dysfunction	Upper motor neuron signs	Lower motor neuron signs	Basal ganglia disorder	Myoclonus	Cerebellar dysfunction	Visual disturbance	EEG	Seizures	Vacuolation	Tangles	Plaques	
T. At.	F	56	15	+	+	+		+	+	+		+	+	+	−	−	⎫
R. Co.	M	35	4	−	+	+		−	+	+		+	−	+	−	−	
E. Ha.	F	51	>9	−	+	+	+	+	+	+	+	+	−	+	+	+	⎬ Transmissible Virus Dementia
C. Ko.	F	50	14	−	+	+	+	+	−	+	−	−	−	+	+	−	
H. Tu.	F	45	20	−	+	+	+	−	+	−	+	+	−	+	−	−	
J. Wo.	M	42	9	−	−	+	−	−	+	−	−	−	−	+	−	+	
A. Yo.	F	42	68	+		+							+	+	+	+	⎭
I. Pu.	F	56	6		+	+		+	+	+	+	+	−	+	−	−	⎫
L. Si.	F	42 (32?)	6 (120?)	+		+		+	+	+			−	+			⎬ Nontransmitted Creutzfeldt-Jakob Disease
M. Wu.	M	51	7		+	+		+	+	+	−	−		+	−	−	
E. Fo.	M	38	60	+	+	+	+	+	+	+		+	+	+	+	+	⎭

number of years before onset of dementia and progression of their illness. In these cases onset was made coincident with the beginning of progressive deterioration.

Duration: Many of these patients survive for months in an akinetic state; the duration of this state depends on medical and nursing care as much as on the disease itself. It has been suggested, therefore, that duration be measured from disease onset to this terminal state. Unfortunately, information is usually not available when terminal status (arbitrarily defined in any case) is achieved. Duration is, therefore, given from estimated disease onset to death. In some cases, because of incomplete information or because the patient is still alive, this is not known and the "minimal" duration is then given. In computing mean duration, this lower bound is used so the mean given is actually less than the true mean.

Behavioral disturbances: The record was searched for evidence of more than the withdrawal, agitation, emotional lability or mild depression found in many demented patients. Evidence was sought for behavior disturbance preceding deterioration of intellectual function.

Higher cortical dysfunction: Evidence for focal cortical disturbances appearing before severe dementia was sought.

Upper motor neuron signs: Decerebrate posturing assumed terminally was not included.

Basal ganglia signs: Rigidity alone without cogwheeling was not included.

Myoclonus: "Myoclonic seizures" were counted as both myoclonus and seizures.

Cerebellar signs: Nystagmus and dysarthria were not included.

Visual disturbances: These included field defects and visual agnosia (both also counted under higher cortical disturbances), difficulty with depth perception, and subjective visual complaints, such as blurring, dyschromatopsia, and objects appearing small, large or simply "funny." Nystagmus, diplopia, ptosis, and abnormalities of pupils and extraocular movements were not included.

EEG: The criterion here was at least one EEG typical of that seen in CJD. Patients differed in the number of EEG's taken and the time in disease course when they were taken.

Seizures: Major motor, focal motor, and "myoclonic" seizures were counted. Reports of "absences" and episodes of psychotic behavior (possibly temporal lobe seizures) without other documentation of seizure activity were not counted.

Pathologic features: Autopsy information was not available on all the patients (Table III). Furthermore, each of the features included here (status spongiosus or vacuolation, neurofibrillary tangles, senile plaques) was searched for in varying degrees. For example, silver stains were not done in all cases. Early spongiform change may be absent in representative sections by light microscopy and a biopsy may miss the localized site of such a process. Neuronal vacuolation is sometimes only apparent with the electron microscope, and the EM study was done only in some of the cases. Amyloid plaques, resembling senile plaques, were considered "present" if at least one was seen. Neurofibrillary tangles were considered present if a "few" or more were seen in at least one section.

CLINICAL AND PATHOLOGIC CHARACTERISTICS OF THE TVD AND CJD PATIENTS

In this section we analyze the clinical and pathologic characteristics of the 56 patients with TVD and the 70 still nontransmitted CJD patients. We also consider a subgroup of the 70 patients, consisting of 8 patients whose tissue was inoculated sufficiently long ago (i.e., more than 4 years ago) into a chimpanzee, squirrel monkey or capuchin monkey that they probably represent "true" failures to transmit. Only cases where the inoculum consisted of fresh frozen brain are included in this "untransmissible" group—cases where the inoculum was *in vitro* tissue culture material are omitted. Data on the 8 apparently untransmissible CJD patients are presented in Table V. The 56 TVD and 70 CJD patients are not separately tabulated. Case histories of 7 of the 8 apparently untransmissible CJD patients are presented in Appendix 3; the history of the remaining untransmissible case, D. St., is given in the section "Differential diagnosis of CJD." Primates inoculated with brain tissue from the still nontransmitted CJD patients have been observed for longer than two years in 25 cases. In one case both inoculated monkeys died without neurologic signs and no inoculum remains for repeating the experiment. Many of the primates still

Table V
Clinical and Pathological Features of 8 Patients with Untransmissible* CJD

Name	Sex	Age at onset (years)	Duration (months)	Behavioral disturbance	Higher cortical dysfunction	Upper motor neuron signs	Lower motor neuron signs	Basal ganglia disorder	Myoclonus	Cerebellar dysfunction	Visual disturbance	EEG	Seizures	Vacuolation	Tangles	Plaques	Family history
J. Ar	M	44	9	+	+	+	−	−	+	−	+	−	−	+	−	−	−
D. Dr	F	43	20	+	−	+	+	−	+	−	+	−	+	+	−	−	−
E. Fo	M	38	60	+	+	+	+	+	+	+	−	+	+	+	+	+	+
A. La	F	68	3	+	+	+	−	−	+	+	+	+	+	+	−	−	−
D. Li	F	51	6	−	+	−	−	−	+	+	+	+	−	+	−	−	−
R. Na	M	52	72	−	−	+	−	+	−	−	−	−	−	+	+	+	−
J. Ob	M	56	13	+	+	+	+	−	−	−	−	−	−	+	−	−	−
D. St	F	52	4	−	+	+	−	−	+	−	−	+	−	+	−	−	−

*Brain (other than in vitro tissue culture) inoculated more than 4 years ago into chimpanzee, squirrel monkey, or capuchin monkey.

105

under observation may eventually develop subacute spongiform encephalopathy.

The total series includes patients from many parts of the world: the United States, France, Britain, Canada, Belgium, Italy, Brazil, Germany, Chile, Japan, Australia, and Austria. No attempt is made here to analyze the geographic distribution.

The data for the three groups are summarized in Table VI. The Student t test was used to determine if mean age of onset and duration was significantly different in TVD, as compared with nontransmitted CJD; the level of significance used was $p < 0.05$. Yates' correction for Pearson's chi square was used to determine if differences between TVD and CJD in sex ratio and in the incidence of other features were significant. Again, the level used was $p < 0.05$.

Comments follow on some of the characteristics. For each characteristic there was no statistically significant difference between the TVD and non-transmitted CJD groups, unless mentioned otherwise.

Sex: In the earlier series, based on 12 transmissions, there was a preponderance of males (85%), which is not present in this larger series of 56 transmitted cases (50% males).

Age of onset: Age of onset in decades is shown in Table VII. The mean is in the fifties for each group, without significant differences between TVD and the nontransmitted group. The figures are all close to the average for May's[62] series of 137 patients: 52.4 ± 10.5.

Our youngest patients had onset at age 26 (Y. Ma., a Japanese woman, and S. Ya., a Papua New Guinea man). May's youngest case (Creutzfeldt's original patient) was even younger. Y. Ma.'s brain had significant numbers of amyloid plaques; her case report is presented below.

Duration: The range of duration for TVD was 1½ months to about 68 months. The 1½ months corresponded to patient J. Gr., whose disease seemed to start about ten days after head trauma. Two of the longest TVD durations, 17 and 68 months corresponded, respectively, to patients D. Ma. and A. Yo. These patients were both atypical in important respects, as discussed below.

The mean duration of TVD is significantly different from that of nontransmitted CJD ($p = 0.05$).

Table VI
Clinical and Pathological Characteristics of TVD, Non-transmitted CJD and Untransmissible CJD

Characteristic	TVD		Non-transmitted CJD		Untransmissible CJD		All TVD and CJD	
Number of patients	56		70		8		126	
males	28		41		4		69	
females	28		29		4		57	
males/females	1.00		1.41		1.00		1.21	
Range age of onset (yrs.)	34-78		26-74		38-68		26-78	
Average age of onset (yrs.)	56.3 ± 9.5		55.7 ± 11.2		20.5 ± 9.2		56.0	
Range of duration (mos.)	1½-68		2-72		3-72		1½-72	
Average duration (mos.)	8.0 ± 9.3		12.1 ± 14.8		23.4 ± 27.1		10.3	
Behavioral disturbance	28/54	52%	26/60	43%	5/8	63%	54/114	47%
Higher cortical dysfunction	30/54	56%	36/62	58%	6/8	75%	67/116	58%
Upper motor neuron signs	43/55	78%	44/61	72%	7/8	88%	88/116	76%
Lower motor neuron signs	14/53	26%	20/36	56%	3/8	38%	34/89	38%
Basal ganglia disorder	29/54	54%	35/64	55%	2/8	25%	64/118	54%
Myoclonus	48/54	89%	50/63	79%	6/8	75%	98/117	84%
Cerebellar dysfunction	35/53	66%	39/62	63%	3/8	38%	74/115	64%
Visual disturbance	24/54	44%	23/59	39%	4/8	50%	47/113	42%
Characteristic EEG	37/53	70%	26/57	46%	4/8	50%	63/110	57%
Seizures	11/53	21%	17/60	28%	3/8	38%	28/113	25%
Neuronal vacuolation	51/52	98%	64/67	96%	8/8	100%	116/119	98%
Neurofibrillary tangles	5/51	10%	5/62	8%	2/8	25%	10/113	9%
Amyloid plaques	6/51	12%	10/62	16%	2/8	25%	16/113	14%
Family history*	7/56	13%	4/70	6%	1/8	13%	11/126	9%

*Of disease suggestive of, or confirmed as, CJD.

Table VII
Age of Onset of CJD Patients

Age	TVD		Non-transmitted CJD*		Untransmissible CJD		All CJD	
21-30	0	0%	2	3%	0	0%	2	2%
31-40	4	7%	5	7%	1	13%	9	7%
41-50	13	23%	12	17%	2	26%	25	20%
51-60	19	34%	22	32%	4	50%	41	33%
61-70	17	30%	25	36%	1	13%	42	34%
71-80	3	5%	3	4%	0	0%	6	5%
All ages	56		69*		8		125	

*Age of onset not known in one of the 70 patients.

Four nontransmitted CJD patients survived more than 48 months from onset. One was Y. Ma., mentioned above; two of the others were patients in the group that has not yet transmitted four years after inoculation.

Lower motor neuron signs: There is a higher incidence of lower motor neuron signs among non-transmitted patients, as observed by Roos et al.;[71] the difference is significant.

Characteristic EEG: The higher incidence of this in TVD patients is significant ($p < 0.01$).

Neuronal vacuolation or status spongiosus: Virtually all the TVD and CJD patients had evidence of spongiform change in gray matter. This contrasts with Kirschbaum's observation of status spongiosus in only two-thirds of the patients he reviewed. The difference may reflect a change in criteria among neuropathologists for diagnosing CJD. It may further reflect the fact that status spongiosus is intensively searched for in patients referred here, especially in those whose disease has been transmitted. Electron microscopy is also now more frequently used than hitherto.

Neurofibrillary tangles and amyloid plaques: The relatively high incidence of these findings in the untransmissible group corresponds to the two patients in that group with mixed pathologic pictures: E. Fo. and R. Na. (see Appendix 3). The tangles and plaques in TVD patient D. Mu. were in number consistent with the patient's age. Two other TVD patients with both of these findings

(E. Ha. and A. Yo.) were originally diagnosed as having Alzheimer's disease and are discussed later. Krücke et al.[58a] have pointed out certain morphological differences between the amyloid-containing plaques in kuru and in Alzheimer's disease, and senility. Most of the pathologists describing the biopsy and autopsy specimens here do not necessarily make this distinction.

Other clinical features in CJD: Certain other features were noted in the records, but were not tabulated. These features, listed below, have been commented upon by other authors:[56,62,71]

(1) vague psychological abnormalities; these occurred early in the course;

(2) peripheral sensory abnormalities: 4 TVD and 2 nontransmitted CJD patients complained of paresthesias. Only one had sensory loss in the limbs without concomitant peripheral nerve disease. One patient may have had decreased sensation in the fifth nerve territory;

(3) headache: this also usually was only noted early in the course and was never well characterized. It occurred in 8 TVD and 7 nontransmitted CJD patients;

(4) dysarthria and dysphagia: these generally occurred in conjunction with other evidence of either upper motor neuron or cerebellar dysfunction. They were especially prominent in 6 TVD and 6 nontransmitted CJD cases;

(5) vestibular and acoustic disturbances: 12 TVD and 10 nontransmitted CJD patients complained of dizziness, vertigo, tinnitus or hearing loss;

(6) eye signs: these included nystagmus, opsoclonus, ptosis, and pareses of extraocular movements. They occurred in 15 TVD and 6 nontransmitted CJD patients. Pupillary abnormalities were observed in one TVD patient (S. Co.). One CJD patient had paresis of vertical eye movements and was originally clinically diagnosed as progressive supranuclear palsy, while a TVD patient also had clinically prominent supranuclear gaze palsy;

(7) bulimia was observed in two TVD patients; one nontransmitted CJD patient was a compulsive cigarette smoker;

(8) primitive reflexes noted in virtually all patients were palmomental, suck, snout and grasp phenomena;

(9) cerebrospinal fluid: none of the patients had increased CSF pressure or pleocytosis. Protein elevation up to 120 mg % was

observed. Ten TVD and 7 nontransmitted CJD patients had a CSF protein greater than 50 mg %. Protein electrophoresis was not available, except in a few cases. One patient had an elevated CSF γ-globulin (22% of CSF protein); and

(10) pneumoencephalogram: this occasionally showed cerebral or cerebellar atrophy or dilated ventricles (sometimes asymmetrically so). Of the 30 TVD patients who had one or more pneumoencephalograms, 22 had an abnormal study. Of the 32 nontransmitted CJD patients who had at least one pneumoencephalogram, 26 had an abnormal study.

Summarizing this section it is seen that the sex ratio, and mean age of onset are approximately the same in the TVD and nontransmitted CJD groups. Disease duration tends to be longer in the nontransmitted group. A characteristic EEG occurs significantly more often in the TVD than the nontransmitted CJD group, while lower motor neuron signs occur less often in the TVD group. Differences in incidence for the remaining characteristics are not significant. The 8 untransmissible patients seem to have a longer duration than the other CJD (including TVD) patients. The small number of these patients does not permit assessment of the significance of this or other differences. In general, the TVD patients do not appear to differ markedly in clinical and pathological features from the nontransmitted CJD cases. However, three very atypical CJD patients do appear in the TVD group. These are discussed in the next section.

THREE ATYPICAL CASES OF TVD

Three of the TVD patients (E. Ha., D. Ma. and A. Yo.) were highly atypical. All three had diagnoses of neurologic disease other than CJD while still alive, one papulosis atrophicans maligna of Köhlmeier-Degos, and the other two familial Alzheimer's disease. The clinical pictures were unusual for CJD and the neuropathologic features were mixed. It is these cases that demonstrate that the spectrum of TVD is not identical with that of CJD.

D. Ma.[27] A 54-year-old neurosurgeon presented with paresthesias in his toes. Within weeks, small red, non-pruritic, crusted, hyperpigmented lesions were noted on the legs. These bled easily and developed shiny white depressed centers with serpiginous borders. Skin biopsy at this time was interpreted as acute vasculitis. Three months after onset he felt dizzy, especially on rapid head motion, and there was a feeling of fullness in the head. At that time he had decreased ankle jerks and decreased vibration sense in the toes. He was hypersensitive to noise and light. A month later there was nystagmus and ataxic gait. Lumbar puncture and EEG were normal. Six months after onset the erythrocyte sedimentation rate was 10; antinuclear antibody, lupus erythematosus preparations and RA latex were normal. In ensuing months he was treated with steroids, azathioprine, cyclophosphamide and cytosine arabinoside, without obvious benefit. Eight months after onset he was depressed, dysarthric and had diplopia. He was unable to walk without support. There was myoclonus during sleep and intermittent palatal myoclonus when awake. He fell asleep while talking. Eye findings included skew deviations, opsoclonus, nystagmus retractorius and bilateral ptosis. There were cerebellar signs, more on the left. Eleven months after onset a peripheral nerve biopsy showed extensive degeneration and a mononuclear infiltrate. He became deaf by the next month. EEG's showed progressive slowing. A pneumoencephalogram showed slight widening of the left lateral ventricle. He died after 17 months of illness. Dementia developed late and was not especially prominent in the early months of his illness.

A skin biopsy two months before death showed focal atrophic dermatitis with epidermal atrophy, disarray and lysis of dermal elastica and collagen with edema, arteritis, hemorrhage and cellular infiltration of dermis. This was felt to be consistent with Köhlmeier-Degos disease. At autopsy, the vascular lesions of Köhlmeier-Degos were found in skin, peripheral nerve, muscle, spinal cord and brain stem. Pathologic findings of CJD were also present in the CNS: neuronal loss (subtle in cerebral cortex, patchy and severe in thalamus, present also in cord), fibrillary gliosis and status spongiosus.

Ten percent autopsy suspensions from D. Ma. have induced, after intracerebral inoculation, experimental CJD in two chimpanzees and a squirrel monkey, with incubation periods of 26, 11, and 19½ months, respectively. The clinical features of the experimental disease in these animals consisted of hemiparesis, somnolence, myoclonus and visual changes; the picture was that of experimental CJD as produced by inoculation of brain from the other TVD patients. Brains of the experimental animals had status spongiosus, but showed no evidence of vasculitis. Disease has been passed from the brain of the primary passage squirrel monkey to 4 additional squirrel monkeys by intracerebral inoculation.

Köhlmeier-Degos disease[75] is a rare disorder of arterioles and medium-sized arteries, in which fibrous tissue is deposited between endothelium and internal elastic lamina, leading to vessel occlusions. Usual sites of lesions are skin and intestine. Central nervous system involvement has been reported[19,32] with vessels having thickened walls infiltrated with lymphocytes and mononuclear cells, and containing fibrin thrombi. In one case,[32] "vacuolization" is commented upon in spinal cord. Electron microscopy of a skin lesion from another patient[67] revealed aggregates of 250-300 Å virus-like particles in the cytoplasm of degenerating endothelial cells.

Some possibilities concerning how D. Ma. came to have TVD were pointed out in the previous report.[27] For example, the presumed viral agent in Köhlmeier-Degos disease may be identical with the CJD agent; by destroying brain or by other mechanisms the vasculitis may have "turned on" infection with the CJD agent; or the patient may have become inoculated with the CJD agent in the course of his profession as a neurosurgeon. The last possibility is of practical importance, especially as the CJD agent may be as resistant to decontamination procedures as the scrapie agent.[33,37,76,76a]

B. Ha. This woman had worked as a nurse's aide for ten years until, at age 51, she insidiously developed difficulty with memory and concentration and inability to perform household chores. She tended to get lost and was apraxic with knife and fork. She complained of nervousness, difficulty with speech and left-sided headaches. Her father died at age 63, having suffered progressive dementia. A 50-year-old sister had "nervous troubles," requiring hospitalization. About five months after onset of the patient's illness, the husband noted his wife having trouble finding words; she also would put her clothes on backwards. An EEG was diffusely irregular with symmetrical 5 Hz waves. A psychiatrist noted perseveration, dysphasia and emotional blunting. Eight months after onset she was disoriented to place and time and could not do calculations. She had severe expressive dysphasia. Deep tendon reflexes were symmetrically hyperactive. A pneumoencephalogram indicated cortical atrophy and dilatation of the lateral ventricles. Following this study, left ankle clonus developed. The CSF protein was 40 mg %. The patient had a left temporal lobe brain biopsy nine months after onset. No information is available to the authors on her course subsequent to the biopsy. Examination of the brain biopsy by Dr. N.B. Rewcastle revealed, with silver stains, prominent flame-shaped neurofibrillary tangles and senile plaques. Some of the plaques were also PAS positive. The specimen was interpreted as indicating Alzheimer's disease. A 10% suspension of the brain biopsy was inoculated intracerebrally and intravenously into squirrel monkey 0-445. After an incubation period of 29½ months, the animal's activity decreased and it became awkward and tremulous. It died after an illness lasting approximately one month. The animal's brain showed spongiform encephalopathy.

A. Yo.[29] This woman had been an excellent student in high school and college. At age 42 she began to have trouble with housework and repeated herself. Examination 40 months after onset showed her to be demented and confused and she misnamed objects. EEG revealed bilateral 2—4 Hz activity of moderate to high voltage. The patient spent her last two years in a state mental hospital, where both jerking movements and tonic convulsions were observed by the nurses. She eventually reached a spastic bed-ridden state and died about 68 months after onset.

Brain biopsy 3½ years after onset revealed numerous neuro-fibrillary tangles and senile plaques. Twisted 800 Å tubules were seen by electron microscopy. There were no spongiform changes and the biopsy was considered diagnostic for Alzheimer's disease.

At autopsy the brain was grossly atrophic, weighing 1080 grams. Senile plaques were found in cerebellum and cerebral cortex. Insular and cerebral cortex and hippocampus showed many neurons with neurofibrillary tangles. These changes were most pronounced in Ammon's horn. There was neuronal loss in basal ganglia and cerebral cortex.

Of great interest is the family history. The patient's father died at age 54 with a dementia. His brother also died with a dementia. A. Yo.'s brother died at age 50 with progressive dementia and convulsions; numerous neurofibrillary tangles and senile plaques were seen in his brain at autopsy. The patient has a living sister now showing signs of dementia.

Autopsy tissues (brain, liver, spleen, heart, and kidney) were inoculated intracerebrally, intravenously and subcutaneously into squirrel monkey 0-1, who died after 23 months. On the day of death myoclonus was noted in limbs, eyelids and lips. This animal's brain showed vacuolation in cerebral cortex and basal ganglia. Special stains revealed neither senile plaques nor neurofibrillary tangles. A 10% suspension of the squirrel monkey's brain was inoculated intracerebrally into squirrel monkey O-142, which developed experimental CJD after 24 months. This animal's brain also showed the changes of experimental spongiform encephalopathy; likewise, no senile plaques or neurofibrillary tangles were seen. Experimental CJD has also been induced in two additional squirrel monkeys, 0-143 and 0-146, after intracerebral inoculation of a 10^{-2} and 10^{-5} suspension, respectively, of squirrel monkey 0-1 brain.

From the above three patients, experimental CJD has been produced in animals by inoculation of brain affected by disease other than CJD itself. In D. Ma., spongiform change was found in the gray matter, in addition to pathological signs of a second recognized CNS disease. Table XII lists these and 15 other cases in which a CJD-like picture developed after some other brain disturbance. All but one brain showed some post-mortem evidence of status spongiosus, or, in one case, "loosening of ground substance." In the three patients from the series of Nevin et al.[66] who had neurosurgery, either neurosurgery itself or the underlying condition could be of significance. The possibility that the CJD agent was introduced from the surgical instruments is an intriguing one; it would give an incubation period in man of TVD by intracerebral inoculation of 17 to 18 months. This is the incubation period observed in the case of a probable human-to-human transmission of CJD via a cornea transplant.[20a]

It is seen that some cases of TVD were not cases of CJD as the latter is usually understood. In the next section we shall consider whether there are cases of CJD that are not TVD.

WHAT FORMS OF CJD ARE TRANSMISSIBLE?

Since CJD has been divided into different clinical types, it is important to ask which ones correspond to transmissible disease. May[62] defines four clinical types of CJD: (1) subacute spongiform encephalopathy; (2) transitional forms; (3) a dyskinetic form; and, (4) an amyotrophic form. The first three types have sufficient overlap that no attempt has been made to classify this series according to types. However, the amyotrophic form is relatively distinctive. To quote May: "This group, in addition to mental deterioration, speech and gait disturbances, and occasional Parkinsonian manifestations, presents *early* with features of typical amyotrophic lateral sclerosis, including fibrillations and muscular wasting. In this group are the cases of longest duration, up to several years." (Italics added). Examples of patients with the amyotrophic form of CJD are W. Ne. and J. O'B., both nontransmitted CJD patients with over four years elapsed since primates were inoculated with their brain tissue (tissue culture inoculum with W. Ne.). Neither had myoclonus or a typical EEG; they survived 60 and 38 months, respectively. W. Ne. had disease onset at age 38; a younger age of onset has been noted with the amyotrophic form.

By the above criteria, none of the 56 TVD patients had the amyotrophic form of CJD; although 14 had lower motor neuron signs, these occurred late. The mean duration for the 14 is 9.7 ± 5.6 months. The mean duration for TVD patients without lower motor neuron signs is only 7.7 ± 10.6 months; the difference is not significant ($p > 0.05$).

It is of interest that TVD patient S. Fe. (Appendix 2) had pathologic changes in the cord indistinguishable from motor neuron disease. Dr. D. Oppenheimer thought that this case represented the amyotrophic form of CJD, but Dr. S. Nevin disagreed and called it "subacute spongiform encephalopathy."[68] One can guess that patients with the "pure" amyotrophic form of CJD are at one end of a spectrum in which destruction occurs in spinal cord and cerebral cortex at different rates. Further study is needed to see if the "pure" amyotrophic form of CJD is transmissible, perhaps using spinal cord as inoculum. Meanwhile, the possibility that some forms of CJD are simply not transmissible must be considered.

Gomori et al.[40] reemphasized that there is an additional type of CJD, an ataxic form, constituting about 10% of published cases. Sixteen of the transmitted patients had relatively early prominent cerebellar symptoms, with the original clinical diagnosis in S. Gr. being cerebellar degeneration. Thus, there is no question about transmissibility of this form of the disease. It is of interest that one of the TVD patients with ataxic CJD also had a large number of amyloid plaques resembling senile plaques.

The above discussion ignores the following crucial possibility: there may be CJD patients whose disease is indistinguishable by *all* clinical and pathologic criteria from that of the typical TVD patients, but who, nevertheless, do not themselves have TVD. In the absence of an immunologic marker for the CJD agent (see the section on Virology of the CJD agent), such a question can only be answered by further inoculation work.

Before discussing the other dementias we shall consider two aspects of CJD that may link it to other conditions: its familial occurrence, perhaps relating it to the other "heredodegenerative" diseases, and the occasional finding of large numbers of amyloid plaques, perhaps linking it to kuru or Alzheimer's disease.

FAMILIAL CJD

Creutzfeldt-Jakob disease has been known to occur on occasion in a familial pattern since Kirschbaum[55] described the Backer family in 1924. Several reports of other families are in the literature. We have recently reviewed the transmission of CJD from patients T. At. and R. Co., described other familial cases, and surveyed the literature on the familial form of the disease.[22]

In this series there are seven TVD patients (T. At. and R. Co., mentioned above; E. Ha., C. Ko., H. Tu., J. Wo., and A. Yo.) and four nontransmitted CJD patients with a family history of a similar disease in close kinsmen (Table IV). The incidence of positive family history for the series as a whole was 9%. A detailed study of the genetics of these cases is beyond the scope of the chapter, but most of the family trees are consistent with an autosomal dominant form of inheritance. There was no known parental consanguinity in any of the cases. The eleven patients with familial disease included 4 males and 7 females. Age range was 35 to 56 years with a mean of 46.2 ± 7.1 years. The mean age of onset is less in the familial patients than in CJD patients as a whole, although the difference is not statistically significant; a similar observation was made by Kirschbaum. The range of duration was 4 to 68 months. The patients with longest duration, 68 and 60 months, corresponded to A. Yo. and E. Fo., respectively, both of whom had features of Alzheimer's disease. The difference in mean duration from that of the entire CJD series is not significant. All of the patients' brains showed vacuolation or status spongiosus.

Explanation for the mode of inheritance of familial CJD and its transmissibility is not obvious. In view of the cases in Table XII, suggesting superimposition of CJD on an underlying process, it is intriguing to speculate that what is actually inherited is not CJD itself, but rather some slowly progressive brain process that allows invasion by or activation of the CJD agent. This might also explain the earlier age of onset in the familial cases.

It is clear that transmissibility of familial CJD implies that an infectious agent may be associated with any of the so-called heredodegenerative diseases. Inoculation experiments are in progress in this laboratory with material from Huntington's chorea, familial Alzheimer's and Pick's diseases, familial myoclonic epilepsy (Lafora body disease), Friedreich's ataxia, and numerous other familial degenerative conditions. Of particular interest is the resemblance clinically of disease in one of the familial TVD patients (H. Tu., also presented as a case 3 in May et al.[63]), and her sister to Huntington's chorea. But for the CJD-typical histopathology, H. Tu., two sisters, and her father might have been considered to have Huntington's chorea, although all had an unusually rapid course for the latter disease.

CJD AND SENILE PLAQUES: A LINK WITH KURU?

Sixteen of the 126 patients with CJD had so-called senile amyloid-containing plaques. Six of these were TVD patients, and 10 were patients whose disease has still not been transmitted. These plaques were seen in significant numbers in three of the TVD patients (T. Ma., E. Ha., and A. Yo.) and in 6 of the nontransmitted patients (E. Fo., E. Gr., Y. Ma., C. Mo., R. Na., and G. Si.). There are several published reports on this phenomenon,[1,16,44,49,77] some corresponding to cases included in this series. It has been suggested that the presence of such plaques in CJD provided a neuropathologic link between CJD and kuru, the latter disease showing large numbers of such plaques in about two-thirds of the cases. It is of interest that virtually none of the animals with either experimental kuru or CJD had a significant number of plaques in their brains. There are those who argue that it is possible to distinguish morphologically between the plaques of kuru and typical amyloid-containing plaques of senility or of Alzheimer's disease. If this distinction can really be made unequivocally, we would have a potent means of differentiating CJD cases with plaques from Alzheimer's disease cases. This has obviously not been done for our 16 cases with plaques, where the pathologists have simply interpreted them as senile plaques similar to those seen in Alzheimer's disease.

E. Ha. and A. Yo. have been discussed above. Of the 7 other patients with significant number of plaques, one has been shown to have transmissible disease: T. Ma. (case 1 in Hirano et al.[44]; see also Gomori et al.[40]). The 7 patients consist of 3 males and 4 females, with age of onset 26 to 68 years (mean 54.8 ± 13.3) and duration 8 to 72 months (mean 32.0 ± 26.5). Only one patient had visual abnormalities. E. Ha., A. Yo., E. Fo., and R. Na. had numerous neurofibrillary tangles, as well as plaques; the latter two patients are presented in Appendix 3. Another patient with plaques, Y. Ma., is of particular interest because of her long clinical course and early age of onset. This case is presented below.

Y. Ma. This Japanese housewife presented with progressive cerebellar ataxia and dysarthria at the age of 26. There was progressive intellectual deterioration with alexia and auditory hallucinations, emotional instability, masked facies and hyperreflexia. After 2½ years she became stuporous and developed muscle atrophy with EMG evidence of denervation. CSF was normal. Death occurred after 4½ years of disease.

A right frontal biopsy 2½ years after onset showed severe status spongiosus and many Alzheimer-type plaques. Because of these plaques and the prominent cerebellar symptoms, a diagnosis of kuru was entertained by the referring physicians, but was rejected in part because the spongiform changes were far more severe than is seen in the frontal lobe in kuru.[20] The interpretation of the biopsy was either CJD or severe Alzheimer's disease. Brain at autopsy showed severe spongiform changes, astrocytic and microglial proliferation and abundant senile plaques. The findings were similar to those of Chou and Martin[16] (G. Si. in this series) and Hirano et al.[44] (T. Ma. in this series).

It was the considerable similarity between kuru and CJD, clinically and pathologically, that led us to investigate the possibility that CJD might have a similar transmissible virus etiology. This similarity was recognized to be more compelling at a cellular level than clinically or in the distribution of lesions in the CNS. We now wonder about the degree of identity of the two agents. We feel that this is a matter that cannot be settled by neuropathologic comparison alone. Even demonstrating identical host ranges for the experimental diseases will not be sufficient. Rather, it requires definitive identification of the agents of the respective diseases, with comparison of their biochemical and antigenic properties.

On the other hand, the relationship, if any, between CJD and Alzheimer's disease is more mysterious. Classical cases of sporadic Alzheimer's disease without prominent myoclonus and with typical Alzheimer's neuropathological changes, but without spongiform change in gray matter, have not transmitted to the chimpanzee or monkey, in spite of periods of several years since inoculation. The transmitted case of A. Yo. of "Alzheimer's disease" is in retrospect atypical because of the relatively rapid evolution to a vegetative state. We feel at present that CJD and Alzheimer's disease represent distinct diseases, but that the CJD agent may perhaps infect a brain damaged by Alzheimer's disease.

PATIENTS WITH DEMENTIAS OTHER THAN CJD

This laboratory has collected material from patients with forms of dementia other than CJD in efforts to find new transmissible dementias. Many such patients were considered by referring physicians originally to have CJD on the basis of clinical course. To date, brain tissue has been inoculated (or suspensions prepared for such inoculations) from 35 patients with Alzheimer's disease, 5 with progressive supranuclear palsy, 2 with Pick's disease, 4 with Parkinsonism-dementia, 7 with familial myoclonic epilepsy (Lafora body disease), 6 with Huntington's chorea, 1 with Hallervorden-Spatz disease, 1 with striatonigral degeneration, 1 with sudanophilic leukodystrophy, 1 with ALS with dementia, 2 with multiple cerebral infarcts, and 33 with progressive dementias in whom clinicopathological information allows no definitive diagnosis (Table III). Some of the latter are alive and may eventually be found to have CJD. Brain from 6 of the above patients was inoculated into chimpanzees more than three years ago (1 Pick's, 1 progressive supranuclear palsy, 3 Alzheimer's and 1 Huntington's chorea), including 2 inoculated more than five years ago. Thus, if these diseases prove to be transmissible, their incubation periods are likely to be longer than that of CJD.

The largest single disease category among these patients was Alzheimer's disease. Data from these patients is summarized in Table VIII according to the 17 characteristics tabulated for CJD patients. Mean age of onset is about the same as for CJD patients, but duration is considerably longer. All of the clinical features tabulated for CJD are found in more than one-fifth of these patients. It should be noted that there were 13 patients with myoclonus. The observation in the earlier report[71] that Alzheimer's patients even with myoclonus have a longer duration than most CJD patients is confirmed here: the mean duration among Alzheimer patients with myoclonus was greater than four years. The figures in Table VIII must not be taken as representative of all Alzheimer patients, since many of our cases were referred because of a clinical suspicion of CJD. Because of the long duration of illness, most of these patients are lost to follow-up or die in a nursing home. This explains why complete clinical and autopsy information is lacking in so many of them.

The group of 33 patients with dementias of unknown etiology is of particular importance, since some of them may be found eventually to have evidence of vacuolation or status spongiosus. The diagnosis of CJD was strongly considered, perhaps correctly, in 11 of these patients and was at least entertained in most of the others. Characteristics of this group are summarized in Table IX.

Table VIII
Summary of Data on 35 Patients with Alzheimer's Disease

Characteristic	Value*	
Number of males	19	
Number of females	16	
Percentage of males	64%	
Age range	27-73 yrs.	
Mean age onset	52.2 ± 9.6 yrs.	
Duration range	12-240 months	
Mean duration	>5 years	
Behavioral disturbance	19/25	(76%)
Higher cortical dysfunction	19/26	(73%)
Upper motor neuron signs	19/23	(83%)
Lower motor neuron signs	9/16	(56%)
Basal ganglia disorder	14/21	(67%)
Myoclonus	13/19	(68%)
Cerebellar dysfunction	7/16	(44%)
Visual disturbance	7/19	(37%)
Characteristic EEG	3/16	(19%)
Seizures	4/17	(24%)
Neuronal vacuolation	2/33	(6%)
Neurofibrillary tangles	31/35	(89%)
Amyloid plaques	33/34	(97%)
Family history	11/27	(41%)

*ratio = number with characteristic/number where information is available.

Of the remaining patients, the diagnosis of CJD was considered in the two with Pick's disease, and one with sudanophilic leuko-dystrophy. Pathologic differentiation of Pick's disease and CJD can at times be difficult: it is, therefore, likely that some of the cases will prove transmissible.

DIFFERENTIAL DIAGNOSIS OF CJD

Roos et al.[71] pointed out that many patients with dementia might have a clinical course highly suggestive of CJD, yet would eventually show pathologic findings necessitating this diagnosis to be abandoned. Examples of final diagnosis in such patients included Alzheimer's disease (some cases familial), striatonigral de-

Table IX
Summary of Data on 33 Patients with Dementia of Unknown Etiology

Characteristic	Value*	
Number of males	21	
Number of females	12	
Percentage of males	64%	
Age range	13-67 years	
Mean age onset	51.5 ± 10.7 years	
Duration range	6 months - 8 years	
Mean duration	>38 months	
Behavioral disturbance	13/19	(68%)
Higher cortical dysfunction	12/19	(63%)
Upper motor neuron signs	20/22	(91%)
Lower motor neuron signs	7/14	(50%)
Basal ganglia disorder	14/17	(82%)
Myoclonus	7/13	(54%)
Cerebellar dysfunction	5/14	(36%)
Visual disturbance	6/11	(55%)
Characteristic EEG	2/10	(20%)
Seizures	11/17	(65%)
Neuronal vacuolation	0 (1?)/33	(0%)
Neurofibrillary tangles	5/33	(15%)
Amyloid plaques	5/33	(15%)
Family history	7/18	(39%)

*ratio = number with characteristic/number where information is available.

generation, Binswanger's disease, glioblastoma multiforme, cerebrovascular disease, Parkinson's disease, sarcoidosis, and unclassified neurologic disease. One patient, E. Fo., had features of both CJD and Alzheimer's disease pathologically, and has been included in the CJD series of this chapter. Clinical features demonstrated by these patients included all of the clinical characteristics tabulated above.

The situation has become even more complex with the recognition of patients in whom CJD was strongly considered, even when conflicting pathologic results were available. The transmissibility of disease from A. Yo., where CJD changes (spongiosus) were subtle compared with striking Alzheimer changes, cautions one against rejecting as irrelevant pathologic indications of CJD in the presence of other neuropathology.

Three cases, S. Co., F. Pe., and D. St., will illustrate the difficulties in the diagnosis of CJD. In all three the diagnosis of CJD was strongly considered on the basis of clinical course and biopsy results; the diagnosis was altered post-mortem in S. Co., and F. Pe., while a glioblastoma was found unexpectedly in D. St.

S. Co. This patient was presented briefly by Vernon et al.[77] as a case of CJD. He was a retired Coast Guardsman. He had decreased vision at age 61; three years later he stopped reading newspapers. About seven years later he was nearly blind, and was withdrawn with deteriorating memory. Myoclonus, dysphagia, speech difficulties, and incontinence appeared. Eight years after onset he was found to be combative and demented. There was bilateral ptosis, bilateral spasticity and atrophy of intrinsic hand muscles. Pupils were equal and reactive, but he seemed to be blind. EEG showed generalized slowing with bursts of high voltage of slower activity, compatible with CJD. A left frontal brain biopsy was done and is reported by Vernon et al.[77] as showing moderate loss of neurons and astrocytosis. Electron microscopy revealed vacuolation in neuropil and a plaque, and virus-like particles were seen. Examination of the post-mortem brain, however, showed abundant neurofibrillary tangles and senile plaques. There was granulovacuolar degeneration in the hippocampus and widespread cortical neuronal loss and gliosis. The picture was that of Alzheimer's disease. There were marked changes in occipital cortex, an unusual finding in Alzheimer's disease.

F. Pe. This man began at age 61 to suffer loss of intellectual function, with urinary incontinence and disorientation. He developed prominent extrapyramidal signs, including akinesia and rigidity; these symptoms improved temporarily with L-Dopa treatment. EEG's became more and more slow. Progressive dementia began. About 14 months after onset, myoclonus appeared. He died about two weeks later. A brain biopsy was thought to be consistent with CJD. At autopsy, the brain was atrophic frontally. There was depigmentation in the substantia nigra and locus ceruleus with extracellular melanin and a few Lewy bodies. The cerebral cortex was essentially normal, except for the presence of a few senile plaques. There were no neurofibrillary tangles and no granulovacuolar degeneration. There was some gliosis in the striatum. The final diagnosis was Parkinsonism-dementia, with stigmata of alcoholic encephalopathy.

D. St. This 52-year-old woman developed confusion, disorientation and apathy progressive over three months. She was noted then to be dysphasic, and a right Babinski sign appeared. Brain scan showed an ill-defined area of uptake in the left temporoparietal region. EEG at the time was diffusely abnormal. The CSF contained five polymorphonuclear cells and 1300 red cells, and had a protein level of 35 mg %. Pneumoencephalography displayed minimal dilatation of the lateral ventricles and mild increase in the width of the third ventricle. Angiography showed a hypoplastic left anterior cerebral artery. Diagnoses of CJD and left hemisphere glioma were entertained. Myoclonus of the right face and body appeared. EEG's evolved periodic complexes, more marked on the left side. A left frontal biopsy showed neuronal loss, astrocytic and microglial proliferation, and a spongy network in the white matter; there was no evidence of tumor. It was read as compatible with subacute spongiform encephalopathy. The patient died after about four months of illness. At autopsy a small glioblastoma multiforme was found in the left parietal subcortical white matter.

This case may be another example of CJD superimposed on a different underlying neurologic disease.

EXPERIMENTAL CJD AND VIROLOGY OF THE CJD AGENT

Inoculation of suspension of brain, brain tissue culture grown in *in vitro* explant culture, liver, kidney, and lymph node by intracerebral and peripheral routes has produced in primates an experimental disease closely resembling human CJD clinically and pathologically. After an incubation period as short as 10 months in the chimpanzee, affected animals develop a progressive subacute illness with hemiparesis, somnolence, myoclonus, visual disturbances and behavioral abnormalities with progression within four months to a helpless, paralyzed, stuporous state, with limbs held in flexion.[24,39] (Such a terminal state is common in man as well.) Pathologic changes are on occasion present in animals dying of intercurrent disease even before onset of clearly recognizable signs. A trained observer can distinguish affected animals with experimental CJD from those with experimental kuru, mainly by the presence of pyramidal tract signs and myoclonus in the former, and ataxia and tremor in the latter. In addition, animals with experimental CJD have more severe somnolence, inanition, and withdrawal than is usual in kuru. There is overlap between the experimental diseases, nonetheless; for example, chimpanzees with experimental CJD may have ataxia and intention tremor. There appears to be no correlation between the clinical pattern in the patient and the animal inoculated with the patient's brain.

Pathologic changes in brains of animals with experimental CJD are found, among other places, in the cerebral cortex, basal ganglia, thalamus and cerebellum.[6,59] Primary changes are confined to gray matter and include neuronal loss and vacuolation, status spongiosus and astrocytic and microglial proliferation. The overall picture resembles closely that in the human disease. The lesions may extend into the brain stem and spinal cord. Pathologic changes may be visible as early as three to four months after inoculation.[61b]

Experimental CJD is now in its fifth serial passage. Unlike kuru, the incubation period has not been shortened in chimpanzees on serial passage. Data on the primary transmissions are summarized in Tables X and XI. Three of the transmissions took place in France, under the auspices of Dr. F. Cathala and her colleagues.[13,15] The disease has been transmitted from humans into the following hosts:

Apes: chimpanzee
New World Monkeys: spider monkey
      squirrel monkey
      capuchin monkey
      marmoset
Old World monkeys: rhesus monkey
      cynomolgus monkey
      mangabey
      bushbaby
      pigtail monkey
      baboon
      African green monkey
      patas monkey
      stumptail monkey
Other: domestic cat
      guinea pig
      mouse

In addition, we have transmitted CJD in serial passage to the woolly monkey. Further, the transmissibility of CJD has been independently confirmed by Zlotnik et al.[79] and Brownell et al.[11] in squirrel monkeys, by Field [22a] to chimpanzees, by Gear [31a] to African green monkeys, and by Schulman et al. [71a] to the rhesus monkey.

Table X
Primary Transmissions of TVD to Laboratory Animals

Patient	Inoculum	Route of Inoculation	Host	Incubation (months)	Duration (months)
V. Ad.	brain aut. 20%	ic	squirrel monkey	30 (died)	
T. At.	brain aut. 10^{-1}	ic	squirrel monkey	19 (died)	
	brain aut. 10^{-1}	ic, iv	chimpanzee	14	2
	brain aut. 10^{-1}	ic	squirrel monkey	22	1
	brain aut. 10^{-1}	ic	capuchin monkey	24	10
	brain aut. tc	ic	capuchin monkey	11	27
	brain aut. tc	ic	capuchin monkey	35	4
	liver aut. 10^{-1}	ic, iv	squirrel monkey	26 (died)	
	liver aut. 10^{-1}	ic	squirrel monkey	40	<1 wk
	knsl aut. 10^{-1}	ic, iv	chimpanzee	18	4
	node aut. 10^{-1}	ic, iv	squirrel monkey	37	2
	kidney aut. 10^{-1}	ic, iv	squirrel monkey	41	2
S. Au.	brain aut. 10^{-1}	ic	*squirrel monkey	21½	½
	brain aut. 10^{-1}	ic	capuchin monkey	35	<1
	liver aut. 10^{-1}	ic	*squirrel monkey	13 (died)	
M. Ba.	brain aut. 10^{-1}	ic	†squirrel monkey	20	2
	brain aut. 10^{-1}	ic	squirrel monkey	20	1½
	brain aut. 10^{-1}	ic	squirrel monkey	20	4
S. Be.	brain aut. 10^{-1}	ic, iv	squirrel monkey	22	<1
E. Br.	brain bx. 10^{-1}	ic, ip	squirrel monkey	25½	1½
R. Bu.	brain aut. 10^{-1}	ic	mangabey	3 (died)	
	brain aut. 10^{-1}	ic, iv	chimpanzee	14	2
	brain aut. 10^{-1}	ic, iv	rhesus monkey	66	4
	brain aut. 10^{-1}	ic	rhesus monkey	56	9
	brain aut. 10^{-1}	ic, iv	rhesus monkey	66	10
P. Ca.	brain aut. 10^{-1}	ic, iv	squirrel monkey	23	<1
	brain aut. 10^{-1}	ic, iv	squirrel monkey	25	1½
	brain aut. 10^{-1}	ic, iv	squirrel monkey	21	3
M. Ch.	brain aut. 10^{-1}	ic, iv	squirrel monkey	29	<1
R. Cl.	brain bx. 10^{-1}	ic, iv	squirrel monkey	25½	<1
	brain bx. 10^{-1}	ic, iv	spider monkey	37½ (died)	
S. Co.	brain aut.	ic, ip	squirrel monkey	11 (died)	
	brain aut. 2×10^{-1}	ic	squirrel monkey	20 (died)	
J. Co.	brain aut. 10^{-1}	ic, iv	squirrel monkey	19 (died)	
J. Col.	brain bx. 10^{-1}	ic	squirrel monkey	22	1½
R. Co.	brain bx. 0.5×10^{-1}	ic, iv	chimpanzee	13	4
R. Cu.	brain bx. 0.5×10^{-1}	ic, iv	squirrel monkey	23	3
S. De.	brain bx. 0.5×10^{-1}	ic	squirrel monkey	18	3½

Table X *Continued*
Primary Transmissions of TVD to Laboratory Animals

Patient	Inoculum	Route of Inoculation	Host	Incubation (months)	Duration (months)
J. Do.	brain aut. 10^{-1}	ic, ip	bushbaby	16	2
	brain aut. 10^{-1}	ic, iv	chimpanzee	11	2
	brain tc	ic, iv	chimpanzee	17½	1½
	brain aut. 10^{-2}	ic	spider monkey	37	3½
	brain aut. 10^{-4}	ic	spider monkey	44	3
	brain aut. 10^{-5}	ic	spider monkey	34	6½
J. Ea.	brain aut. 10^{-1}	ic, iv	squirrel monkey	28	1
	brain aut. 10^{-1}	ic, iv	squirrel monkey	30	1½
L. Er.	brain bx. 0.5×10^{-1}	ic, iv	chimpanzee	14	1
	brain bx. 0.5×10^{-1}	ic	spider monkey	25	4
S. Fe.	brain aut. 10^{-1}	ic, ip	squirrel monkey	13	1
A. Fl.	brain aut. 10^{-1}	ic, iv	squirrel monkey	27	1
P. Ga.	brain aut. 10^{-1}	ic, iv	chimpanzee	23½	6
J. Gr.	brain aut. 10^{-1}	ic, iv	*chimpanzee	14	1*
S. Gr.	brain aut. 10^{-1}	ic, ip	squirrel monkey	28	2
	brain aut. 10^{-1}	ic, iv	spider monkey	38 (died)	
	brain aut. 10^{-1}	ic, iv	chimpanzee	34	5
	brain aut. 10^{-1}	ic	spider monkey	41½	2
	brain aut. 10^{-1} 450 nm filtrate	ic, ip	squirrel monkey	19	3
	brain aut. 10^{-6} 450 nm filtrate	ic, ip	squirrel monkey	14	<1
B. Ha.	brain bx. 10^{-1}	ic, iv	squirrel monkey	29½	<1
H. Ha.	brain aut. 10^{-1}	ic, ip	squirrel monkey	22	<1
R. Ia.	brain aut. 10^{-1}	ic, iv	squirrel monkey	23	1
J. Ja.	brain aut. 10^{-1}		chimpanzee	13	2
	brain aut. 10^{-1}		cat	30	2
V. Je.	brain bx. + aut. 10^{-1}	ic	capuchin monkey	29	11
	brain bx + aut. 10^{-1}	ic	capuchin monkey	39	8
	brain bx + aut. 10^{-1}	ic, iv	chimpanzee	12	1½
	brain bx + aut. 10^{-1}	ic	cynomolgus monkey	52½	7
	brain bx 10^{-1}	ic	spider monkey	23	1
	brain bx 10^{-1}	ic, iv	baboon	47½ (died)	
G. Jo.	brain aut. 10^{-1}	ic, iv	squirrel monkey	23	<1
K. Kn.	brain aut. 0.5×10^{-1}	ic	squirrel monkey	14	<1
	brain aut. 0.5×10^{-2}	ic	squirrel monkey	18	<1
	brain aut. 0.5×10^{-3}	ic	chimpanzee	13	<1

Table X *Continued*

Primary Transmissions of TVD to Laboratory Animals

Patient	Inoculum	Route of Inoculation	Host	Incubation (months)	Duration (months)
R. Ko.	brain aut. 0.5×10^{-1}	ic	capuchin monkey	44½	<1
C. Ko.	brain bx 0.5×10^{-1}	ic, iv	squirrel monkey	20	1½
L. Kr.	brain aut. 10^{-1}	ic, im	squirrel monkey	20	2
C. Lo.	brain aut. 10^{-1}	ic, im	squirrel monkey	26 (died)	
T. Ma.	brain aut. 10^{-1}	ic, iv	squirrel monkey	29½	<1
M. Ma.	brain bx 2×10^{-1}	ic	squirrel monkey	22	1
	brain bx 2×10^{-1}	ic	capuchin monkey	34½	1½
D. Ma.	brain aut. 10^{-1}	ic,iv,ip,sc,im	chimpanzee	26	5½
	brain aut. 10^{-1}	ic	squirrel monkey	19½	6½
	brain aut. 10^{-1}	im	chimpanzee	11	<1
D. May.	brain aut. 10^{-1}	ic, iv	capuchin monkey	34 (died)	
	brain aut. 10^{-1}	ic, iv	squirrel monkey	22½	1½
C. Mo.	brain aut. 10^{-1}	ic	spider monkey	26½	7½
D. Mu.	brain aut. 0.5×10^{-1}	ic, iv	chimpanzee	11	1
	brain aut. 0.5×10^{-1}	ic	spider monkey	25	4½
	brain aut. tc	ic,iv,sc	chimpanzee	26½	<1
E. Ne.	brain aut. 10^{-1}	ic	squirrel monkey	23	1
	brain aut. 10^{-1}	ic	squirrel monkey	24½	<1
F. Ni.	brain aut. 10^{-1}	ic	spider monkey	50	3½
R. Po.	brain bx 10^{-1}	ic, iv	spider monkey	23	1½
	brain bx 10^{-1}	ic, iv	squirrel monkey	23	<1
	brain aut. 10^{-1}	ic, iv	squirrel monkey	28	<1
R. Re.	brain bx 0.5×10^{-1}	ic, iv	chimpanzee	13	1
	brain bx 0.5×10^{-1}	ic, iv	chimpanzee	12	2½
	brain bx 0.5×10^{-1}	ic, ip	marmoset	43	<1
	brain bx 0.5×10^{-1}	ic, ip	capuchin monkey	31	6½
T. Se.	brain bx 10^{-1}	ic, iv	chimpanzee	12	<1
	brain bx 10^{-1}	ic	squirrel monkey	16	<1
	brain aut. 10^{-1}	ic, iv	squirrel monkey	23 (died)	
E. Sp.	brain bx 0.5×10^{-1}	ic, iv	chimpanzee	12	1
	brain bx 0.5×10^{-1}	ic, iv	mangabey	41½	2½
	brain bx 0.5×10^{-1}	ic	spider monkey	25½	2½
	brain bx 0.5×10^{-1}	ic	rhesus monkey	60	1
E. St.	brain aut. 10^{-1}	ic, iv	squirrel monkey	25	5
	brain aut. 10^{-1}	ic, iv	squirrel monkey	32½ (died)	

Table X *Continued*
Primary Transmissions of TVD to Laboratory Animals

Patient	Inoculum	Route of Inoculation	Host	Incubation (months)	Duration (months)
B. Sy.	brain aut. 10^{-1}	ic, iv	squirrel monkey	22	3½
	brain aut. 10^{-1}	ic, iv	squirrel monkey	30½	4½
	brain aut. 10^{-1}	ic, iv	spider monkey	25½	1½
A. Ta.	brain aut. 10^{-1}	ic, iv	chimpanzee	14	1
	brain aut. 10^{-1}	ic	squirrel monkey	25	1½
	brain aut. 10^{-1}	ic	stumptail monkey	60	12
W. Tr.	brain aut. 10^{-1}	ic	squirrel monkey	28½	2½
	brain aut. 10^{-1}	ic, iv	chimpanzee	36	1
	brain bx + aut. 10^{-1}	ic, sc	chimpanzee	71	3½
H. Tu.	brain aut. 0.5×10^{-1}	ic, iv	squirrel monkey	14	<1
	brain aut. 10^{-1}	ic, im	squirrel monkey	18	1
N. Wi.	brain aut. 10^{-1}	ic, iv	squirrel monkey	23½	2
	brain aut. 10^{-1}	ic, iv	squirrel monkey	28	<1
J. Wo.	brain aut. 10^{-1}	ic	squirrel monkey	20	1½
M. Wo.	brain aut. 2×10^{-1}	ic, iv	spider monkey	26	1
	brain aut. 2×10^{-1}	iv, ip	chimpanzee	16	2
	brain aut. 10^{-1}	ic, iv	chimpanzee	12	1½
	brain aut. 10^{-1}	ic, iv	rhesus monkey	67	1
	brain aut. 10^{-1}	ic, ip	capuchin monkey	36	2
	brain aut. 10^{-1}	ic, iv	rhesus monkey	66	2
	brain aut. 10^{-1}	ic, iv	rhesus monkey	68	6
A. Yo.	brain - lshk	ic, iv, sc	squirrel monkey	23 (died)	

Footnotes and Abbreviations:
* Inoculations in France by Dr. F. Cathala et al.[13,15]
† Inoculations in England by Zlotnik et al.[79]
  ic - intracerebral   iv - intravenous   ip - intraperitoneal
  im - intramuscular   sc - subcutaneous
  tc - tissue culture (in vitro)
  knsl - kidney, node, spleen, liver
  lshk - liver, spleen, heart, kidney

Disease has been transmitted from one patient solely by peripheral routes of inoculation (M. Wo.). The highest titer in human brain yet found is 10^6 infectious doses/gm tissue, although end points have not been reached in titrations.

Table XI shows also the incubation times in the different hosts

Table XI

Incubation Periods to Onset of Clinical Disease for Experimental
TVD in Laboratory Animals After Inoculation of
Human Brain Tissue[+]

Host	Range of incubation period (months)	n	Mean incubation period (months)
chimpanzee	11 - 71	22	18.6 ± 13.8
squirrel monkey	13 - 30½	50	22.5 ± 4.6
spider monkey	23 - 50	13	31.2 ± 9.1
capuchin monkey	24 - 44½	8	34.1 ± 6.3
rhesus monkey	56 - 68	7	64.1 ± 4.4
bushbaby	16	1	16
mangabey	41½	1	41½
cynomolgus monkey	52½	1	52½
cat	30	1	30

[+]Animals dying before development of clinical disease are excluded. Inoculations of
in vitro tissue culture specimens are excluded.

for the primary transmissions. Chimpanzees have the shortest
incubation period of 11 to 71 months. The incubation period seems
to be a characteristic of the experimental host. Further, incubation
period does not seem to depend on the titer of inoculum. It is
important to note that conventional neurotropic agents, such as
poliomyelitis virus, are often not recovered from brain suspensions
from well-diagnosed cases. A failure to transmit CJD may represent
a similar phenomenon.

The CJD agent has been shown in two experiments to persist
in tissue culture. In the first experiment brain cells from a chimpanzee dying with the R. Re. strain of the agent were maintained
in explant culture for one month; they produced experimental CJD
in a chimpanzee after intracerebral and peripheral inoculation. In
the second experiment, brain cells from the biopsy of J. Do. were
maintained in explant culture for 255 days, with 14 changes of
medium. They induced experimental CJD in a chimpanzee with an
incubation period of 16 months. The property of persisting in

explant systems is shared by the agents of the other spongiform encephalopathies.[28,41]

The CJD agent survives storage at $-70°C$ for at least three years. It passes through a 220nm filter, but has not yet passed a 100nm filter. This is true also of the kuru agent, but the scrapie and TME agents seem to be smaller.[33] Experiments are in progress to determine the density of the CJD agent in sucrose gradients.[72]

Some observers have seen virus-like particles in CJD brains with the electron microscope.[77] These have not been found consistently. We believe that these do not represent the CJD agent itself, in view of their absence in experimental infection and in view of the large number of latent viruses isolated from human and primate brain tissue.[30,46]

Attempts to link the CJD agent to known viruses by demonstrating a specific serologic response to these viruses have yielded negative results. Brown et al.[10] examined sera from CJD patients and chimpanzees for antibody to viruses and Bedsoniae of the following types: influenza, parainfluenza, measles, mumps, RSV, NDV, Echo, Coxsackie, polio, herpes simplex and zoster, CMV, adenovirus, reovirus, certain arboviruses, vaccinia, rabies, LCM, rubella, SV-40, psittacosis, E-B and Australia Antigen. No consistent pattern of high titers was found. Similar negative results have been obtained with kuru sera.[7]

A virus resembling the RNA-oncogenic viruses has been isolated from the brain biopsy of S. Gr.[45,47,48] This man had "typical" CJD as seen below:

S. Gr. This 61-year-old retired Navy officer, an air pollution specialist, presented with gait imbalance and loss of mental acuity. After one month he had limb dysmetria and ataxic gait, and the diagnosis of cerebellar degeneration was considered. Dementia was progressive and myoclonus, right Babinski sign, and dysphagia appeared. EEG showed bursts of slow activity; these were not periodic. He became comatose and died after six months of illness. A brain biopsy midway through his course showed some swollen astrocytes and vacuolation. The brain at autopsy showed general depletion of cortical neurons. Astrogliosis and status spongiosus were seen. In addition, a small psammomatous meningioma was found in the pituitary gland. Inoculation of autopsy brain suspensions at dilutions of 10^{-1} and 10^{-6} has induced experimental CJD in 3 squirrel monkeys, a chimpanzee, and two spider monkeys (Table X). Two of these suspensions were cell-free, having been filtered through 450nm membranes.

Brain biopsy cells from S. Gr. grown *in vitro* showed altered morphology after 60 days in explant culture.[45] On the 5th subculture, all cells were transformed and had lost contact inhibition. Cells were shown to be definitely of human origin. Most had 75 chromosomes. Plating efficiency was extremely high. Electron microscopy showed virus particles resembling RNA oncogenic viruses, in particular, Mason-Pfizer monkey virus (MPMV); some were budding at the cell membrane. The agent was passed to a human sarcoma cell line in which it produced an RNA-dependent DNA polymerase immunologically cross-reactive with that of MPMV. Chimpanzees and monkeys inoculated with S. Gr. tissue culture materials 24 to 39 months ago remain well.

Similar particles resembling MPMV have not been seen in other human or experimental CJD brains. Numerous viruses have been isolated in this laboratory from primate tissues, including foamy viruses productive of RNA-dependent DNA polymerase.[46,69] These isolates are all distinct from the S. Gr. agent. The relationship of the S. Gr. agent to CJD remains obscure.

THE NATURAL SPREAD OF TVD

The natural mode of spread of TVD remains unknown. Absence of a serologic test for antibody to the CJD agent makes it impossible to determine how frequently people and animals are exposed to the virus. Data reviewed in this chapter do allow some reasonable speculation, however. Familial CJD has already been discussed.

TVD has probably been transmitted from human to human via a cornea transplant.[20a] Since the donor's eye was enucleated prior to removal of the cornea, the cornea was almost certainly contaminated with optic nerve (i.e., brain). Thus, this case may represent transmission of TVD via peripheral inoculation of brain. (Marsh et al. have demonstrated, however, the presence of the TME agent in corneal epithelium.)[61a] In addition, the neurosurgical cases of Nevin et al.[66] in Table XII also suggest that TVD may be trans-

Table XII

Association of CJD or CJD-Like Picture with Other Disturbances of the Central Nervous System

Primary neurological disturbance	Age of onset of primary disturbance (year)	Time from onset primary disturbance to appearance of CJD picture	Duration "CJD"	Clinical Features	Neuropathologic Features
CVA (Reference: Case 3, Nevin et al.[66])	53	2 years	3½ months	memory loss, clumsiness, myoclonus, EEG: synchronous sharp waves	neuronal loss, suggestion of status spongiosus
Surgical removal of meningioma (Reference: Case 1, Nevin et al.[66])	57	15 months	5 months	blindness, rigidity, myoclonus, CJD-typical EEG	neuronal loss, astrocytosis, vacuolation
Surgical removal of brain abscess (Reference: Case 2, Nevin et al.[66])	67	17 months	3½ months	memory loss, aphasia, myoclonus, blindness, CJD-typical EEG	neuronal loss, astrocytosis, suggestion of status spongiosus
Bilateral frontal leucotomy (Reference: Case 7, Nevin et al.[66])	46	17 months	2 months	confusion, myoclonus, typical EEG	neuronal loss, astrocytosis, loosening of "ground substance"
Familial Alzheimer's disease (Reference: A. Yo., this series (TVD))	44	unclear	unclear	dementia, emotional instability	senile plaques, neurofibrillary tangles, one area of spongiosus in insular cortex

Table XII *Continued*

Association of CJD or CJD-Like Picture with Other Disturbances of the Central Nervous System

Primary neurological disturbance	Age of onset of primary disturbance (year)	Time from onset primary disturbance to appearance of CJD picture	Duration "CJD"	Clinical Features	Neuropathologic Features
Familial Alzheimer's disease (Reference: B. Ha., this series (TVD))	51	unclear	>6 years	dementia, dysphasia, increased deep tendon reflexes	senile plaques, neurofibrillary tangles
Köhlmeier-Degos' disease (Reference: D. Ma., this series (TVD))	54	unclear	<17 months	brain stem signs, sleep disturbance, myoclonus, ataxia	vasculitis, neuronal loss, astrogliosis, status spongiosus
Glioblastoma (left parietal) (Reference: D. St., this series)	<53	unknown	4 months	dementia, myoclonus, right-sided weakness EEG typical but with left-temporo-parietal focal features	Bx: neuronal loss, astrocytosis, spongy network in white matter
Hereditary ataxia (Reference: Case 1, Skre & Löken[73])	16 (?34)	25 years (7 years)	9-10 months	dementia, seizures, myoclonus, ataxia, peripheral neuropathy, EEG typical	spongy changes, neuronal loss in cortex, spinocerebellar degeneration, lower motor neuron lesions

Hereditary ataxia (Reference: Case 3, Skre & Löken[73])	20	1 year	6 years	seizures, myoclonus, cerebellar signs, peripheral neuropathy, EEG not typical	cortical neuronal loss, astrocytosis, spongy changes cerebellum, olivo-ponto-cerebellar and spinal degeneration, peripheral nerve degeneration
Hepatocerebral degeneration (Reference: Case 5, Victor, Adams & Cole[78])	37	13 years	9 years	confusion, ataxia, dysarthria, athetosis, mild dementia	cortical and putaminal status spongiosus, diffuse hyperplasia of protoplasmic astrocytes
Head trauma (Reference: A.H., Brownell & Oppenheimer[12])	55	8 months	8 months	ataxia, dysphasia, hyperreflexia, chorea, myoclonus, dementia	neuronal degeneration, astrocytosis, minimal status spongiosus
Head trauma (Reference: J. Gr., this series (TVD))	51	10 days	5 weeks	catatonia, pyramidal tract signs, myoclonus	neuronal loss, status spongiosus
Head trauma (Reference: R. Cu., this series (TVD))	59	c. 1 year	5 months	dementia, bulimia, field cut, myoclonus	astrocytosis, microspongiosus
Alzheimer's disease (Reference: E. Fo., this series)	38	4 years	4 years	delusions, seizures, myoclonus, amyotrophy, EEG typical	senile plaques, neurofibrillary tangles, microspongiosus cavity by EM (Bx)

Table XII *Continued*

Association of CJD or CJD-Like Picture with Other Disturbances of the Central Nervous System

Primary neurological disturbance	Age of onset of primary distrub-ance (year)	Time from onset primary disturbance to appearance of CJD picture	Duration "CJD"	Clinical Features	Neuropathologic Features
Alzheimer's disease (Reference: S. Co., this series)	61	7-8 years	<1 year	blindness, myoclonus, spasticity, typical EEG	senile plaques, neurofibrillary tangles, vacuolation in neuropil by EM (Bx)
Meningioma (pituitary) (Reference: S. Gr., this series (TVD))	unknown <61	unclear	6 months	dementia, myoclonus, cerebellar signs	neuronal loss, astrocytosis, status spongiosus
Neurofibromatosis (Reference: P. Ca., this series (TVD))	childhood	c. 56 years	5 months	dementia, myoclonus, ataxia, seizures	status spongiosus, astrocytosis

missible to man by direct inoculation. The case of the neuro-surgeon, D. Ma., again raises this possibility. These cases, together with the known transmissibility to primates of at least some CJD and the presence of the CJD agent in visceral tissue, have important practical implications. First, it is unwise to transplant tissues, including skin, kidney and cornea, from any patient with presenile dementia.[20a] Second, because of the presumed stability of the CJD agent by analogy with the scrapie agent,[33] tissues from presenile dementia patients may pose a hazard to neurosurgeons, pathologists and others coming in contact with them.[76] We know, however, of no cases to date, other than those mentioned above, for which there is evidence of contact with CJD-contaminated material.

Transmissibility to the domestic cat raises the possibility of an animal reservoir for TVD, although there seems to be no natural disease of cats resembling experimental feline CJD. Of interest in this connection is M. Wo., a mink rancher with TVD. L. Herzberg has noted that two of the CJD patients referred to us kept ferrets, and one case known to us was a furrier. An epidemiologic study,[8] however, found no difference in animal exposure between CJD patients and controls; the observation that one-third of patients and controls ate brains may be important, however. This matter remains open. Jellinger et al.[43,53] described CJD appearing in husband and wife within four months of one another, suggesting a possible common contact; the nature of this proposed contact is unknown. The focus of CJD among Libyan Jews also remains to be explained.

Finally, we have made the proposal that perhaps the CJD agent can "invade" or be activated from latency in an already diseased brain. If this is correct, the diagnosis of CJD in a patient with presenile dementia does not exclude all other diagnoses. CJD might thus be an opportunistic infection which can occur *de novo* or as a complication in an altered host.

SUMMARY

A series of 56 Transmissible Virus Dementia patients is presented and their clinical and pathologic features are compared with those of 70 CJD patients whose disease has not yet transmitted. A subgroup consisting of 8 patients whose brain was inoculated more than four years ago in a chimpanzee, squirrel monkey, or capuchin monkey, is also selected as likely to represent "true" nontransmissions. The features of these 8 untransmissible patients are also considered.

Except for the incidence of lower motor neuron signs and of a CJD-characteristic EEG, there is no statistical difference between the TVD patients as a whole, and the nontransmitted CJD patients as a whole, with respect to the incidence of the various clinicopathologic features. Mean age is almost identical for the two groups. The nontransmitted CJD patients seem to have a longer disease duration (but the standard errors are large, so that the meaning of this is not clear).

In spite of this, the spectrum of TVD is not identical with that of CJD. First, the TVD group included three patients with a different underlying neurologic disease, i.e., with a mixed neuropathologic picture, and in whom the diagnosis of CJD was not even considered during life. Second, no patient with amyotrophic CJD has yet been shown to have transmissible disease.

Virtually all of the TVD and CJD patients reported here had status spongiosus, in contrast to the two-thirds of cases reported by Kirschbaum. This may reflect in part a change in the neuropathologic criteria for diagnosing CJD. Every one of the TVD patients showed evidence of status spongiosus or vacuolation, but this could easily have been missed in several without a careful search. In addition, all animals with experimental CJD showed status spongiosus. (Thus, it is still possible that Nevin[65] is correct in his contention that TVD represents a distinct entity from the classical, amyotrophic form of CJD.)

The transmission of spongiform encephalopathy to primates from three patients with different underlying neurological diseases (Köhlmeier-Degos syndrome and Alzheimer's disease), and the presence of CJD changes in association with other chronic CNS diseases in 18 patients, leads us to suggest that the CJD agent may occur as a secondary pathogen in an already diseased brain. Neurosurgery, consumption of animal brain, and contact with ferrets may also be involved in spread of the disease. It is emphasized that CJD tissue may pose a hazard to man and that tissue from any patient with presenile dementia should not be used for transplantation,[20a,76] nor should their blood or blood products be used for transfusion.

The positive family history in seven of the TVD patients is of special interest and necessitates search for transmissible agents in other "heredodegenerative" diseases.

Creutzfeldt-Jakob disease, at least the transmissible form, is one of the subacute spongiform encephalopathies, others being kuru, scrapie and TME. All are progressive subacute CNS diseases caused by atypical viruses, producing gliosis, neuronal loss and vacuolation and status spongiosus. There are particular links between the two human diseases, including the existence of an ataxic form in both (10% of CJD, and 100% of kuru) and the presence of amyloid-containing "senile" plaques in significant numbers in both (about 14% in CJD, and about 70% in kuru).

The virology of the CJD agent is discussed. Incubation periods in the chimpanzee are generally shorter with TVD than kuru, and the clinical features of the experimental syndromes somewhat different. What little is known, however, about the properties of the two agents is consistent with the hypothesis that the CJD and kuru agents may be different strains of very similar viruses.

Future investigations depend upon gathering material from patients with atypical forms of presenile dementia. Research will be aided by finding an experimental host easier and less expensive to work with than primates and with shorter incubation than the 30 months in the domestic cat. In this regard, the incubation period of 19 months for second passage CJD in the cat is promising, as is current work on the transmission of CJD to guinea pigs and mice. Finding an immunologic marker for the CJD agent is also of the utmost importance. Work is meanwhile in progress to concentrate the CJD agent by sucrose gradient zonal centrifugation.

ADDENDUM

Since the last revision of this paper the number of cases of transmissible virus dementia which we have identified has increased to 78. Of the additional transmitted cases 21 were confirmed cases of CJD, 1 with a history of familial occurrence of similar dementia;

1 additional transmission was from a patient suffering from progressive supranuclear palsy. These 22 patients have caused illness in 1 chimpanzee and 21 squirrel, 3 capuchin, 2 spider, and 1 African green monkeys.

Of the 21 CJD patients, 17 were included in the 70 yet untransmitted cases reported above, and only one of these, namely A. La., was in the series of 8 "untransmissible" cases. Two monkeys were affected from the inoculation of 10% brain from this patient (A. La.): a capuchin monkey with 47½ months incubation and 2 months duration of illness, and an African green monkey with 44½ months incubation and 6 months duration. The nature of their progressive illness was not recognized as TMV at the time of the previous summary. In addition, 1 non-CJD case has transmitted as a subacute spongiform encephalopathy to a spider monkey after 31 months incubation: this was from a patient with classical clinical and pathological signs of progressive supranuclear palsy and with no sign of neuronal vacuolation or status spongiosus on neuro-pathological examination of the brain at autopsy. Three newly transmitted cases of CJD are "new cases", not inoculated at the time of the last summary.

In addition, there have been 35 further transmissions from tissues from 26 of the 56 patients with TMV reported above. These have occurred in 1 chimpanzee and 11 squirrel, 7 capuchin, 4 spider, 3 rhesus, 2 patas, 6 African green monkeys, and 1 marmoset. One of these transmissions has been from one of the patients (B.H.) with familial Alzheimer's disease, who remains alive in advanced disease 7 years after the onset of her illness. A further transmission to the African green monkey,[31a] to the guinea pig [59a] and to squirrel monkeys[11,79] has also been reported.

Brain tissue from one of the 21 newly transmitted CJD patients had been stored at room temperature in 10% formal saline (4% formaldehyde) for six months before inoculation into a chimpanzee (Gajdusek, Gibbs, Traub and Collins, 1976).[*]

Another CJD patient with senile plaques has come to our attention. We also have inoculated tissue from a new patient with familial CJD, where Huntington's chorea had been considered in the differential diagnosis.

---

[*]Gajdusek, D.C., Gibbs., C.J. Jr., Traub, R.D., and Collins, G. Survival of Creutzfeldt-Jakob disease virus in formol-fixed brain tissue. *New England Journal of Medicine* 294: 10 (March 4), 553, 1976.

Acknowledgments

The authors wish to acknowledge the efforts of all referring physicians who supplied tissue and information for this study (Appendix 1). We also wish to acknowledge the efforts of the following workers in contacting physicians, collecting tissue, and gathering and organizing data: Drs. Raymond Roos, David Asher, Paul W. Brown, Richard Ferber, Stephen Wiesenfeld, and Richard Yanagihara. We wish also to thank Drs. E. French, L. Herzberg, and D. Asher for their critical comments. Many of the pathological observations were made by Drs. Peter Lampert, Byron Kakulas, and Kenneth Earle. We also wish to thank Mr. Michael Sulima for valuable technical assistance and Mrs. Marion Poms for her secretarial assistance.

REFERENCES

1. Adams, H., Beck, E., and Shenkin, A.M.: Creutzfeldt-Jakob disease: further similarities with kuru. *J. Neurol. Neurosurg. Psychiat.*, 37: 195–200, 1974.

1a. Adornato, B., and Lampert, P.: Status spongiosus of nervous tissue. *Acta Neuropath.* (Berlin), 19: 271–289, 1971.

2. Alpers, M.: Kuru: a clinical study. Mimeog., Dept. of Medicine, Univ. of Adelaide, 38 pp.

3. Amyot, R., and Gauthier, C.: Sur la maladie de Creutzfeldt-Jakob deux observations anatomo-cliniques: conception unicist. *Rev. Neurol.*, 110: 473–478, 1964.

4. Asher, D.M., Gibbs, C.J., Jr., David, E., Alpers, M.P., and Gajdusek, D.C.: Experimental kuru in the chimpanzee. In *Nonhuman Primates and Human Diseases*, W. Montagna and W.P. McNulty, eds. *Symp. IVth Int. Congr. Primat.*, 4: 43–90. S. Karger, Basel, 1973.

5. Baringer, J.R.: Personal communication.

6. Beck, E., Daniel, P.M., Matthews, W.B., et. al.: Creutzfeldt-Jakob disease: the neuropathology of a transmission experiment. *Brain*, 92: 699–716, 1969.

7. Benfante, R.J., Traub, R., Lim, K.A., et al.: Immunological reactions in kuru: Attempts to demonstrate serological relationships between kuru and other known infectious agents. *Am. J. Trop. Med. Hyg.*, 23: 476–488, 1974.

8. Bobowick, A.R., Brody, J.A., Matthews, M.R., et al.: Creutzfeldt-Jakob disease: a case control study. *Am. J. Epidem.*, 98: 381–394, 1973.

9. Bonduelle, N., Escourolle, R., Bouygues, P., et al.: Maladie de Creutzfeldt-Jakob familiale. Observation anatomo-clinicque. *Rev. Neurol.*, 125, 197–209, 1971.

10. Brown, P., Hooks, J., Roos, R., et al.: Attempt to identify the agent for Creutzfeldt-Jakob disease by CF antibody relationship to known viruses. *Nature New Biol.*, 235: 149–152, 1972.

11. Brownell, D.B., Campbell, M.J., Greenham, L.W. et al.: Experimental transmission of Creutzfeldt-Jakob disease. *Lancet*, 2: 7926, 186–187, 1975.
12. Brownell, D.B., and Oppenheimer, D.R.: An ataxic form of subacute presenile polioencephalopathy (Jakob-Creutzfeldt disease). *J. Neurol, Neurosurg. Psychiat.*, 28: 350–361, 1965.
13. Cathala, F.: Experience with the transmission of kuru and Creutzfeldt-Jakob disease in France. *Ninth Int. Congr. Trop. Med. Malaria*, Athens, Oct. 14–21, 1973.
14. Cathala, F., and Brown, P.: La maladie de Creutzfeldt-Jakob. Une "encephalopathie spongiforme à virus" de l'homme. *Path. Biol.*, 21: 299–308, 1973.
15. Cathala, F., Hauw, J.J., Escourolle, R., et al.: Transmission of experimental subacute spongiform encephalopathy (Creutzfeldt-Jakab disease) from chimpanzee to chimpanzee. *Biomedicine*, 18: 328–335, 1973.
16. Chou, S.M., and Martin, J.D.: Kuru-plaques in a case of Creutzfeldt-Jakob disease. *Acta Neuropath.* (Berlin), 17: 150–155, 1971.
17. Crémieux, A., Recordier, M., Boudouresques, J., et al.: Degenerescence spino-cerebelleuse familiale et maladie d'Alzheimer. Étude anatomo-clinique d'un cas. *Rev. Neurol.*, 109: 45–54, 1963.
18. Creutzfeldt, H.G.: Über eine eigenartige herdformige Erkrankung des Zentralnervensystems. *Z. Ges. Neurol. Psychiat.* 57: 1–18, 1920.
19. Culicchia, C., Gol, A., and Erickson, E.E.: Diffuse central nervous system involvement in papulosis atrophicans maligna. *Neurol.*, 12: 503–509, 1962.
20. Daniel, P., and Beck, E.: Personal communication.
20a. Duffy, P., Wolf, J., Collins, G., et al.: Person-to-person transmission of Creutzfeldt-Jakob disease. *New Eng. J. Med.*, 299: 692–693, 1974.
21. Earle, K.: Personal communication.
22. Ferber, R.A., Wiesenfeld, S.L., Roos, R., et al.: Familial Creutzfeldt-Jakob disease. Transmission of the familial disease to primates. In *Proc. Xth Inter. Cong. Neurol.*, Series 319, A. Subirana, J.M. Espadaler, and E.H. Burrows, eds., pp. 358–380, 1973. Excerpta Medica, Amsterdam.
22a. Field, E.J.: Transmission experiments and degenerative conditions of the central nervous system. In *Viral Diseases of the Central Nervous System*, L.S. Illis, ed., pp. 175–213, 1975. Ballière Tindall, London.
23. Gajdusek, D.C.: Spongiform virus encephalopathies. *J. Clin. Path.*, 25: Suppl. (Roy. Coll. Path.) 6: 78–83, 1972.
24. Gajdusek, D.C., and Gibbs, C.J., Jr.: Transmission of two subacute spongiform encephalopathies of man (kuru and Creutzfeldt-Jakob disease) to New World monkeys. *Nature*, 230: 588–591, 1971.
25. Gajdusek, D.C., and Gibbs, C.J., Jr.: Transmissible virus dementias and kuru. The two subacute spongiform virus encephalopathies of man. *Bull. de l'Inst. Pasteur*, 70: 117–144, 1972.
25a. Gajdusek, D.C., and Gibbs, C.J., Jr.: Familial and sporadic chronic neurological degenerative disorders transmitted from man to primates.

In Primate Models of Neurological Disorders, B.S. Meldrum and C.D. Marsden (eds.), *Advances in Neurology*, 10: 291–317. New York, Raven Press, 1975.

26. Gajdusek, D.C., Gibbs, C.J., Jr., and Alpers, M.: Experimental transmission of a kuru-like syndrome to chimpanzees. *Nature*, 209: 794–796, 1966.

27. Gajdusek, D.C., Gibbs, C.J., Jr., Earle, K., et al.: Transmission of subacute spongiform encephalopathy to the chimpanzee and squirrel monkey from a patient with papulosis atrophicans maligna of Köhlmeier-Degos. In *Proc. Xth Inter. Cong. Neurol.*, Series 319, A. Subirana, J.M. Espadaler and E.H. Burrows, eds., pp. 390–392, 1973. Excerpta Medica, Amsterdam.

28. Gajdusek, D.C., Gibbs, C.J., Jr., Rogers, N.G., et al.: Persistence of viruses of kuru and Creutzfeldt-Jakob disease in tissue cultures of brain cells. *Nature*, 235: 104–105, 1972.

29. Gajdusek, D.C., Gibbs, C.J., Jr., Zeman, W., et al.: Transmission of subacute spongiform encephalopathy to monkeys from a patient with familial Alzheimer's disease. In preparation.

30. Gajdusek, D.C., Rogers, N.G., Basnight, M., et al.: Transmission experiments with kuru in chimpanzees and the isolation of latent viruses from the explanted tissues of affected animals. *Ann. N.Y. Acad. Sci.*, 162: 529–550, 1969.

31. Gajdusek, D.C., and Zigas, V.: Degenerative disease of the central nervous system in New Guinea. The endemic occurrence of "kuru" in the native population. *New Eng. J. Med.*, 257: 974–978, 1957.

31a. Gear, J.H.S.: Personal communication.

32. Gever, S.G., Freeman, R.G., and Knox, J.M.: Degos' disease (Papulosis atrophicans maligna): report of a case with degenerative disease of the central nervous system. *South. Med. J.*, 55: 56–60, 1962.

33. Gibbs, C.J., Jr., and Gajdusek, D.C.: Transmission and characterization of the agents of spongiform virus encephalopathies: kuru, Creutzfeldt-Jakob disease, scrapie and mink encephalopathy. In *Immunologic Disorders of the Nervous System*. Res. Publ. ARNMD, 49: 383–410, 1971.

34. Gibbs, C.J., Jr., and Gajdusek, D.C.: Isolation and characterization of the subacute spongiform virus encephalopathies of man: kuru and Creutzfeldt-Jakob disease. *J. Clin. Path.*, 25: Suppl. (Roy. Coll. Path.) 6: 84–96, 1972.

35. Gibbs, C.J., Jr., and Gajdusek, D.C.: Experimental subacute spongiform virus encephalopathies in primates and other laboratory animals. *Science*, 182: 67–68, 1973.

36. Gibbs, C.J., Jr., and Gajdusek, D.C.: Biology of kuru and Creutzfeldt-Jakob disease. In W. Zeman and E.H. Lennette (eds.) *Slow Virus Diseases*. Proc. AAPB Symp., Washington, D.C., pp. 39–48, 1974.

37. Gibbs, C.J., Jr., and Gajdusek, D.C.: Scrapie virus. In preparation.

38. Gibbs, C.J., Jr., and Gajdusek, D.C.: Unpublished data.

39. Gibbs, C.J., Jr., Gajdusek, D.C., Asher, D.M., et al.: Creutzfeldt-Jakob disease (spongiform encephalopathy): transmission to the chimpanzee. *Science,* 161: 388–389, 1968.

40. Gomori, A.J., Partnow, M.J., Horoupian, D.S., et al.: The ataxic form of Creutzfeldt-Jakob disease. *Arch. Neurol.,* 29: 318–323, 1973.

41. Gustafson, D.P., and Kanitz, C.L.: Evidence of the presence of scrapie in cell cultures of brain. In D.C. Gajdusek, C.J. Gibbs, Jr., and M. Alpers (eds.), *Slow, Latent, and Temperate Virus Infections.* NINDB Monograph #2, U.S. Govt. Print. Off., pp. 221–236, 1965.

42. Hanson, R.P., Eckroade, R.J., Marsh, R.F., et al.: Susceptibility of mink to sheep scrapie. *Science,* 172: 859–861, 1971.

43. Hess, W.D., and Jellinger, K.: Conjugal appearance of Jacob-Creutzfeldt's disease. Abstract in 10th Inter. Cong. Neurol., Barcelona, Sept. 8–15, 1973.

43a. Hirano, A.: Progress in the pathology of motor neuron diseases. In H.M. Zimmerman (ed.), *Progress in Neuropathology,* Vol. 2, pp. 181–215. Grune & Stratton, New York, 1973.

44. Hirano, A., Ghatak, N., Johnson, A., et al.: Argentophilic plaques in Creutzfeldt-Jakob disease. *Arch. Neurol.,* 26: 530–542, 1972.

45. Hooks, J.J., Gibbs, C.J., Jr., Chopra, H., et al.: Spontaneous transformation of human brain cells grown in vitro and description of associated virus particles. *Science,* 176: 1420–1422, 1972.

46. Hooks, J.J., Gibbs, C.J., Jr., Cutchins, E.E., et al.: Characterization and distribution of two new foamy viruses isolated from chimpanzees. *Arch. Ges. Virusforsch.,* 38: 38–55, 1972.

47. Hooks, J.J., Gibbs, C.J., Jr., and Gajdusek, D.C.: Reply to letter to editor. Transformation of cell cultures derived from human brain. *Science,* 179: 1019–1020, 1973.

48. Hooks, J.J., Gibbs, C.J., Jr., et al.: Relationships of the Griswald oncornavirus to the Mason Pfizer viruses. In preparation.

49. Horoupian, D.S., Powers, J.M., and Schaumberg, H.H.: Kuru-like neuropathological changes in a North American. *Arch. Neurol.* 27: 555–561, 1972.

50. Jacob, H.: Muscular twitchings in Alzheimer's disease. In G.E.W. Wolstenholme and M. O'Connor (eds.), *Alzheimer's Disease,* pp. 75–93. London, Churchill, 1970.

51. Jakob, A.: Uber eigenartige Erkrankungen des Zentralnervensystems mit bemerkenswertem anatomischen Befunde (spastische Pseudosclerose-encephalomyelopathie mit disseminierten Degenerationsherden). *Z. Ges. Neurol. Psychiat.,* 64: 147–228, 1921.

52. Jakob, A.: Uber eine der multiplen Sclerose klinischnahestehende Erkrankung des Zentralnervensystems (spastische Pseudosclerose) mit bemerkenswertem anatomischen Befunde, *Med. Klin.,* 17: 372–376, 1921.

53. Jellinger, K., Seitelberger, F., Hess, W., et al.: Konjugale form der

Subakuten spongiose Encephalopathie. *Wien. Klin. Wschr.*, 84: 245–249, 1972.

54. Kahana, E., Alter, M., Braham, J., et al.: Creutzfeldt-Jakob disease: a focus among Libyan Jews in Israel. *Science*, 183: 90–91, 1974.

55. Kirschbaum, W.R.: Zwei eigenartige Erkrankungen des Zentralnerven-systems nach Art der spastischen Pseudosclerose (Jakob). *Z. Ges. Neurol. Psychiat.*, 92: 175–220, 1924.

56. Kirschbaum, W.R.: *Jakob-Creutzfeldt Disease*. New York, Elsevier, 1968.

57. Kirschbaum, W.R.: Jakob-Creutzfeldt disease. In J. Minckler (ed.), *Pathology of the Nervous System*, Vol. 2, 1971. New York, McGraw-Hill.

58. Klatzo, I., Gajdusek, D.C., and Zigas, V.: Pathology of kuru. *Lab. Invest.* 8: 799–847, 1959.

58a. Krücke, W., Beck, E., and Vitzthum, H.: Creutzfeldt-Jakob disease. Some unusual morphological features reminiscent of kuru. *Z. Neurol.*, 206: 1–24, 1973.

59. Lampert, P.W., Gajdusek, D.C., and Gibbs, C.J., Jr.: Subacute spongiform virus encephalopathies. Scrapie, kuru and Creutzfeldt-Jakob disease. *Am. J. Path.*, 68: 626–646, 1972.

59a. Manuelidis, E.E.: Transmission of Creutzfeldt-Jakob disease from man to the guinea pig. *Science*, 190: 571–572, 1975.

60. Marsh, R.F., Eckroade, R., ZuRhein, G., et al.: A preliminary report on the experimental host range of the transmissible mink encephalopathy agent. *J. Inf. Dis*, 120: 713–719, 1969.

61. Marsh, R.F., and Hanson, R.P.: Physical and chemical properties of the transmissible mink encephalopathy agent. *J. Virol.*, 3: 176–180, 1969.

61a. Marsh, R.F., and Hanson, R.P.: Transmissible mink encephalopathy: Infectivity of corneal epithelium. *Science*, 187: 656, 1975.

61b. Masters, C.L., Kakulas, B.A., Alpers, M.P., Gajdusek, D.C., and Gibbs, C.J., Jr.: Preclinical lesions and their progression in the experimental spongiform encephalopathies (kuru and Creutzfeld-Jakob disease in primates). *J. Neuropath. Exper. Neurol.*, 35:6 (Nov.), 593–605, 1976.

62. May, W.W.: Creutzfeldt-Jakob disease. I. Survey of the literature and clinical diagnosis. *Acta Neurol. Scand.*, 44: 1–32, 1968.

63. May, W.W., Itabashi, H.H., and De Jong, R.: Creutzfeldt-Jakob disease. II. Clinical, pathologic, and genetic study of a family. *Arch. Neurol.* 19, 137–149, 1968.

64. Neumann, M.A., Gajdusek, D.C., and Zigas, V.: Neuropathologic findings in exotic neurologic disorders among natives of the Highlands of New Guinea. *J. Neuropath. Exp. Neurol.*, 23: 486–507, 1964.

65. Nevin, S.: Jakob-Creutzfeldt disease. *Brit. Med. J.*, 1: 847, 1969.

66. Nevin, S., McMenemey, W.H., Behrman, S., et al.: Subacute spongiform encephalopathy. A subacute form of encephalopathy attributable to vascular dysfunction (spongiform cerebral atrophy). *Brain*, 83: 519–564, 1960.

67. Nishida, S., and Howard, R.O.: Is Degos' disease of viral origin? *Lancet*,

2: 1200–1201, 1968.
68. Oppenheimer, D.R.: Personal communication.
69. Parks, W., Todaro, G., Scolnick, E., et al.: RNA dependent DNA polymerase in primate synctytium forming (foamy) viruses. *Nature*, 229: 258–260, 1971.
70. Roos, R., Gajdusek, D.C., and Gibbs, C.J., Jr.: Liver disease in Creutzfeldt-Jakob disease (subacute spongiform encephalopathy). Abstract in Program 23rd Ann. Meeting, Am. Acad. Neurol., New York, April 26-May 1, 1971, p. 34.
71. Roos, R., Gajdusek, D.C., and Gibbs, C.J., Jr.: The clinical characteristics of transmissible Creutzfeldt-Jakob disease. *Brain*, 96: 1–20, 1973.
71a. Schulman, S., Vick, N.A., Blank, N.K. et al.: Transmission of Jakob-Cruetzfeldt disease from man to rhesus monkey. *Journal of Neuropathology and Experimental Neurology*, 35: 117, 1976.
72. Siakotos, A.N., Gajdusek, D.C., Gibbs, C.J., Jr., et al.: Partial purification of the scrapie agent from mouse brain by pressure disruption and zonal centrifugation in a sucrose-sodium chloride gradient. *Virology*, 70: 230–237, 1976.
73. Skre, H., and Löken, A.C.: Myoclonus epilepsy and subacute presenile dementia in heredo-ataxia. *Acta Neurol. Scand.*, 46: 18–42, 1970.
74. Steele, J.C., Richardson, J.C., and Olszewski, J.: Progressive supranuclear palsy. *Arch. Neurol.*, 10: 333–359, 1964.
75. Strole, W.E., Jr., Clark, W.H., Jr., and Isselbacher, K.L.: Progressive arterial occlusive disease (Köhlmeier-Degos). *New Eng. J. Med.*, 276: 195–201, 1967.
76. Traub, R.D., Gajdusek, D.C., and Gibbs, C.J., Jr.: Precautions in conducting biopsies and autopsies on patients with presenile dementia. *J. Neurosurg.*, 41: 394–395, 1974.
76a. Traub, R.D., Gajdusek, D.C., and Gibbs, C.J., Jr. Precautions in autopsies on Creutzfeldt-Jakob disease. *Am. J. Clin. Pathol.*, 64: 287, 1975.
77. Vernon, M.L., Horta-Barbosa, L., Fucillo, D.A., et al.: Virus-like particles and nucleo-protein-type filaments in brain tissue from 2 patients with Creutzfeldt-Jakob disease. *Lancet*, 1: 964–967, 1970.
78. Victor, M., Adams, R.D., and Cole, M.: The acquired (non-Wilsonian) type of chronic hepatocerebral degeneration. *Medicine*, 44: 345–396, 1965.
79. Zlotnik, I., Grant, D.P., Dayan, A.D., et al.: Transmission of Creutzfeldt-Jakob disease from man to squirrel monkey. *Lancet*, 2: 435–438, 1974.

Appendix I

Referring Physicians

Physicians referring TVD patients cited in text:

V. Ad.:	P. LeCompte, S. Kimball, Boston, Massachusetts
T. At.:	K. Johnson, Cleveland, Ohio
S. Au.:	F. Röhmer, F. Cathala, Paris, France
M. Ba.:	D. Tyrrell, P. Slack, Middlesex, England
S. Be.:	J. Wilson, R.S. Dow, Portland, Oregon
E. Br.:	E. Beck, M. Swash, A. Dayan, London, England
R. Bu.:	A. Pope, Belmont, Massachusetts
P. Ca.:	M. Salon, S. Hicks, Ann Arbor, Michigan
M. Ch.:	C. Plank, Boston, Massachusetts
R. Cl.:	J. Miller, W. Brannon, Bethesda, Maryland
J. Co.:	L.J. Williams, Houston, Texas
J. Col.:	T.A. Knauss, H. Leffman, Seattle, Washington
S. Co.:	F. Cathala, J. LeBeau, J. Foncin, Paris; Dr. F. Tayot, Rouen, France
R. Co.:	J.C. Ribadeau-Dumas, M. Bonduelle, R. Escourolle, F. Cathala, Paris, France

R. Cu.:	F. Lhermitte, R. Escourolle, F. Cathala, Paris, France
S. De.:	E.P. Palmer, Boston, Massachusetts
J. Do.:	M. Baldwin, J. Roth, H. Kaufman, J. Wilson, Bethesda, Maryland
J. Ea.:	J.M. Walker, Decatur, Georgia; D. Pearl, Atlanta, Georgia
L. Er.:	A. Lowenthal, Antwerp, Belgium
S. Fe.:	D. Oppenheimer, J. Spalding, E. Beck, London, England
A. Fl.:	D. Porter, Los Angeles, California
P. Ga.:	P. Duizabo, J. Barbizet, J. Poirer, Y. Pinaucet, F. Cathala, Paris, France
J. Gr.:	F. Cathala, F. Rohmer, N. Heldt, Paris, France
S. Gr.:	E. Diamond, Bethesda, Maryland
B. Ha.:	N.B. Rewcastle, Toronto, Ontario, Canada
H. Ha.:	E. Beck, P. Kahn, London, England
R. Ia.:	C. Plank, V. Perlo, Boston, Massachusetts
J. Ja.:	N.B. Rewcastle, Toronto, Ontario, Canada
V. Je.:	J. Deck, Toronto, Ontario, Canada
G. Jo.:	F. Cathala, J.J. Hauw, Paris, France
K. Kn.:	L. Kurland, J. Grabow, H. Okazaki, Rochester, Minnesota
R. Ko.:	F. Cathala, Paris, France
C. Ko.:	J. Deck, Toronto, Ontario, Canada
L. Kr.:	F. Cathala, R. Escourolle, Paris, France
C. Lo.:	F. Cathala, J. Floquet, Paris, France
T. Ma.:	J. French, A. Hirano, New York, New York
M. Ma.:	M.J. McArdle, P.M. Daniel, E. Beck, London, England
D. Ma.:	G.J. Dammin, W.C. Schoene, Boston, Massachusetts
D. May.:	M.P. Alpers, S.S. Gubbay, B.A. Kakulas, Perth, Australia
C. Mo.:	A. Woolfe, D. Cowen, New York, New York
D. Mu.:	P. Hoekstra, P. Bradford, Grand Rapids, Michigan
E. Ne.:	J.R. Baringer, San Francisco, California
F. Ni.:	D. Oppenheimer, D.B. Brownell, J. Spalding, P.M. Daniel, E. Beck, London, England
R. Po.:	J.-M. St. Hilaire, Montreal, Quebec, Canada
R. Re.:	W.B. Matthews, P.M. Daniel, E. Beck, London, England
T. Se.:	K. Bogart, LaCrosse, Wisconsin
E. Sp.:	P. Kahn, W.H. McMenemey, E. Beck, London, England
E. St.:	K. Sadjadpour, Omaha; W.O. Brown, Scottsbluff; W.J. Gentry, Gering, Nebraska
B. Sy.:	N. Popoff, R. Lopez, Miami, Florida
A. Ta.:	W.B. Matthews, P.M. Daniel, E. Beck, London, England
W. Tr.:	L. Forno, Palo Alto, California

H. Tu.:	W. Tourtellotte, Los Angeles, California
N. Wi.:	P. Steinlaus, G. Dauzier, Patterson, New Jersey
J. Wo.:	D. Porter, Los Angeles, California
M. Wo.:	E.R. Ross, Chicago, Illinois
A. Yo.:	W. Zeman, Indianapolis, Indiana

Physicians referring Non-CJD patients cited in text:

A.L. Amacher, London, Ontario, Canada
M. Ambler (3 patients), Providence, Rhode Island
P. Augustin, Paris, France
M.J. Ball (2), Edmonton, Alberta, Canada
H.J.M. Barnett (3), London, Ontario, Canada
H.W.K. Barr, London, Ontario, Canada
H. Bauer, Göttingen, Germany
E. Beck (2), London, England
A. Bignami (6), Stanford, California
S. Brion, Paris, France
Dr. Buge, Paris, France
F. Cathala (10), Paris, France
S. Chou, Morgantown, West Virginia
R.M. Clark, Florida
P.M. Daniel (2), London, England
F. Dekaban, Bethesda, Maryland
F. Diamond, New York, New York
P.M. Dreyfuss, Davis, California
R.N. Eidem, Edmonton, Alberta, Canada
W.G. Ellis, Davis, California
R. Escourolle (7), Paris, France
T.E. Feasby, Canada
B. Festoff, Miami, Florida
L. Forno, Palo Alto, California
J. French, Bronx, New York
S. Gendelman, New York, New York
H.H. Goebel, Göttingen, Germany
J. Griffith (2), Boston, Massachusetts
J. Guinane, Boston, Massachusetts
Dr. Happer, Denver, Colorado
J.J. Hauw, Paris, France
A. Hudson, London, Ontario, Canada
H. Huntington, Portland, Oregon
F.S. Jannotta, Washington, D.C.
I. Janota (2), England

M. Jones, East Lansing, Michigan
R. Jutkowitz, New York, New York
M. Kassirer, Boston, Massachusetts
R. Katzman (2), New York, New York
J.C.E. Kaufman (2), Canada
A. Kertesz, London, Ontario, Canada
R. Kim, Vancouver, Washington
M. Koslow, Bethesda, Maryland
K. Kugler, Kansas City, Missouri
J. Kurtzke (2), Washington, D.C.
P. Lampert, LaJolla, California
Dr. LaPlane, Paris, France
N. Lombardi, Boston, Massachusetts
A. Lowenthal, Antwerp, Belgium
R. Lynde, Texas
G. Mathieson, Montreal, Quebec, Canada
Dr. Mattern, Göttingen, Germany
W.F. McCormick, Iowa City, Iowa
L. McDonald, Davis, California
W.P. McInnis (2), London, Ontario, Canada
M. Menkin, Miami, Florida
G. Miner, Minneapolis, Minnesota
T.J. Murray, Halifax, Nova Scotia, Canada
L. Pearce (2), Winston-Salem, North Carolina
Y. Ponchon, Strasbourg, France
N. Popoff, Miami, Florida
N.B. Rewcastle, Toronto, Ontario, Canada
Dr. Rim (2), Detroit, Michigan
E.A. Rodin (2), Detroit, Michigan
S. Rosen, Boston, Massachusetts
M. Samsson, Rouen, France
S.S. Schochet (2), Iowa City, Iowa
G.E. Schumaker, Burlington, Vermont
C.R. Smith, Washington, D.C.
K.R. Smith, St. Louis, Missouri
M. Smout (2), London, Ontario, Canada
J.C. Steele, Toronto, Ontario, Canada
R. Steng, Texas
J. Strom (3), Providence, Rhode Island
D. Tarsy, Massachusetts
I. Tellez-Nagel, Bronx, New York
R.D. Terry, Bronx, New York

R.R. Wade, Toledo, Ohio
J.D. Waggener, Phoenix, Arizona
I. Watanabe, Kansas City, Missouri
M. Weintraub, Chelsea, Massachusetts
S.L. Wiesenfeld, Sacramento, California
N. Wexler, Ann Arbor, Michigan
J.H. Williams, Columbus, Ohio
B.K. Williamson, Rock Island, Illinois
S.M. Wolf, Los Angeles, California
W. Zeman (2), Indianapolis, Indiana
D.K. Ziegler (2), Kansas City, Kansas

Physicians referring CJD patients cited in text:

T. Am.:	J.R. Baringer, San Francisco, California
E. Fo.:	F. Cathala, J. LeBeau, J. Foncin, J. Barbizet, Paris, France
E. Gr.:	D.S. Horoupian, Winnipeg, Manitoba, Canada
D. Li.:	W.B. Matthews, P.M. Daniel, E. Beck, London, England
Y. Ma.:	H. Namiki, M. Takamori, Nagasaki, Japan
C. Moo.:	M. Swash, P.M. Daniel, E. Beck, London, England
R. Na.:	J. Brody, Bethesda, Maryland; A. Hirano, Bronx, New York
W. Ne.:	W. Zeman, J. Wayne, Indianapolis, Indiana
J. O'B.:	I. Allen, E. Dermott, J. Connolly, P.M. Daniel, E. Beck, London, England
G. Si.:	S. Chou, D. Martin, Morgantown, West Virginia
D. St.:	P. Kahn, London, England
S. Ya.:	R. Hornabrook, Papua New Guinea

Physicians referring Other patients cited in text:

S. Co.:	J.R. Baringer, San Francisco, California
F. Pe.:	F. Cathala, P. Augustin, R. Escourolle, Paris; M. Samsson, Rouen, France
C. Th.:	S. Appel, A.V. Escueta, Durham, North Carolina
M. Wa.:	E. Beck, J. Pearce, London, England

Physicians referring CJD patients not cited in text:

M. Alpers, Perth, Australia
J. Barbizet, Creteil, Seine, France
J.R. Baringer, San Francisco, California
R.O. Barnard, London, England
E. Beck (3 patients), London, England

A. Bignami, Stanford, California
F. Borikowski, Florida
G. Boudin, Paris, France
S. Brion, Paris, France
W.O. Brown, Scottsbluff, Nebraska
Dr. Buge, Paris, France
J. Burks, Denver, Colorado
H. Butler, Urbana, Illinois
F. Cathala (7), Paris, France
S.M. Chou (3), Morgantown, West Virginia
J. Conomy, Cleveland, Ohio
P.M. Daniel (3), London, England
J. Deck (2), Toronto, Ontario, Canada
R. Dow, Portland, Oregon
J.M. Eaton, Burlingame, California
B. Eig, Silver Spring, Maryland
R. Escourolle (4), Paris, France
R. Feldman, Boston, Massachusetts
K. Fisher, Miami Beach, Florida
M. Fleming, Brighton, Massachusetts
J. Foncin (2), Paris, France
W.J. Gentry, Gering, Nebraska
D. Gilden, Philadelphia, Pennyslvania
M.L. Hanson, Alexandria, Virginia
D.G.F. Harriman, England
J. Hauw, Paris, France
S. Heller, Porte Allegre, Brazil
D. Henderson, Woodville, S. Australia
R. Herndon, Baltimore, Maryland
S.P. Hicks, Ann Arbor, Michigan
L. Horta-Barbosa, Bethesda, Maryland
H.W. Huntington, Portland, Oregon
F. Isaacs, Richmond, Virginia
F.S. Jannotta, Washington, D.C.
K. Jellinger, Vienna, Austria
P.A. Kahn, London, England
A. Kertesz, London, Ontario, Canada
S. Kimball, Boston, Massachusetts
T. Knauss, Seattle, Washington
L. Kurland, Rochester, Minnesota
B. Larke, Hamilton, Ontario, Canada

J. LeBeau (2), Paris, France
P. LeCompte, Boston, Massachusetts
N. Leopold, Boston, Massachusetts
N.L. Levy, Durham, North Carolina
E. Lewin, Denver, Colorado
R. Lopez, Miami, Florida
F. Lublin, New York, New York
A.V. Marasigan, Syracuse, New York
D. Martin, Morgantown, West Virginia
R. Masland, New York, New York
G. McKhann, Baltimore, Maryland
R. McPhedran, Toronto, Ontario, Canada
J. Mundall (2), Denver, Colorado
Dr. Okazaki, Rochester, Minnesota
E.P. Palmer, Boston, Massachusetts
J. Parr, Philadelphia, Pennsylvania
D. Pearl, Atlanta, Georgia
R. Penn, New York, New York
V. Perlo, Boston, Massachusetts
C. Plank (2), Boston, Massachusetts
M. Platt, Toronto, Ontario, Canada
R. Platt, Boston, Massachusetts
N. Popoff (2), Miami, Florida
D. Porter (3), Los Angeles, California
L. Protass, Bronx, New York
R.A. Rischbeith, Woodville, S. Australia
J.T. Roberts, Canada
R. Roos, Baltimore, Maryland
W. Rosenblum, Richmond, Virginia
I. Ross, Canada
K. Sadjadpour, Omaha, Nebraska
M. Salon, Ann Arbor, Michigan
D. Sax, Boston, Massachusetts
P. Scheinberg, Miami, Florida
S.A. Schneck, Denver, Colorado
J. Sever (4), Bethesda, Maryland
R. Shebert, Miami, Florida
P.M. Slack, Middlesex, England
E.M. Stadtlan, Minneapolis, Minnesota
J.-M. St. Hilaire, Montreal, Quebec, Canada
S. Staunton, Schenectady, New York

K. Sullivan, Denver, Colorado
M. Swash, London, England
Dr. Tayot, Rouen, France
W.W. Tourtellotte, Los Angeles, California
D.A.J. Tyrrell (2), Middlesex, England
J. Walker, Decatur, Georgia
A.R. Watts, Regina, Saskatchewan, Canada
C.K. Williams, Canada
L.J. Williams, Houston, Texas
J. Wilson, Portland, Oregon
B.W. Zaias, Miami, Florida
D.K. Ziegler, Kansas City, Kansas

Appendix II

Thirty-six TVD patients not presented in other publications* or in the text: clinical and pathological summaries

V. Ad. This patient developed episodes of confusion at age 69. He would forget to go to work or would sit behind the wheel of his car and forget to get out. Two weeks later his right arm became weak and had jerky movements. This was shortly followed by leg weakness. One month after onset he was unable to talk. Deep tendon jerks were increased. An EEG showed repetitive triphasic waves and slow spikes. He was placed on diphenylhydantoin. The patient had been thought to have cholelithiasis one week before onset of his confusion. Ten days before death he developed projectile vomiting and abdominal distension. He became jaundiced and had a total bilirubin of 4.3 mg%, direct bilirubin of

---

*The following 12 patients are presented in Roos et al.:[71] R. Bu., R. Co., J. Do., L. Er., J. Ja., V. Je., D. Mu., R. Re., E. Sp., T. Se., A. Ta., M. Wo. Familial CJD patients T. At. and R. Co. are discussed in Ferber et al.[22] Patients S. Gr., E. Ha., D. Ma., and A. Yo. are discussed in the text in this chapter. Patient H. Tu. is patient 3 in May et al.[63] Patient T. Ma. is case 1 in Hirano et al.[44] Patient M. Ba. is discussed in Zlotnik et al.[79]

2.4 mg%. He died three months after onset. At autopsy the liver weighed 1350 grams and appeared passively congested. The gallbladder contained no calculi. Microscopically the liver showed areas of focal necrosis, cholestasis and leukocytic infiltrates. The lesions were attributed to circulatory factors or to diplenyl-hydantoin treatment. The brain weighed 1400 grams. There were spongiform changes and astrocytic and microglial proliferation in the gray matter of the cerebral cortex and basal ganglia.

S. Au. This woman presented with headaches, insomnia and trouble with equilibrium at the age of 59 years. She developed vertigo on changing position and a clumsy gait. EEG showed slowing, mainly right posterior. Three months after admission she became easily frightened on stimulation, had visual hallucinations and dyschromatopsia, showed aphasia, apraxia and agnosia, and had truncal and limb incoordination. Progressive dementia, pyramidal and extrapyramidal signs, myoclonus, and typical EEG appeared. CSF was normal. She died after six months of illness. A left frontal brain biopsy done one month before death showed neuronal loss and some gliosis and vacuolation. (Autopsy results are pending).

S. Be. This woman had trouble controlling her right hand in skilled activities at the age of 60. There was also lower abdominal cramping that slowly improved. After three months she was unable to write. At that time her speech was slow, monotonous and difficult to understand, but she was well oriented. She was deaf in the right ear. Horizontal nystagmus was noted. There were tremors in all limbs and the tongue. There was incoordination in all limbs. Deep tendon reflexes were depressed. EEG showed diffuse bilateral slow activity with isolated sharp waves. Disease progressed with incontinence, dementia, choreic movements, and myoclonic jerks appearing. She died after eight months of illness. During the last three months she appeared to see, but was uncommunicative. The brain had widespread cortical neuronal loss, spongy changes and gliosis. Similar changes were seen in the basal ganglia and thalamus. There was a loss of granular cells in the cerebellum with glial proliferation in the granular layer.

E. Br. This 48-year-old man felt depressed and inadequate and his gait became first unsteady and then stiff and shuffling. He lost the ability to dress himself. Three months after onset, myoclonus, bilateral focal seizures, dystonic posturing, incoherent speech and incontinence appeared. He could still respond to simple commands. The legs were spastic and there were bilateral Babinski signs. An EEG showed repetitive complexes of triphasic waves on a slow background. The CSF was normal. He died 4 months after onset. No autopsy was done. A brain biopsy performed a week before death showed fine status spongiosus with neuronal loss and loss of axons in the white matter.

P. Ca. This male custodian had lifelong neurofibromatosis. He had a skull fracture at an unknown age. At the age of 56 he developed involuntary movements and ataxia of the right arm. Shortly after this he was noted to have decreased tone and ataxia of the right side with slightly increased reflexes on the right. He had multiple subcutaneous tumors, cafe au lait spots, and multiple telangiectasias and punctate hemangiomas. One month later he made many mistakes on serial sevens. There was right patellar clonus and a broad-based retropulsive gait. Right internal carotid and vertebral angiograms were normal. An EEG was "diffusely abnormal". The CSF was normal. The patient became progressively demented and dysarthric over the next weeks. Ataxia appeared in the left arm. Fasciculations were noted in the right arm. About two months after onset myoclonic jerks and increased startle response occurred. Dementia progressed relentlessly. Generalized convulsions with tonic-clonic movements appeared. An EMG demonstrated fibrillation potentials. Serial EEG's displayed focal slowing in the left frontotemporal region, then generalized slowing with spikes and spike and wave together with paroxysmal responses to sound. Four months after onset bilateral electrical status epilepticus appeared. The patient died of pneumonia 5 months after onset. At autopsy, neurofibromatosis was confirmed. The cerebral cortex was found to be thinned and uneven. Spongy vacuolization and astrocytic gliosis were seen microscopically.

M. Ch. The family of this 62-year-old woman noted difficulties with memory progressive over a period of 2 months. After this interval she would fall asleep easily, could not guide a fork, and had abnormal rhythmic movements of the left elbow and shoulder. She was admitted to a psychiatric service, but was transferred after a week to a general hospital. Rhythmic jerking of fingers, arms, legs and mouth was noted. She did not respond to commands. Retinitis pigmentosa was observed in the optic fundi. The liver was palpated 8cm below the right costal margin. The CSF protein was 20 mg%. An EEG contained generalized slow and sharp activity. The patient was treated with amantidine, but died 2 1/2 months after onset. At autopsy the liver weighed 1500 grams; it contained centrilobular congestion and hepatocellular necrosis. Hepatocytes bordering congested areas showed mild fatty changes. Some hepatocytes contained large and vacuolated nuclei. The brain weighed 1080 grams. The cerebral cortex had some spongy change and gliosis, most marked in the calcarine cortex. Spongiosus and gliosis were also noted in basal ganglia and the molecular layer of the cerebellum. There was also gliosis and cell loss in the thalamus. The spinal cord was normal.

R. Cl. This 53-year-old housewife and former accountant noted difficulty walking with falling to both sides. Over the past two months she also had trouble understanding people who spoke to her and asked to have statements repeated. There was flattening of affect, difficulty with calculations and weight loss. Three weeks after onset the CSF, including protein electrophoresis, was normal. She had a paralysis of upward gaze, horizontal nystagmus, hypomimetic facies and bilateral cerebellar signs. Tremors appeared in the arms which were at times choreoathetotic in appearance. Gait became festinating. Two months after onset she was demented and unable to stand. EEG showed periodic bursts of high amplitude slow waves followed by suppression. A pneumoencephalogram demonstrated dilatation of the lateral ventricles. She became progressively rigid, with grimacing and dyskinesias and died about 7 months after onset. A right frontal biopsy taken two months before death revealed diffuse spongiform changes with mild gliosis and neuronal loss. At autopsy the brain weighed 1250 grams. The cerebral cortex showed spongiform changes, shrinkage and degeneration of neurons and gliosis. The cerebellum showed also spongiform changes, degeneration of Purkinje cells, loss of cellularity in the granular layer and gliosis. There were similar changes in the midbrain and hippocampus.

S. Co. This 62-year-old seamstress developed morning headaches and depression with abdominal pains. She became irritable and had some trouble sleeping. A month later she complained of visual fatigue and saw an ophthalmologist. Five months after onset she began to have progressive trouble walking, so that after one month she had to cling to her husband. Six months after onset there was increased muscle tone on the right and decreased tone on the left. There was left facial paresis with a right ptosis. Tendon reflexes were slightly increased on the right. Anisocoria was noted, with the left pupil larger. She rapidly became obtunded and developed a left hemiparesis with a left Babinski sign. An EEG displayed diffuse slowing with a right temporal delta focus. A right carotid arteriogram was consistent with ventricular dilatation. Six months after onset a right frontal brain biopsy was performed. Six days after biopsy an EEG displayed diffuse paroxysmal activity typical of CJD. The patient became first mute and then comatose with fists and eyes clenched shut and diffuse hypertonus. Ventriculography was normal. Convulsive movements appeared in the left leg. A repeat brain biopsy was done one month after the first. Two weeks later myoclonic jerks appeared, first in the arms and later in the face. An EEG one year after onset showed generalized slowing with disappearance of the periodic activity. She died after disease lasting one year, having been comatose the last six months.

The first brain biopsy showed vacuoles and neuronal atrophy with abundant lipofuscin. Electron microscopy of the two biopsies was interpreted to show probably nonspecific neuronal changes.

J. Co. This man became lethargic and apathetic at age 67, one month after an upper respiratory tract infection. He drove his car into a pole on the left side of the street. Within a week he was unable to care for himself. He was ataxic and tended to stagger to the left. A week later he was restless and disoriented and had a left hemianopsia. A pneumoencephalogram showed bilateral ventricular enlargement, slightly more prominent on the left. He rapidly became unresponsive. Bilateral Babinski signs appeared. Two months after onset he began having seizures and bouts of myoclonic jerking. He died eight months after onset, having been in a chronic care facility for the last 5 1/2 months. A left parieto-occipital biopsy done two months after onset showed pyknotic degeneration of cortical neurons with satellitosis and neuronophagy. There was vacuolation of neurons, astrocytes and oligodendrocytes. No gliosis was seen. At autopsy the brain weighed 1025 grams. There was diffuse gliosis with neuronal vacuolation, satellitosis and neuronophagy.

J. Col. This 47-year-old man noticed some weakness of his right side; he also had to "look to see what the right side was doing." His wife noticed jerking of his hand. One month after onset he still had only mild weakness and impaired position sense of the right side. The CSF was normal. Nystagmus on right lateral gaze and mental vagueness appeared over the next weeks, together with mild right-sided dysmetria. A pneumoencephalogram and ventriculogram were interpreted as being normal, except for a questionably dilated fourth ventricle. Myoclonus was noted in the right arm and a right Babinski sign appeared. An EEG taken about five weeks after onset suggested burst suppression. A week later he was clearly demented and had intention myoclonus of tongue, jaw and hands. Soon after, he seemed to be cortically blind and required a feeding tube. Two months after onset he was comatose and responded to painful stimulation with right decerebrate and left decorticate posturing. There were conjugate roving eye movements and frequent myoclonic jerks. An EEG revealed biphasic and tri-phasic sharp waves. A right parietal brain biopsy was performed 10 weeks after onset. An EMG demonstrated fibrillation potentials. He died after a course of seven months. The brain biopsy contained severe status spongiosus and gliosis. Sections of frontal and occipital cortex taken at autopsy also contained wide-spread status spongiosus and severe gliosis.

R. Cu. This 60-year-old man was hypertensive for many years and had head trauma about one year prior to onset. He presented with irritability, loss of interest and bulimia. Two months later slightly increased deep tendon reflexes were noted, together with rotary nystagmus and a left homonymous hemianopia. CSF protein was 60 mg%. Mental deterioration was rapid. Four months after onset myoclonus appeared. There was a 30 second focal seizure involving the face. EEG showed low amplitude bilateral delta waves with some sharp waves on the right. He died after five months of illness. A right fronto-parietal biopsy done three weeks before death demonstrated microspongiosis and astrocytosis. At autopsy there was a moderate subdural hematoma under the biopsy scar. (Microscopic findings are pending).

S. De. This 66-year-old man developed personality changes, became irritable and complained of trouble with vision. An ophthalmologic examination was normal. A month later he had a left homonymous hemianopia and was hospitalized. He became rapidly demented and rigid and developed myoclonus. A pneumoencephalogram was normal. An EEG was interpreted as being consistent with CJD. A brain biopsy was performed three months after onset. The patient was subsequently lost to follow-up. The biopsy revealed status spongiosus and astrocytic and microglial proliferation. A few neurons contained eccentric nuclei and ballooned cytoplasm with chromatolysis.

J. Ea. This 57-year-old man became restless and complained of insomnia. His wife noted trouble making decisions. Three weeks later he had trouble speaking. The CSF and a pneumoencephalogram were normal. An EEG demonstrated an asymmetric alpha rhythm and a focus of left anterior medium amplitude delta activity. One month after onset his speech contained jargon and he perseverated. He was disoriented to place and could not obey two step commands. A tentative diagnosis of CVA was made. Seven weeks after onset he had developed a fever of 101°F and was semi-comatose. The right side moved less than the left; there was decorticate posturing and a snout reflex was present. A chest x-ray film was interpreted as consistent with aspiration pneumonia. An EEG revealed bursts of sharp and slow waves occurring about once per second. Myoclonus and calf fasciculations appeared. He died after a course of two months. At autopsy the brain weighed 1390 grams. Meninges were thickened and dull. There was moderate frontal lobe atrophy. Microscopically, status spongiosus and increased neuronal lipofuscin were observed.

S. Fe. This housewife stopped keeping her house as spotless as usual at the age of 35. Two months later she was forgetful and had diplopia and headaches. She developed a voracious appetite, incongruous mood, stiff limbs and a broadbased gait. Schizophrenia was considered. Ten months after onset she walked with the right shoulder higher than the left and she was clearly demented. Limbs became stiff and wrist drop and positive Babinski signs appeared. She died after 12 months of illness. EEG was never typical and there was no myoclonus. At autopsy there was severe status spongiosus and astrocytic proliferation in the putamen, caudate nucleus and amygdalas. The lateral corticospinal tracts were degenerated in the cord. There was mild loss of anterior horn cells. Muscles showed changes consistent with recent denervation. It was considered that the cerebral changes were those of CJD, while those in the spinal cord were indistinguishable from motor neuron disease. Dr. D. Oppenheimer felt this was amyotrophic CJD, but Dr. S. Nevin felt that it was "subacute spongiform encephalopathy."[68]

A. Fl. This 39-year-old woman became progressively hyperirritable and anxious. Over the next 18 months she developed unreasonable fears and paranoid delusions. In addition, 14 months after onset she began to have difficulty with motor activities. There was trembling, sometimes to the point of violent shaking of the entire body. She complained of dizziness and vomiting. Hydroxyzine, carbamazepine, biperiden and estrogens were administered without benefit. Eighteen months after onset, because of increasing agitation, the patient was given 50 mg of intramuscular chlorpromazine. She became temporarily unresponsive and was admitted to a hospital. At this time there were violent shaking tremors and an increased startle response to noise. An EEG contained generalized 1-2hz activity. A brain scan showed generalized increased uptake. Two lumbar punctures, both traumatic, had proteins of 47 and 63 mg%, respectively. CSF protein electrophoresis was normal. Ice water calorics were abnormal in that the phase of tonic deviation was followed by coarse upward nystagmus, greater on the right side. Tone was increased in the arms and snout and grasp reflexes were present. The patient had seizure-like clonic movements of all extremities. A repeat EEG demonstrated periodic triphasic sharp waves. A pneumoencephalogram was normal. The patient died of pneumonia 19 months after onset. At autopsy the brain weighed 1160 grams. Frontal cortical atrophy was noted. There was diffuse cortical neuronal loss and gliosis. The cortex had a spongy appearance, created by occasionally confluent microcysts up to 30 nm in diameter.

P. Ga. This 49-year-old woman presented with peculiar behavior, mistakes at work and weight loss. She developed alexia, visual agnosia and memory loss. Eleven months after onset there was coprophagia, incontinence and extrapyramidal hypertonus. Voluntary eye movements were lost. There was rapidly progressive dementia. Groping hand movements, myoclonus, pyramidal signs and amyotrophy appeared. EEG was slow with paroxysmal "seizure" activity. CSF was normal. She died after 14 months of illness. The brain at autopsy showed severe neuronal loss, astrocytosis and status spongiosus.

J. Gr. At the age of 51 this woman was struck on her occiput without loss of consciousness. This was followed by headache; ten days later she had trouble concentrating and was confused. There was a mild left hemiparesis. EEG was slow, espeically anteriorly on the right. Two weeks after head trauma, she was "slow" and appeared catatonic. She had a left grasping reflex and a right Babinski sign. CSF was normal. She rapidly became mute and hyperreflexic and EEG showed paroxysms on a slow background. Jerking movements appeared in the hands. She died six weeks after falling. Brain biopsy (frontal) showed neuronal loss and status spongiosus. The relation of head trauma to the onset of dementia in this case is unclear.

H. Ha. This 64-year-old man complained of a "muzzy" feeling in his head. He became confused, talked gibberish, behaved bizarrely and ceased to recognize his wife. About a month later he was confused, dysphasic, incoordinated in the right arm, and had impaired position and vibration sense in the legs. Two months after onset there was apraxia of the hands. Deep tendon reflexes were increased on the right and there was a right Babinski sign. An EEG was interpreted as being consistent with CJD. Myoclonus appeared. He deteriorated rapidly, becoming mute, and died four months after onset. A brain biopsy taken two months after onset showed neuronal loss, astrocytic proliferation and spongiosus. At autopsy the brain weighed 1262 grams. The lateral ventricles were moderately dilated. The cerebellar folia were atrophic. There was slight cerebral atrophy. In the cere-

bral cortex there were foci of fine spongiosus, neuronal loss and astrocytic proliferation. In the cerebellum there was loss of Purkinje cells and granule cells. The
spinal cord was normal.

R. Ia. This woman began to feel tired at age 50. About six months later
she began making paraphasic errors and complained of visual blurring beginning
in the right eye. The next month she had occipital headaches and began to fall,
initially to the left. There was tinnitus and incoordination in the right hand. Over
the next few weeks she could not find food on her plate, and she had difficulties
with walking; speech and memory impairment progressed rapidly. One month
before death there was myoclonic lid blinking and the tongue deviated slightly
to the right. She could not follow two-step commands. CSF was normal. EEG
contained prominent bilateral delta activity with slow spikes. Myoclonus increased, together with her startle response. An EEG three weeks after the above
showed typical burst suppression. There was decorticate posturing. She died
after about eight months' illness. At autopsy the brain weighed 1350 grams. In
the cerebral cortex there were severe spongiform changes and astrocytic and
microglial proliferation.

G. Jo. This woman had Sydenham's chorea at the age of seven and developed hypertension at age 69. At age 73 she became confused, her degree of confusion varying from one moment to the next. At times she would appear euphoric.
There was diffuse hypertonus with akinesia and tendency to retropulsion. Tendon reflexes on the right side were increased with a positive right Babinski sign.
An EEG about one month after onset contained a left front-temporal slow wave
focus. CSF was normal. She rapidly progressed to a state of bedridden akinetic
mutism with lower limbs extended and upper limbs flexed. Involuntary movements appeared in the limbs that were sometimes choreic, but more often
myoclonic. These movements increased after sensory stimulation. A brain biopsy
was done about six weeks after onset. The patient became comatose and died
two months after onset. The brain biopsy was said to be typical of CJD. At
autopsy the brain weighed 1150 grams. In the cerebral cortex were status
spongiosus, astrocytic proliferation and neuronal loss. These lesions were not
prominent in occipital and temporal cortex. There were also some neuronal
ischemic changes. Status spongiosus and gliosis were also noted in basal ganglia,
thalamus, the molecular layer of the cerebellum and the anterior horn of the
spinal cord. Rare perivascular inflammatory infiltrates were noted throughout
the neuraxis.

K. Kn. This 48-year-old man developed a respiratory infection while visit-
ing overseas. A few days later he was restless and had involuntary twitching of
the right side at night. Four weeks later, back in the U.S., he was dizzy. Two
months after onset he noted difficulty finding words. Three weeks later he was
noted to speak slowly. There was slight nystagmus on the right lateral gaze and
mild right arm tremor with some dysmetria. Fasciculations were seen, first in

the arms and later in the calves. The CSF had a protein of 71 mg% and contained no cells. An EEG showed slowing in the left frontal region. A pneumoencephalogram showed dilatation of the ventricular system. Over a period of weeks, all speech was lost and myoclonus appeared. He became rigid, with increased deep tendon reflexes and bilateral Babinski signs. There were dystonic movements of the limbs. He died 7 1/2 months after onset. The brain at autopsy showed changes compatible with spongiform encephalopathy.

R. Ko. This woman at age 64 developed over a period of days an unsteady, broad-based gait. Two weeks later she complained of horizontal diplopia and parieto-occipital headaches. Horizontal nystagmus was noted. Over the next few days she became confused, had delusional ideas and began losing weight. Six weeks after onset she had dysmetria in all limbs, left-sided weakness, a left homonymous hemianopia and a left third nerve palsy; she was bedfast. Over the next week her speech became incomprehensible, profound left hemiplegia appeared with generalized limb hypertonus in flexion, and myoclonus was noted. An EEG contained periodic spikes on a slow background. A ventriculogram was normal. Nine weeks after onset she was mute, incontinent and apparently cortically blind. Lower limbs were extended and upper limbs were flexed. Opisthotonus developed when she was disturbed. Deep tendon reflexes were increased, but there was no extensor plantar response. CSF was normal, with a protein of 22 mg%. She died ten weeks after onset. A brain biopsy one week before death and autopsy were said to be consistent with Creutzfeldt-Jakob disease; details are not available.

C. Ko. This 50-year-old woman developed headaches, dizziness, staggering gait, confusion and forgetfulness, and difficulty with speech and vision. Three sisters living in Hungary had been admitted to mental hospitals in middle age; no further information on their clinical course or pathologic findings is available. Three weeks after onset of the patient's illness, she seemed cortically blind and displayed myoclonus. Within another three weeks she was severely demented. SGOT was elevated, but other tests of liver function were normal. A pneumoencephalogram at this time was suggestive of cerebral atrophy. An EEG contained bursts of spike activity followed by slow wave activity. The CSF contained no cells; protein was 14 mg% and CSF protein electrophoresis was normal. A right parietal brain biopsy was performed about one month after onset. Subsequently she developed truncal and limb ataxia, supranuclear gaze palsy, hyperreflexia, and later decorticate and decerebrate posturing. She died after 13 months of illness. The brain biopsy contained cortical spongiform change. At autopsy, the brain was severely atrophic, weighing only 820 grams. The cerebral cortex and basal ganglia contained widely distributed neuronal loss and gliosis. The corticospinal tracts were degenerated. The pretectal area was gliotic and contained degenerating neurons. The cerebellar cortex was atrophic. Purkinje cells were not significantly reduced in number, but the granular layer of the cerebellum showed neuronal loss, vacuolation and gliosis. The spinal cord contained some neuronal loss and gliosis in the anterior horns.

L. Kr. This 61-year-old man became dysphasic and dyspraxic with his hands. For one to three months previously he had been making mistakes at his work. In the month after the onset of dysphasia, he became aggressive, began speaking less and less, developed hypertonus of the right upper extremity, and possibly had a seizure. Over the next week he became confused and developed dystonic movements of the right arm and hand. The CSF was normal. An EEG contained a slow and disorganized background superimposed on which were pseudo-periodic paroxysms, the latter more prominent on the left. The patient became progressively more rigid and lost all spontaneous eye movements; the eyes did not move during passive rotation of the head. A right central facial paresis developed. The patient became comatose and died ten weeks after the onset of dysphasia. At autopsy the brain weighed 1300 grams. Multiple areas of cerebral cortex contained spongiosus and glial proliferation. Similar findings were found in the putamen and caudate nucleus.

D. Lo. This woman at age 59 had a "grippe-like" illness and simultaneously noted bilateral decrease in vision, the latter worsening over the next few days. In ensuring weeks dysarthria appeared and a neurologist observed her to suffer some loss of memory; gait was careful and broad-based. The patient became rapidly demented and myoclonus and cerebellar signs appeared. An EEG demonstrated bursts of triphasic waves and spikes. The patient became blind, mute and incontinent. She died nine weeks after onset. At autopsy lesions were found throughout the cerebral cortex, basal ganglia and thalamus; neuronal loss, gliosis and moderate status spongiosus. Gliosis was seen in the inferior olives and the cerebellar white matter.

M. Ma. This 34-year-old woman had a long psychiatric history, including alcoholism and depression. Because of this, disease onset is difficult to determine, but it may have coincided with onset of forgetfulness and paresthesiae. At that time there was a right facial weakness, jerky facial movements and dysarthria. Mood was labile. Both arms were ataxic. CSF protein was 97 mg%. Reflexes were brisk. Dementia, ataxia and dysarthria progressed. Limb myoclonus appeared and EEG showed repetitive complexes. She died about 4 to 5 months after onset of paresthesiae. A left frontal biopsy done six weeks after onset showed chromatolysis of most neurons, astrocytosis and vacuolation. At post-mortem the brain weighed 980 grams. Microscopic appearance of the cortex was the same as in the biopsy.

D. May This 47-year-old man was admitted to a hospital for investigation of dementia. No history was available. On examination his speech consisted of only an occasional "yes" or "no." He had intention tremor in the limbs of both sides. His gait was shuffling and unsteady. Minimal weakness on the right side was noted. The CSF was normal; protein was 36 mg%. A pneumoencephalogram revealed widening of some of the cerebral sulci. The patient deteriorated steadily, becoming completely demented and incontinent with diffuse rigidity and hyperactive deep tendon reflexes. One month after admission myoclonic jerks were noted. He died six weeks after admission. The fixed weight of the brain was 1090 grams. There was some widening of cerebral sulci and ventricular dilatation. The cerebral cortex contained widespread neuronal degeneration, spongiform change and astrocytic proliferation. Similar changes were seen in the basal ganglia and the cerebellum. Degenerative changes were seen also in midbrain, pons and medulla.

C. Mo. This 61-year-old male clerk presented with mild confusion and decrease in memory. This progressed slowly for about seven months, then progressed rapidly. His gait became unsteady six months after onset and there was progressive decrease in vision. Nystagmus on lateral gaze appeared, together with bilateral limb dysmetria. EEG showed slowing punctuated by repetitive discharge. He rapidly developed fasciculations and myoclonus. Coincidentally, he had an acute anteroseptal myocardial infarction. He died after nine months of illness. Post-mortem findings included a healing myocardial infarction and acute splenitis. The cerebral cortex showed neuronal degeneration in all layers; the cortex had a "porous" appearance. There was moderate astrocytosis. The anterior horns of the cord showed neuronal loss and astrocytosis; long tracts were intact.

E. Ne. This 60-year-old housewife noted trouble spelling and writing. She felt uncoordinated, had difficulty opening locks, and put golf clubs in the bag upside down. She complained of forgetfulness, dizziness and blurring of vision. A diagnosis of multiple sclerosis had been made at the age of 28 on the basis of fatigue, nystagmus and slurred speech, but these had apparently resolved. An EEG two weeks after onset of the dysgraphia showed slow wave foci in the left frontal and central areas and in the right temporal area. An EEG one month after onset displayed eruptions of high voltage sharp waves and diffuse high voltage slow activity. The CSF, including protein electrophoresis, was normal. Six weeks after onset she had expressive dysphasia and was apraxic. The right hand was postured abnormally during walking and also would show jerking movements. There was a mild right hemiparesis. A pneumoencephalogram displayed diffuse slowing with triphasic sharp waves. The patient deteriorated progressively and died three months after onset. The brain contained neuronal loss and increased astrocytic nuclei throughout most of the cerebral cortex. There was only a hint of spongiform change.

F. Ni. This woman presented with vertigo at the age of 60. She developed progressive limb and truncal ataxia with nystagmus, left ptosis and possibly dysarthria. In addition, there was decreased sensation in the left fifth nerve territory. She had progressive mental deterioration with Parkinsonian features (rigidity, immobile facies and abnormal non-myoclonic movements).

EEG showed bursts of slow wave complexes. She died after four months of illness. The brain showed astrocytic proliferation in the corpus striatum, cerebral cortex, thalamus, hypothalamus, midbrain, and cerebellum. There was nerve cell loss, particularly in the corpus striatum and of granule cells in the cerebellum. There was mild status spongiosus in the cerebral cortex. This case was read as CJD by Dr. Brownell. Cerebellar signs were particularly prominent.

R. Po. This woman at age 60 developed episodes of confusion and irritability. Four and one half months later she had difficulty walking; after an additional month she could not stand unsupported. She complained of trouble with vision. Six months after onset she was slightly demented; upward gaze was limited; there was an intention tremor in each arm; there was hypertonus and some limb dystonic posturing and the deep tendon reflexes were slightly increased. The EEG contained paroxysmal activity with diffuse slowing. CSF was normal. PEG showed enlargement of the sulci at the sylvian fissure. She became rapidly demented and developed myoclonus. Seven months after onset she was stuporous and then comatose with eyes deviated to the left. She died after eight months of illness. A right frontal biopsy done two weeks before death demonstrated severe status spongiosus, astrocytic proliferation and pigmentary degeneration of nerve cells. Post-mortem, the brain weighed 1150 grams. There was status spongiosus in the cerebral cortex, greatest in the occipital lobe. There was marked astrocytic proliferation in the cerebral cortex, basal ganglia and thalamus. Status spongiosus was also noted in the molecular layer of the cerebellum.

E. St. This 64-year-old woman developed a pill-rolling tremor in both hands, more marked on the left. She complained also of shortness of breath. Within two weeks she noted difficulty moving her limbs, a problem that came on over one day. Over the next month she lost the ability to walk without assistance. Six weeks after onset she was found to be bradykinetic and to have Parkinsonian tremors and cogwheel rigidity in all extremities. The clinical impression was Parkinson's disease. She was not demented at this time. The patient became confused and developed bilateral facial weakness, more marked on the left. L-Dopa was administered without benefit, other than possibly to relieve some neck stiffness. A sacral decubitus appeared. She died after four months of illness. At autopsy, pulmonary atelectasis, purulent bronchitis and pulmonary foreign body granulomata were found. There were bilateral subdural hematomata. The brain weighed 1150 grams and showed moderate cortical atrophy. Spongiform changes, mild neuronal loss and gliosis were seen in cerebral cortex and basal ganglia.

B. Sy. This 61-year-old male businessman had an apparent viral syndrome with malaise, lassitude and myalgia. About two weeks later there were subtle personality changes and difficulty with memory and thinking. Within another two or three weeks he was acting strangely and was disoriented. A month after onset of the mental changes, a pneumoencephalogram revealed cerebral atrophy. After an additional two weeks he was found to perseverate in speech and was inattentive and emotionally labile. He was dyspraxic in all skilled motor activities. There was mild left facial paresis and marked dysarthria. There was considerable Gegenhalten and deep tendon reflexes were increased in the upper extremities. Snout, suck, rooting and grasp reflexes were noted. RISA cisternography was suggestive of early low pressure hydrocephalus. Myoclonic jerks, repeated abnormal posturing of the neck and oculogyric crises appeared. The patient had a brain biopsy with placement of a ventricular shunt two months after onset of the mental changes. He died a month later. The brain biopsy showed severe astrocytic proliferation, some microglial proliferation, and severe status spongiosus. The brain after death was found to contain widespread cerebral cortical status spongiosus, neuronal loss and astrocytic proliferation. Several senile plaques were seen in the temporal lobe. Neuronal loss was also noted in basal ganglia, thalamus, dentate nucleus, pontine nuclei, inferior olives and anterior horns of the spinal cord. A few neurofibrillary tangles were seen in the locus ceruleus.

W. Tr. This man presented suddenly, at age 57, with tremor, unsteady gait and mental changes. He developed rapidly progressive dementia and cerebellar signs. CSF protein was 91 mg%. EEG was slow, but without specific features of CJD. He developed cogwheel rigidity and positive Babinski signs. He died of aspiration pneumonia after four months of illness. Right frontal brain biopsy three months after onset showed vacuolation and diffuse nerve cell loss. The post-mortem brain showed nerve cell loss in cerebral cortex, basal ganglia and cerebellum. There was status spongiosus in the cerebral cortex and molecular layer of the cerebellum. There was some degree of astrocytic gliosis in all of the above areas. A few neurofibrillary tangles were seen in the hippocampus.

N. Wi. This 78-year-old woman had been somewhat depressed for five years, but functioned normally. Over a period of weeks she became confused and would periodically interrupt her activities. After an additional three weeks she required help in cleaning house and she refused to eat. She was usually mute, except for occasional echolalia. She had motor perservation and was unable to find her way about her apartment. Six weeks after onset she developed tremors in the right arm and showed bizarre posturing. Objects appeared big to her. She maintained postures in catatonic fashion. She required assistance in walking, her gait consisting of small shuffling steps. EEG showed periodic discharges of spikes and spike and wave activity on a slow background. CSF was normal. She became combative and developed a right hemiparesis. About two months after onset myoclonus appeared. She assumed a flexed posture during the last two weeks and died after three months of illness. The brain was frozen prior to fixation, so no statement can be made about status spongiosus. Cerebral cortical neurons were shrunken and diminished in number. There was astrocytic proliferation. No senile plaques or neurofibrillary tangles were seen.

J. Wo. Thirteen relatives in the patient's own and two preceding generations had died of neurologic disease with clinical diagnoses including multiple sclerosis, premature senility, and Pick's disease. Another living male relative (two of whose great-grandparents are the patient's grandparents) has been told he has cerebral atrophy. The patient himself was a 42-year-old male department store buyer who became tired and irritable and complained of a sore back. About a month later he felt aching in the right shoulder. He noted flashing bright colors in the morning and complained of blurred vision in the evening. He felt dizzy for a few days. He became increasingly irritable, complained of headaches and resigned from work four months after onset. The next month, while driving, he almost had a head-on collision. He also misjudged distances. His gait became staggering and five months after onset a diagnosis of multiple sclerosis was made. He developed delusional ideas, e.g., that he was dead and that blood was spilled over him. Six months after onset he lost his ability to taste food. He perseverated in speech. Voluntary eye movements were absent. Snout and glabellar reflexes and bilateral Babinski signs were noted. The CSF was normal. A pneumonencephalogram demonstrated cortical atrophy and dilated ventricles. An EEG displayed diffuse slowing with triphasic waves, spikes and spike-and-wave forms. An EMG demonstrated denervation in the right hand and leg. He deteriorated steadily. Ten months after onset he was unresponsive to painful stimuli and was curled up into a ball. Myoclonic jerks were noted. He died 11 months after onset. A brain biopsy performed six months after onset showed spongiform degeneration. At autopsy, the brain showed diffuse cortical atrophy. It weighed 1010 grams. Severe status spongiosus was noted in cerebral cortex, cerebellum and cranial nerve nuclei.

Appendix III

Seven* CJD patients likely to be true untransmissible cases: clinical and pathological summaries†

J. Ar. This 44-year-old male accountant developed trouble with balance and difficulty judging depth. He also complained that his left arm did not feel attached to his body. He would walk in circles, turning toward the left. His movements became slowed. Within weeks he began to miss appointments and his work became disorganized. He became unable to sign his name. His wife noted jerking movements of his left arm. An EEG was normal. Ten weeks after onset he was apraxic in the use of objects such as a key. There was some very slight weakness on the left. The patient deteriorated steadily, developing bilateral Babinski signs 6 months after onset. He died 9 months after onset. A

---

*The remaining untransmissible case (D. St.) is presented in the body of the text.

†Five of the 8 patients were in the non-transmitted group of Roos et al.[71] (All except E. Fo., D. Li. and D. St.). E. Fo. was listed as "Alzheimer's disease" in that paper, but is included under CJD here because of microspongiosus in his brain. He is also included in the Alzheimer group in this paper.

brain biopsy performed 4 months after onset contained severe spongiform changes and astrocytic and microglial proliferation. No information is available on the post-mortem findings.

D. Dr. This 43-year-old housewife became lethargic, depressed, irritable and confused over a period of months. Her speech became slurred and her handwriting deteriorated. Four months after onset, a pneumoencephalogram was found to be "abnormal." Eight months after onset she was agitated and appeared to be hallucinating. Wasting of small hand muscles and myoclonic jerks in the hands were noted. The deep tendon reflexes were very brisk and there were questionable Babinski signs. The CSF contained one red cell and no white cells; the CSF protein was 123 mg%. CSF serology was weakly reactive at 1/4 dilution. An EEG revealed diffuse slowing. Nine months after onset (3 weeks after a brain biopsy) she had a single generalized convulsion. She died 20 months after onset. The brain biopsy displayed neurons containing a moderate amount of lipofuscin; no neurofibrillary tangles or senile plaques were seen. The changes were considered nonspecific. At autopsy, the brain weighed 1330 grams. There was focal thinning of cortical gray matter and the ventricles were widely dilated. The cerebral cortex contained extensive vacuolation in both white and gray matter. In the white matter, reactive gliosis, gemistocytic astrocytes and Alzheimer type II cells were seen. The gray matter also contained an increased number of glia with occasional gemistocytic astroctyes. Many neurons were pyknotic and contained increased lipofuscin. There was rare perivascular lymphocytic cuffing. Both hippocampi showed extensive neuronal loss, microcystic change and astrocytosis in the cerebellum. There was extensive loss of Purkinje cells and focal depletion of cells in the granular layer.

E. Fo. This man had progressive dementia of onset at age 38. He had delusions of persecution and generalized convulsions. At age 42 CSF protein was 120 mg%; EEG showed left-sided slowing and there was a mild right hemiparesis; the diagnosis of tumor was considered. Myoclonus, dysarthria, Wernicke aphasia and apraxia, limb dysmetria and pyramidal tract signs appeared. EEG became diffusely slow with some sharp waves, occasionally periodic. Truncal amyotrophy appeared. The patient died at age 43 after five years of illness. The patient's father died at age 51 after an illness of unknown duration with memory disturbance and apraxia, with diffuse cerebral atrophy found after death. E. Fo. had left and right frontal biopsies, 11 and 9 months before death, respectively. The first biopsy was read as showing Alzheimer's disease. The second, interpreted by Dr. Foncin, showed many senile plaques and probable neurofibrillary degeneration; with the electron miscroscope, a microspongious cavity was seen. Autopsy results are pending. This patient had the family history, the long course and the mixed pathologic features of A. Yo., a TVD patient.

A. La. This 69 year old woman, over a period of weeks, lost her ability to sign her name and had difficulty naming objects. She complained of generalized headaches and was noted to be confused, emotionally labile, anorexic and insomniac. A month after onset she tended to stagger to the right and had decreased swing of the right arm. A mild snout reflex was present. An EEG contained a left fronto-central-temporal slow wave focus. A pneumoencephalogram showed some widening of the frontal sulci. The CSF protein was 26 mg%. The patient deteriorated rapidly. Another EEG, 2 weeks after the first, contained generalized slowing with periodic biphasic and triphasic discharges. Myoclonic jerks appeared in the right arm. The patient became mute and pseudobulbar and developed multifocal seizures. She died about 3 months after onset. No autopsy was performed. A left frontal brain biopsy performed two months after onset contained severe spongiform changes and gliosis.

D. Li. D. Li. was a 51-year-old woman who presented with vertigo. She developed limb ataxia, reading difficulty and myoclonus. CSF protein was 75 mg%. EEG showed typical CJ features. She had a declining level of consciousness and died after 6 months of illness. At autopsy there was status spongiosus in the cortex and caudate nucleus and putamen. There was diffuse cortical astrocytic proliferation; the cerebellum showed loss of granule and Purkinje cells. There were no senile plaques or neurofibrillary changes. The final diagnosis was Creutzfeldt-Jakob disease (cortico-striato-cerebellar variant).

R. Na. This patient is discussed by Hirano 43a (p. 203, pathology on p. 206). This man was a Filipino, born in the Philippines, who had moved to Guam at age 39. He developed masked facies and rigidity at age 52, with onset of progressive dementia six months later. By age 55 there were pyramidal tract signs. Dementia and debilitation continued and he died at age 58. The brain was atrophic. It weighed 950 grams. Neurons in the cerebral cortex had perinuclear vacuolation. There was neuronal loss and astrocytic gliosis in the cerebral cortex, globus pallidus, substantia nigra and vestibular nuclei. There was also gliosis in inferior olive and dentate nucleus. There were some senile plaques in the frontal and parietal lobes. There were neurofibrillary tangles in Sommer's sector, amygdaloid nucleus, periaqueductal gray, pontine tegmentum and vestibular nuclei. There was descending degeneration of the pyramidal tract; cerebral white matter was also the site of considerable destruction. Neuronal loss was particularly severe in the substantia nigra and locus ceruleus. There were no Lewy bodies. This case was considered to have features of both CJD (neuronal loss, vacuolation and gliosis) and the Guamanian type of ALS-Parkinsonism Dementia found in the Chamorros (long course, distribution of neurofibrillary tangles). However, if the patient had the Guamanian disease, he would be the first non-Chamorro on record to do so; thus, this case is unique.

J. O'B. This seaman presented at age 56 with arm weakness, wasting and fasciculations. He confabulated and was apraxic; reflexes were brisk. Mental deterioration continued and bulbar palsy appeared. There was no myoclonus and EEG's were not typical of CJD. CSF protein was 20 mg%. He died after (at least)

13 months of illness. A right frontal biopsy 11 months before death (taken at the time of aspiration of a chronic subdural hematoma) was normal-looking by electron microscopy. The post-mortem brain showed spongiform changes in some areas of cerebral cortex, confirmed by EM. There was neuronal loss and gliosis, severe in cerebral cortex, but also present in the anterior horns, caudate nucleus and thalamus. There was pallor by myelin staining in the lateral columns of the spinal cord. Like W. Ne., this man had the amyotrophic form of CJD.

6

Intellect and Personality in the Aged

R. D. SAVAGE

This rather brief article will present some recent developments in the understanding of intellectual functioning and personality in the aged. More comprehensive reviews of these topics can be found in H.J. Eysenck, *Handbook of Abnormal Psychology*, second edition (1973), Savage et al. *Intellectual Functioning in the Aged* (1973), and the well-known *Handbook of Ageing and the Individual* by Birren (1959, 1972), as well as in a number of issues of the *Annual Review of Psychology*. Generally speaking, there has been much more work on cognitive functioning than in the area of personality, and an unfortunate lack of longitudinal studies in both areas until quite recently.

Several earlier studies of intellectual ability over wide age ranges suggested, and most people accepted, the view that intellectual functioning declines slowly from the third decade of life to the sixth and more abruptly thereafter. However, in spite of the above findings, intelligence, when appraised by other, broader criteria than the well-known intelligence tests, does not always manifest the same decline with age. For example, with increasing age, experience plays an ever-increasing role in the individual's capacity to deal effectively with his environment, a criterion basic to many definitions of intelligence. General intelligence, as evaluated by pragmatic environmental criteria, appears to maintain itself unimpaired over a much greater portion of adult life, and to decline at a much slower rate than do the mental abilities assessed in some types of intelligence test. Furthermore, one may now show that general intelligence is a multivariate construct. There may be differences in how we define and measure intelligence, in the rates at which it changes, or the nature of its influence on other things at different ages.

It is clear from recent research that the popular conception that, after a certain age, one is too old to learn has no basis in fact below age 60, and much more needs to be known of the role of motivational and personality factors in the learning process. More crucial, however, is the fact that this so-called popular view has dominated supposedly scientifically respectable theories and investigations, particularly in the field of cognitive functioning and mental illness. What in fact does happen to intellectual functioning and personality after 60? Do their structures change? Are they affected by organic and functional psychiatric illness? How do the data from cross-sectional and longitudinal investigations of functioning in the elderly compare? Are normal and pathological changes in the aged similar or divergent? One may, of course, ask the same questions in relation to personality and all aspects of behavioral functioning in the aged.

THE STRUCTURE AND MEASUREMENT OF INTELLECT IN THE AGED

Much of the confusion in the results of intellectual measurement on normal and abnormal aged individuals and groups will remain until a more satisfactory theory or analysis of the structure of intellect in the aged is available. How then can we understand cognitive functioning and change in the aged?

Several investigations in the fields of aging and senility have accounted for their findings by contrasting the results from techniques which measure the stored experiences of subjects with those from measures of learning or problem-solving ability. The former are said to be more resistant to the effects of aging and brain damage than the latter. Thus, Wechsler (1944, 1958) distinguishes between "hold" and "don't hold" subtests on his measures of intellectual functioning; Cattell (1963) suggests a distinction between fluid and crystallized ability, in which fluid ability (GF) is said to show itself best in novel or culture-free material, while crystallized ability (GC) has its highest loading in acquired, familiar, cultural activities. In the same vein, Reed and Reitan (1963b) have differentiated between tests that demand immediate adaptive ability and tests that tap stored information. Furthermore, research work reviewed by Payne (1960, 1972) and Savage (1973) indicates that this distinction between already acquired, crystallized ability or intellectual level and fluid or learning ability to cope with new materials or situations is not only crucial to normal intellectual development, but has important implications for intellectual change associated with functional and/or organic pathological processes.

One can suggest from the Newcastle upon Tyne studies of the community and hospitalized aged a theory for intellectual functioning and impairment in the aged and appropriate methods of assessment. Analysis of work carried out between 1963 and 1972 by Drs. Savage, Britton, Bolton and Hall (1973) gave a sound, mathematical-statistical and psychological solution for understanding the structure of intellect in the aged which appears to have considerable potential. Their solution produced a structure for cognitive functioning in the aged which makes a strong distinction between *intellectual level and intellectual learning*. These are illustrated in Tables I and II. The major first factor or aspect found was one of *general intellectual level*, but not represented in the Learning measures. The *levels of Verbal and Performance* intellectual functioning and deterioration of the Wechsler type were represented by Factors 2 and 3. *Intellectual learning* is seen in the 4 and 5 factors as *performance learning* and *verbal learning*. Figure 1 extends the paradigm to allow specialized experimental studies of the major perceptual and learning aspects where detailed analysis is needed. The aspects of intellectual functioning highlighted by

Table I
Mental Illness and the Structure of Intellect
Newcastle upon Tyne Hospital Aged III
Principal Component Factor Analysis of WAIS, MWLT, PALT

	Factor 1	Factor 2	Factor 3	Factor 4
Full Scale IQ	0.95	−0.09	0.07	0.10
Verbal IQ	0.92	−0.03	0.29	0.08
Performance IQ	0.91	−0.16	−0.22	0.12
Information	0.89	0.18	0.14	−0.03
Comprehension	0.89	0.24	0.06	0.05
Arithmetic	0.83	−0.20	0.16	0.11
Similarities	0.86	−0.02	0.18	−0.08
Digit Span	0.60	−0.48	0.32	0.30
Vocabulary	0.87	0.16	0.26	0.03
Digit Symbol	0.79	−0.16	−0.23	0.05
Picture Completion	0.87	0.09	−0.25	0.16
Block Design	0.82	−0.24	−0.13	−0.03
Picture Arrangement	0.81	−0.04	−0.27	0.10
Object Assembly	0.80	−0.13	−0.32	0.09
Verbal/Performance IQ Discrepancy	0.11	0.22	0.93	−0.04
WAIS Deterioration Quotient	−0.11	0.81	−0.23	0.23
Wechsler-Bellevue Deterioration Quotient	0.34	0.76	−0.25	0.14
Reynell's Index	0.31	0.77	−0.13	−0.16
Hewson Ratios	0.19	−0.56	−0.32	−0.19
Allen's Index	0.50	0.72	0.09	−0.20
MWLT	−0.54	−0.00	0.03	0.63
PALT	−0.63	0.12	0.06	0.55
Latent Root	11.41	3.31	1.85	1.09
Percentage of Variance	51.87	15.04	8.44	5.00

this solution are orthogonal with measures of each showing fortunately very low loadings on the other. This particular breakdown of the nature or types of intellectual functioning on the aged was gaiend from the analysis of the Newcastle upon Tyne information on psychometric assessment which has included over 350 normal and mentally ill aged, over nine years of research.

Savage's proposed solution or explanation of the structure of intellect in the aged is extremely helpful both theoretically and practically. In effect, it *breaks down intellectual functioning in the aged into level and learning components which are orthogonal*

Table II
The Structure of Intellect
Combined Aged IV
Principal Component and Varimex Rotated Factor Analysis

N = 94	Principal Component				Varimax Rotation			
Factors	I	I	III	IV	I	I	III	IV
WAIS								
Comprehension	0.89	0.33	0.08	0.07	0.69	0.62	0.03	0.20
Vocabulary	0.91	0.26	−0.02	0.09	0.74	0.57	0.08	0.17
Block Design	0.82	−0.27	0.01	0.10	0.87	0.08	0.03	0.01
Object Assembly	0.81	−0.43	0.00	−0.09	0.90	−0.13	0.00	0.14
Verbal Score	0.95	0.31	0.03	0.08	0.75	0.63	0.03	0.19
Performance Score	0.90	−0.42	−0.01	−0.02	0.99	−0.06	0.03	0.10
Full Scale Score	0.99	0.00	0.02	0.05	0.91	0.36	0.03	0.16
Verbal IQ	0.95	0.28	0.03	0.08	0.77	0.60	0.03	0.19
Performance IQ	0.89	−0.43	−0.01	−0.03	0.98	−0.08	0.03	0.11
Full Scale IQ	0.99	−0.03	0.02	0.03	0.92	0.33	0.03	0.17
Verbal/Performance IQ Discrepancy	0.11	0.98	0.05	0.15	−0.27	0.95	0.01	0.12
MWLT	−0.46	−0.35	0.15	0.80	−0.20	−0.21	−0.04	−0.95
BDLT	0.09	0.04	−0.99	0.14	0.04	0.02	0.99	0.04
Latent Root	8.54	2.04	1.01	0.73	7.45	2.30	1.01	1.16
Percentage of Variance	65.71	15.72	7.73	5.61	57.33	20.75	7.77	8.92

or independent of one another and specifies both verbal and performance aspects of these two components. Furthermore, the solution is consistent with the previous theoretical decisions of Cattell (1963) and others who have stressed the breakdown between crystallized and fluid abilities, and is consistent with information regarding known effects of functional illness and organic lesions, accidental or natural, on cognitive functioning (Payne, 1960, 1972; Savage, 1970; Yates, 1966). It is also meaningful in terms of the longitudinal changes observed in our work, particularly the differential rate of change in verbal and performance levels in the WAIS, and in the development of learning impairment in the aged.

The importance of this theory of the structure or nature of intellect for psychometric assessment of intellectual functioning in the aged is obvious. *Intellectual level* of functioning consisting of acquired or crystallized intellectual ability is probably more

The Structure and Measurement of Intellect in the Aged

GENERAL INTELLECTUAL LEVEL (1)
(FSIQ)

VERBAL INTELLECTUAL LEVEL (2)
(VIQ)

PERFORMANCE INTELLECTUAL LEVEL (3)
(PIQ)

Measured by Full or Short WAIS
(Wechsler 1955, Britton & Savage
1966)

Intellectural Level Impairment
estimated by WAIS DQ[
(Wechsler, 1958, Savage, 1971)

VERBAL LEARNING (4)
measured by MWLT
(Walton & Black, 1957,
Bolton et al. 1967)

PERFORMANCE LEARNING (5)
measured by BDLT
(Savage & Hall, 1973)

VERBAL LEARNING PARAMETERS
by Experimental Psychology Techniques
(Welford, 1958, 1968; Honig, 1966;
Sidowski, 1966)

PERCEPTUAL-MOTOR LEARNING PARAMETERS
by Experimental Psychology
(Welford, 1958, 1968; Honig, 1966;
Sidowski, 1966)

resistant to the normal aging changes or processes of senility and may well be impaired less rapidly by generalized cerebral injury than fluid intelligence. What is also of practical importance is that this *level* of intellectual ability in terms of both verbal and performance may be adequately assessed in the aged by a short form of the Wechsler Adult Intelligence Scale (1958) especially standardized for the aged (Britton and Savage, 1966). *Learning ability,* both verbal and performance, is probably affected more quickly by the normal organic changes or natural processes of aging, and such deficiencies may be expected to appear before loss of acquired intellectual level occurs. The *verbal learning* aspect of intellectual functioning can be assessed by the Modified Word Learning Test of Walton and Black (1957) with the appropriate age norms presented by Bolton et al. (1967). *Performance or motor-perceptual learning* may be measured by the Block Design Learning Test developed by Savage and Hall (1973). Differences between Verbal and Performance levels and Verbal and Performance Learning can be measured and evaluated by the norms for the aged presented by Savage et al. (1973). An initial comprehensive, yet time-saving, assessment of intellectual functioning in the aged is, therefore, possible, and changes over time or due to illness can be monitored.

If it is felt necessary to give the full WAIS, Wechsler's *Deterioration Quotient* can be calculated to estimate the loss in intellectual functioning level. Despite criticisms by Payne (1960) and Yates (1954, 1966) of the Wechsler Deterioration Quotient concept, it can be very helpful if correctly used and evaluated. Changes in intellectual level and learning as well as the internal subject variability of cognitive functioning can also be traced for individuals and evaluated against adequate peer group norms provided in several sources, such as Savage et al. (1973). Comparative subtest or subscale analysis of the WAIS for individuals with the appropriate statistical evaluation is occasionally useful, but rarely, and in any case only gives hypotheses which might be further investigated. It seems likely, however, that those elderly people whose levels of performance intelligence remain unimpaired should be healthier and probably better adjusted to the difficulties of old age and more likely to be normal and live in the community. Furthermore, the maintenance of a reasonable level of the ability to cope with new verbal and performance material is also associated with the continued survival in both normal and psychiatrically ill aged (Savage et al. 1973).

In summary, then, the structural analysis of intellect in the aged developed from our Newcastle upon Tyne investigations suggest that applied psychology practice in the clinic or in society may be well served by a view of the structure or nature of intellect in the aged, stressing the level and learning components of cognitive processes, both having verbal and performance aspects. Fairly well-standardized, reliable and valid measures to assess these functions in the aged have been presented, and intellectual difficulties associated with functional, treatable psychiatric disorders, such as in the affective states and with more severe degenerative senile processes, indicated (Savage, 1971; Savage et al. 1973). Above all, however, the assessment of cognitive functioning in itself is stressed as extremely important in that it has implications for the way in which we might advise and handle people; we would hope to help them generally to cope more effectively in a variety of situations. Accurate, reliable knowledge of the intellectual functioning of an individual can help us advise that person or family on how to cope in society, at home and in numerous personal and family situations. This should help towards having the best possible personal and social adjustment for the individual aged person and for those who surround him or her. It can also have important implications for the advice given to society on social care, on needs—personal, social and physical—of the elderly in relation to the community at large; to what extent community care, hospitalization, etc., are necessary.

THE STRUCTURE AND MEASURE OF PERSONALITY IN THE AGED

The identification, description and presentation of adequate techniques for the measurement of personality characteristics in the aged has lagged behind those for cognitive assessment in the elderly. The development of more adequate personality assessment procedures by Cattell, Eysenck and others gives hope for the future, but one cannot help but be disappointed by the small amount of research in this field on old people. It is an area of investigation, for example, where latitudinal studies, because of the problems of sampling and natural selection, could give extremely misleading results. The difficulties, particularly the considerable expense of longitudinal studies, must be accepted if we are to make any real progress. Even now, few methods of measuring personality have any, let alone satisfactory, normative data for the elderly. The personality theorists have given only limited attention to changes in old age or even to adequately describing old age personality until very recently. Watson, in a review of the situation in 1954, suggested that research of personality in the elderly was in a naturalistic, exploratory stage rather than at a theoretically or experimentally based level. There has been some but not a great deal of progress since.

Investigations using *projective techniques of personality measurement* have been reported. Indeed, the developmental changes accompanying increasing age were mentioned rather briefly by Rorschach (1942), who commented that "the older individual loses the capacity for introversion and becomes more coarted or constricted." He described further influences of age as an increase in stereotype and a decrease in the freedom of association and claimed that the protocols of normal subjects 70 to 80 years of age closely resembled those of younger cases of dementia simplex.

The Thematic Apperception Test (Murray, 1943) has also been used on the aged, though very little, in an effort to describe and understand their personality. A series of studies from the Kansas City project followed up and generally substantiated the view that there are no statistically significant age differences in the analysis of ratings of flexibility, recollection, mental flexibility, ego transcendence, body transcendence, body satisfaction or sexual integration from six T.A.T. cards with 40–64-year-olds.

In other studies, moreover, they looked at the hypothesis that four dimensions of ego functioning diminish in effectiveness with age. The Thematic Apperception Test was used on 144 subjects aged 40–71 year, divided by age, sex and social class: the older subjects showed fewer extra characteristics in their stories, used less conflict, less strong emotion and described less vigorous activities. Neugarten (1963) concluded that personality does change significantly with age to give way to passive mastery of the situation in 60–70-year-olds and that important sex differences remain at this age level.

Recent years have seen the introduction of *psychometric personality questionnaires* into research on old age personality measurement. This work is still in its infancy, but has immense potential, though the practical and financial difficulties in this area of investigation are considerable. The Minnesota Multiphasic Personality Inventory (Hathaway and McKinley, 1951, 1969) has been used in several investigations and has highlighted the need for caution when applying tests to the aged which have not been specifically standardized on the appropriate populations. Application of this large Inventory to old people is in itself a somewhat difficult task. This no doubt accounts for the limited extent of publications in this area, thought one has the impression that the MMPI enjoys extensive clinical use with all adult age groups, particularly in the United States.

British normative data on the MMPI were published from a community investigation carried out on a sample of the aged (70+) resident in the Newcastle upon Tyne by Britton and Savage (1965). The full card form of the MMPI was administered to 83 subjects, representing both sexes, who were selected at random from the aged community. The questionnaire items were read to each subject during two sessions in his own home.

The means and standard deviations in terms of the standard K corrected T scores for each of the validity and basic clinical scales for the investigation showed statistically significant deviations on all except the Pd and Si scales from the standard MMPI normative data. The means of the K, D and Sc scales are raised by more than one and the means of Hs and Hy by more than two standard deviations. A comparison of the Swenson (1961) and Kornetsky (1963) and Britton and Savage (1965) data showed the British sample as having higher scores than those obtained by the American subjects, but the profile pattern to be similar. Even allowing for any possible sampling bias, the results presented confirmed the suggestion that the standard manual normative data for the MMPI should not be applied to aged subjects.

However, our work in Newcastle upon Tyne leads us to the opinion that the full MMPI, as it stands, has little to recommend itself for use with the aged on either theoretical or practical grounds. Greater understanding of the underlying processes of personality and its changes with age is necessary before one would or could expect the diagnostic efficiency of the MMPI or new scales derived from it to be of much practical value. For example, on the basis of their factor analysis of the MMPI, Britton and Savage (1967) have proposed a screening measure for Mental Illness in the Aged. It consists of a simple yes–no answer, 15 item scale, assessing general mental illness or psychopathology. A cut-off point of 6+ suggests that mental illness is present. The scale was validated against psychiatric diagnosis: 95% of those diagnosed mentally ill on clinical criteria by an independent psychiatric opinion were identified as such by the Britton and Savage Mental Health Scale. We would welcome more extensive information on this measure. A major advantage of the scale is that it can be easily and efficiently used by doctors, nurses, health visitors, social workers, etc., as a preliminary screening device on a large scale—for example, to give an indication of the extent of the problem in an area.

The paucity of studies on the aged with Cattell's and Eysenck's well-developed measures of personality assessment is of some considerable concern to researchers and clinicians. Lynn (1964) discussed the implications of Eysenck's theory of personality and age, and evidence on the responses of 144 normal and mentally ill aged to the Maudsley Personality Inventory questionnaire (Eysenck, 1959) measure of neuroticism and extraversion is provided by Bolton and Savage (1971). The aged had generally slightly higher neuroticism and similar extraversion scores than the younger subjects used in the test standardization. Surprisingly, the Maudsley Personality Inventory data showed that the E scale scores for normals, affectives, schizophrenics and organics were not significantly different from one another, nor were organics distinguishable even from normals on extraversion. On the other hand, organics did differ from both the normal and schizophrenic groups on the neuroticism scale. The high N scores for the affectives is not surprising, as the group was mainly aged affective depressives—reactive and endogenous. One can reasonably assume that the new Eysenck

Personality Inventory and the P.E.N. (Eysenck and Eysenck, 1964) would show similar age and mental illness effects. We await work with this instrument.

The application of Cattell's theory and methods of measurement of personality to the aged have not been very extensive, as the previous review by Savage (1971) revealed. It may be of interest to add here, however, that an attempt by Britton and Savage to administer the Cattell 16 PF scale to 20 elderly people living in the community, but diagnosed "organic," showed that only six were able to complete the inventory, even though it was read to them.

Some very recent work from the Newcastle upon Tyne community aged investigations highlights the possibility of a structure for the understanding of personality in the aged and its relationship to adjustment and self-concept. Four personality groups (Table III) are described on the basis of cluster analysis of data from Cattell's 16 Personality Factor Questionnaire (Gaber, 1974). These are:

GROUP I: The "Normal or Silent Majority." This, the largest group, comprised 44 individuals (54% of the sample population) whose mean age was 78.8 year. As the name implies, this group seems to represent the bulk of the older individuals residing within the community.

This normal group of people tends to be somewhat more intense and apprehensive than younger age groups. They are shown to be suspicious of outward interference in matters concerning themselves and rather wary. These old people are not very happy with changes, are self-sufficient and can be intolerant. Coupled with this, however, they are fairly deliberate in their actions and quite shrewd, analytic and calculating.

GROUP II: The "Introverted." The Aged group consists of 16 individuals whose mean age is 83.8 years. The 16 people were 19.5% of the total sample population. This group is clearly very sober and taciturn. They are reserved, introspective, conscientious people who stick to their inner sense of values. Sometimes, however, they have a tendency to be apprehensive and even melancholic. These elderly people do not enjoy meeting people, are not adventurous, but shy and withdrawn, preferring one or two friends to large groups. Self-restraint and serious-mindedness typify the group,

Table III
Personality Types in the Aged
Cattell Dimension Scores for the Four Aged Personality Groups

	Factor Description	Normal Group I N = 44		Introverted Group II N = 16		Perturbed Group III N = 9		Mature Group IV N = 13	
		Mean	S.D.	Mean	S.D.	Mean	S.D.	Mean	S.D.
A	Reserved v. Outgoing	4.72	1.89	3.50	1.90	6.22	1.54	4.92	1.77
C	Affected by Feelings v. Emotionally Stable	4.00	1.56	5.06	1.47	2.77	1.22	6.53	1.90
E	Humble v. Assertive	5.79	1.43	5.18	1.18	5.55	1.43	5.61	0.92
F	Sober v. Happy-go-Lucky	4.84	2.07	2.62	1.45	3.33	1.76	4.15	1.16
G	Expedient v. Conscientious	6.29	1.19	7.18	1.70	7.33	1.88	6.46	1.82
H	Shy v. Venturesome	5.15	1.50	3.37	1.05	4.44	1.83	5.07	1.20
I	Tough-minded v. Tender-minded	6.13	1.15	6.43	1.53	7.44	1.16	3.23	1.42
L	Trusting v. Suspicious	7.34	1.44	5.75	2.01	9.11	0.73	6.00	1.92
M	Practical v. Imaginative	5.18	1.91	5.06	1.34	6.66	1.56	3.46	1.27
N	Forthright v. Shrewd	7.15	1.53	4.75	1.71	6.33	1.15	7.23	1.31
O	Placid v. Apprehensive	7.13	1.65	6.93	1.14	8.77	0.91	5.23	1.76
Q_1	Conservative v. Experimenting	4.88	1.56	4.68	1.40	3.44	1.25	4.69	1.53
Q_2	Group-dependent v. Self-Sufficient	6.50	1.50	5.62	1.89	3.88	1.72	7.92	1.68
Q_3	Undisciplined Self-confict v. Controlled	5.52	1.72	3.68	1.57	2.55	0.86	7.00	1.24
Q_4	Relaxed v. Tense	6.47	1.65	6.50	1.83	8.55	1.34	5.23	1.36

along with sensitivity to others and some tension in themselves.

GROUP III: The "Perturbed." This type, whose mean age is 76.4 years, made up 11% of the sample population under investigation. As a group, they seem rather perturbed, very suspicious and difficult to get along with. They have very weak ego-strength, and are to a marked degree emotionally unstable and uncontrolled. Likewise, they demonstrate considerable undisciplined self-conflict with consequent personal and interpersonal problems. These people tend to be emotionally immature and get emotionally upset. They aspire to be conscientious, but also exhibit inner apprehension and self-reproach. Irrational worry, tenseness, irritability, anxiousness and being in an inner state of turmoil also characterize this group.

It is of interest that almost all of these individuals in the Perturbed group were independently and blindly assessed by a psychiatrist as being sufficiently disturbed to require psychiatric treatment. Although there are only a small number of these individuals in our sample, these people with functional disorders would tend to loom large in any psychiatric population.

GROUP IV: The "Mature." This type or group is comprised of 13 individuals, 16% of the sample population, whose mean age is 79.1 years. They are highly self-sufficient and resourceful people, enjoying their independence and taking pride in their ability to make their own decisions. This mature-tempered group exhibits considerable ego-strength in terms of emotional stability. They are shrewd, wordly and tough-minded.

The importance and validity of these groups were then further established in terms of their adjustment and self-concept characteristics. The Introverted group whose personality is typified by their tendency toward social interaction and the Normal Majority both demonstrate adequate personal adjustment as defined by LSI B. The Mature Group IV are also well adjusted, while the Perturbed Group III of 11% showed evidence of personal maladjustment on the Havighurst scale.

When considering the four aged personality groups—the Normal Majority, the Introverted, the Perturbed, and the Mature—in relation to self-concept in old age, it also becomes rather evident that such aspects of self-concept as defensiveness and variability of self-concept, conflict in self-definition and various facets of self-esteem are essential in gaining a fuller understanding of the personality in the elderly and figure prominently in the way in which the four groups achieve personal satisfaction (Savage et al., 1976).

This work is most interesting, but considerably more work is needed, particularly longitudinal investigations of personality in the aged. The integration of the cognitive and personality models outlined here is theoretically evident, but the empirical research on this and its implications is essential if we are to help the aged in future generations, or perhaps even our own. To a small extent, research work along these lines is under way in Newcastle upon Tyne.

REFERENCES

Birren, J.E. (ed).: *Handbook of Aging and the Individual*. Chicago, Univ. of Chicago Press, 1959, 1972.

Bolton, N., Savage, R.D., and Roth, M.: The MWLT on an aged psychiatric population. *Brit. J. Psychiat.*, 113, 1139–1140, 1967.

Bolton, N., and Savage, R.D.: Neuroticism and Extraversion in elderly normal and psychiatric patients: Some normative data. *Brit. J. Psychiat.*, 118, 545, 473–474, 1971.

Britton, P.G., and Savage, R.D.: The MMPI and the Aged—Some normative data from a community sample. *Brit. J. Psychiat.*, 112, 941–943, 1965.

Britton, P.G., and Savage, R.D.: A short form of the WAIS for use with the aged. *Brit. J. Psychiat.*, 112, 417–418, 1966.

Britton, P.G., and Savage, R.D.: A short scale for the assessment of mental health in the community aged. *Brit. J. Psychiat.*, 113, 521–523, 1967.

Cattell, R.B.: The theory of fluid and crystallised intelligence: A critical experiment. *J. Educ. Psychol.*, 54, 1–22, 1963.

Eysenck, H.J.: *The Maudsley Personality Inventory Questionnaire*. London, London Univ. Press, 1959.

Eysenck, H.J.: *Handbook of Abnormal Psychology*. London, Pitman Medical Publications, 1973.

Eysenck, H.J., and Eysenck, S.B.G.: *Eysenck Personality Inventory*. London, London Univ. Press, 1964.

Eysenck, H.J., and Eysenck, S.B.G.: The measurement of psychoticism: A study of factor stability and reliability. *Brit. J. Soc. Clin. Pschol.*, 7, 286–294, 1968.

Gaber, L.B.: Personality Dimensions, Self-Concept and Adjustment in the Aged. Unpublished Ph.D. thesis, University of Newcastle upon Tyne, England, 1974.

Hathaway, S.R., and McKinley, J.C.: *Minnesota Multiphasic Personality Inventory Manual*. New York, Psychological Corporation, 1951.

Hathaway, S.R., and McKinley, J.C.: *MMPI Manual (Form R)*. New York, Psychological Corp., 1969.

Honig, W.K.: *Operant Behaviours:Areas of Research and Application*. New York, Appleton Century Crofts, 1966.

Kornetsky, C.: Minnesota Multiphasic Personality Inventory: Results obtained from a population of aged men. In Birren, J.E., Butler, H.N., Greenhouse, S.W., Boroloff, L., and Yarrow, M.R. (eds.), *Human Aging: A Biological and Behavioural Study*, Chap. 13. U.S. Department of Health, Education and Welfare, Bethesda, Maryland, 1963.

Lynn, R.: Personality changes with aging. *Beh. Res. Ther.*, 1, 343–349, 1964.

Murray, H.A.: *Thematic Apperception Test (3rd Revision)*. Cambridge, Mass., Harvard University Press, 1943.

Neugarten, Bernice L.: In Williams, R.H., Tibbits, C., and Donahue, Wilma (eds.), *Processes of Aging, Vol I*. New York, Atherton Press, 1963.

Payne, R.W.: Cognitive abnormalities. In Eysenck, H.J. (ed.), *Handbook of Abnormal Psychology*, 1st and 2nd eds. London, Pitman, 1960, 1972.

Reed, H.B.C., and Reitan, R.M.: Changes in psychological test performance associated with the normal ageing process. *J. Gerontol.*, 18, 271–274, 1963.

Rorschach, H.: *Psychodiagnostics*. New York, Grune & Stratton, 1942.

Savage, R.D.: Intellectual Assessment. In Mittler, P. (ed.), *The Psychological Assessment of Mental and Physical Handicaps*. London, Methuen, 1970.

Savage, R.D.: Psychometric Assessment and Clinical Diagnosis in the Aged. In May, D.W.K., and Walk, A. (eds.), *Recent Advances in Psychogeriatrics*. London, Royal Medico Psychological Association, 1971.

Savage, R.D.: Old age. In Eysenck, H.J. (ed.), *Handbook of Abnormal Psychology*. (2nd Ed.) London, Pitman, 1973.

Savage, R.D., Britton, P.G., Bolton, N., and Hall, E.H.: *Intellectual Functioning in the Aged*. London, Methuen & Co., 1973.

Savage, R.D., Gaber, L.B., Britton, P.G., Bolton, N., and Wilkinson, A.: *Personality Functioning in the Aged*. London, Academic Press, 1976.

Savage, R.D., and Hall, E.H.: A performance learning measure for the aged. *Brit. J. Psychiat.* 122, 721–3, 1973.

Swenson, W.M.: Structured personality testing in the aged: An MMPI study of the geriatric population. *J. Clin. Psychol.*, 17, 302–304, 1961.

Walton, D., and Black, D.A.: The validity of a psychological test of brain damage. *Brit. J. Med. Psychol.*, 30, 270–279, 1957.

Wechsler, D.: *The Measurement of Adult Intelligence*. (3rd ed.) Baltimore, Williams & Wilkins, 1944.

Wechsler, D.: *Manual for the Wechsler Adult Intelligence Scale*. New York, Psychological Corporation, 1955.

Wechsler, D.: *The Measurement and Appraisal of Adult Intelligence*. Baltimore, Williams & Wilkins, 1958.

Welford, A.T.: *Ageing and Human Skill*. London, Nuffield Foundation, O.U.P., 1958.

Welford, A.T.: *Fundamentals of Skill*. London, Methuen & Co., 1968.

Yates, A.J.: Validity of some psychological tests of brain damage. *Psychol. Bull.*, 51, 359–379, 1954.

Yates, A.J.: Psychological deficit. *Ann. Rev. Psychol.*, 17, 111–114, 1966.

7

Cognition in Dementia Presenilis

L.R.C. HAWARD

*Das Gebiet der Präsenile Psychosen ist heute
vielleicht das dunkelste der ganzen Psychiatrie.*
—Kraepelin

INTRODUCTON

It is now 76 years since the concept of dementia presenilis
was first introduced by Binswanger and yet we seem to have made
little progress in what Kraepelin has called "the darkest area in
the whole of psychiatry." Why should this be so? It is certainly
not because the problems of presenile dementia have been overlooked, much less ignored, for they have never lacked investigators;
yet, as we look back over the seven decades since the original and
now-famous report of Alzheimer, we cannot honestly say that this
group of diseases is clearly classified or even fully understood.

The many difficulties encountered in the scientific study of the
syndrome known as dementia presenilis may be subsumed under
two headings: *low incidence* and *differentiation difficulties.* Of the

former, it will be appreciated how difficult it is to obtain cases for comparison, when the incidence of dementia presenilis among psychiatric cases (in which group all dements will eventually find themselves) has been put as low as 0.12% (Moffie, 1953). Even greater difficulties, however, center on the fact that there is no simple relation between the character and degree of the dementia and the histo-neurological picture; it has been found that patients with an almost identical picture clinically produce quite distinct microscopic and even macroscopic appearances post-mortem, while other patients with similar pictures of cerebral pathology may show markedly dissimilar pre-mortem behavior.

Thus it may not be obvious that these diseases are discrete entities, and some clinicians and pathologists have questioned, on completely different grounds, whether they are, in fact, entities at all. The clinical course progresses through a broad and very varied spectrum of behavior, which even when quantified, bears no simple or linear relation to the morbid anatomy revealed at post-mortem examination.

The situation is not quite so pessimistic as one may consider, however, for in the last decade there has been a number of fresh attacks made upon some of the facets of this intensely interesting nosological problem. In Scandinavia, the genetic and clinical aspects have been receiving close study since the end of the last war, and a number of pathological institutes in the Netherlands have been particularly concerned with the morbid anatomy of dementia. Perhaps the most elaborate work to date has been that of Mansvelt (1954) who, in addition to a longitudinal study of his own cases, has tabulated and analyzed in detail the 196 cases of Pick's Disease which have been fully described in the world's medical literature.

The methodology of investigators also differs widely, both in the area of study and in the source of the material under investigation. Some are concerned with macroscopic changes, some with microscopic. Some ignore the clinical picture entirely, feeling with Valentine (1955) that "it is doubtful whether the presenile psychoses can be diagnosed apart during life." Others again ignore the pathological picture, taking up the view at the other extreme exemplified by Mayer Gross et al. (1954), who maintain that "the disorders in this group (the presenile dementias) can only be defined with any consistency in clinical terms." In the temporal dimension, some patients are seen as outpatients when the behavior disturbance only is apparent, others on admission as requiring hospital care; some are seen in mental hospitals after many years of institutionalization when the dementia is already advanced, others only at post-mortem examination. This bewildering variety of periods after onset must surely prevent an even and universal picture of the disease from being obtained. It is possible to obtain a really comprehensive picture only by a longitudinal study as soon after onset as possible and continuing until a full post-mortem analysis can be made.

When we come to the problem of diagnosis itself, the term "presenile dementia" does not suggest that there should be anything difficult in the diagnosis of such a condition—one would merely suppose that it referred to any condition characterized by the symptom of dementia occurring in the presenium. This simplification is more apparent than real, for there exists a wide divergence of opinion on what the age range of the presenium actually is, what is really meant by dementia, and what particular types of disease should either be included or excluded from the group as a whole.

The onset of the physical state called senility varies from individual to individual, and any demarcation of the presenium must therefore, by its very nature, be arbitrary. Bini (1948), for example, designates the presenile period as existing between the ages of 45 and 65 years. Valentine (1955) defines it as the 40–60 age group. Many writers mention cases which seem to have had their onset very early in adult life, while a number of cases unequivocally diagnosed as Morbus Alzheimer have been described as commencing in ripe old age.

It seems unlikely that any good purpose can be served either by attempting to delineate a lower age limit, or by criticizing limits which have already been stated. The upper limit is, of course, of less importance in diagnosis and prognosis, since neurologically the presenile dementias tend to merge with the senile organic conditions. Nevertheless, Raskin and Ehrenberg (1956) describes cases of Pick's and Alzheimer's Disease which can be diagnosed unequivocally and yet have their onset in the late 60's or even the late 70's.

INCIDENCE

Most authorities agree that presenile dementia is a comparatively rare condition, and as we have seen, its low incidence has been a major obstacle in the path of progress into the understanding of this group of diseases. Yet it seems that there is no general agreement on just how rare they actually are, for the incidence figures vary very considerably between one investigator and another. Sjoegren and his co-workers (1952), for example, suggest that the relatively *high* frequency of occurrence of Morbi Pick and Alzheimer has not been appreciated. These authors conclude that no less than 8% of all senile and presenile psychoses fall into the Pick-Alzheimer category. On the basis of their extensive genetic studies, this finding gives a morbidity risk for these two diseases in their population of 0.1%.

Mayer Gross et al. (1954) believe that presenility is useless as a purely chronological concept, remarking that some individuals are senile before they are 60, while others are only "middle-aged" in appearance at 70; they prefer as their criterion a discrepancy between mental decline and physical preservation, weighted in significance by certain pathological signs. Nevertheless there is obviously something to be said for lowering the borderline age and thereby increasing the significance of the symptomatology.

With ascending age, signs of deterioration are no longer clinically abnormal and a cause of anxiety for the individual, but are merely expected evidence of a decline in mental powers matched to some extent with that of the patient's physical condition. The age of 65, which represents the age of general retirement in the United Kingdom, appears to be a popular choice as the dividing line between senility and presenility.

It could be argued that the problem is semantic rather than clinical and that the diseases subsumed under the title of the presenile dementias have existence and clinical validity in their own right irrespective of the age of the patient. Nevertheless, the diagnosis becomes increasingly important in the younger patient, and the concept of presenility appears to be worth preserving. Since the psychological aspects are so important in this group, as will be seen later, 65 years has been set as the upper age limit for the purposes of this study. After retirement, the individual seems more prepared to accept evidence of failing functions without undue emotional reaction than he was before this age. Retirement age therefore has some logical validity and justification as a dichotomizing criterion. However, since retirement is tied to age by official regulation, it seems more convenient to use age as the separator between the senium and the presenium when defining a research sample.

SAMPLING:

This study covered a five-year period and was based upon a county mental hospital of 2,000 beds and its associated psychiatric outpatient departments. During this period 49 patients were provisionally diagnosed as having presenile dementia and underwent a full psychometric examination, including a psychophysiological assessment. The age range was 40–62 inclusive, mean 52.4 years and the age distribution of this sample was as follows:-

40-44	45-49	50-54	55-59	60-64	Total
5	15	10	14	5	49.

The sex distribution was 36 females and 13 males, a sex ratio rather more in favor of women than is commonly reported in the literature, but an explanation for this follows in the discussion. The distribution of socioeconomic status of the patients did not differ significantly from that of the population as a whole.

METHOD

The patients were referred for this long-term research project, which was originally planned to cover at least a decade, on the basis of showing symptoms of intellectual deterioration before the age of 65. The referring psychiatrists were asked to avoid including in the study any patients showing intellectual impairment believed at the time to be temporary and due to functional processes of their psychopathology. They were not required to be positive about the diagnosis of dementia, but were asked to refer only those patients for whom this probability was greater than other alternatives. It was hoped by this method of selection that the sample would include some patients who could be diagnosed post-mortem on histological evidence even in the absence of an unequivocal clinical picture, and such proved to be the case. All patients were seen by the author within a fortnight of coming to the attention of the psychiatric service, and received a comprehensive assessment spread over three sessions. The first session was devoted to a personality assessment, since it represented the least threatening task of the three sessions, and utilized a variety of both objective and subjective measures, including questionnaires, and projective techniques. In the second session the patient participated in a battery of cognitive tests, including the Wechsler Bellevue Intelligence Scale, the Wechsler Memory Scale, Tien's Organic Integrity Test and the Kahn Test of Symbol Arrangement. The third session was conducted at the psychological laboratory and consisted of a stress-inducing psychomotor task with visual and auditory distraction, together with monitoring of the autonomic nervous response by means of heart rate, respiration, skin temperature and galvanic skin response. For the ANS variables standard sensors were used, and incorporated an earlobe photoelectric pulse detector, a sub-nostril airflow temperature thermometer attached to the microphone boom of the headset used for supplying the auditory stimulus, a skin thermister located over the prominence of the cheekbone, and stainless steel mesh finger electrodes on the first and third finger of the sub-dominant hand for measuring skin resistance. The task itself called for a two-way manual response to a 7 light display according to instructions of increasing complexity. At the simplest level one of two lights would indicate the direction of movement to be made, while at the most complex level additional lights would signal simultaneously a code which canceled, modified or reversed the code of neighboring lights. The patient was handed a card with instructions printed in large type which could be referred to at any time during the task, and all patients were allowed to practice until they could complete the sequence correctly, no time limit being imposed at this stage. The program was then speeded up until at least one error per sequence was recorded, thus setting the stimulus input at a point just above the channel capacity of the individual patient. A five-minute run of the program was then given and a basic score derived. After a five-minute rest period in which the patient was engaged in relaxing and reassuring conversation, a second run of the program was made. This time, stress was induced by supplying auditory distraction in the form of randomly given instructions: "Left" and "Right" which bore no overall relationship with the correct direction the lever was required to be moved. At the same time visual distraction was provided by the random illumination of extraneous but logically oriented lights, and the program itself was speeded up. It has been the author's contention (see, for example, Haward, 1970) that only by overloading the channel capacity of the cerebral processing circuits can the real differences between the cerebral functioning of one patient and another be detected. As long as channel capacity is not fully utilized, there will always be some individuals who can absorb an otherwise stressful increment in information input. Indeed, in complex psychomotor tasks the hypoactive and under-aroused patient often does better under stressful conditions than he does at a so-called "resting level." Scoring was in units of the logarithm of the sum of the errors, the error distribution being a J-curve. The basic score, which correlated significantly and positively with intelligence quotient, was not used by itself but the stress-effect was quantified by the formula:

$$S = 100 \ (logE_b - logE_s).(logE_b)^{-1}$$

where S = stress effect, E = total number of errors per run,, Suffix b = basic conditions and suffix s = stress conditions. This transformation produced an approximately gaussian distribution and made some allowance for the level of intellectual efficiency existing at the time of the testing.

RESULTS

Of the 49 patients who entered the study, 17 produced a psychometric picture incommensurate with an organic state and suggestive of an endogenous depression, and under the appropriate treatment showed a reversal of the apparent cognitive impairment they had exhibited earlier. The differentiation of early dementia from the less obvious depressive conditions met with in the late middle-aged and elderly patient has been a notoriously difficult psychometric task, but the newer forms of stress inducing psychomotor procedures using saturated channel capacity appear to make an effective contribution to the resolution of these diagnostic difficulties. Only 9 of this group had died by the time of writing, and these patients showed no specific abnormal changes in cerebral pathology under histological examination at post-mortem, the condition of the cerebrum being commensurate with the age of the patient. In none of these patients was the cause of death recorded as due to brain pathology. In the tabulated data this group is designated Group I. Histologically the brains of patients who antemortem have shown symptoms of presenile dementia can be placed in one of four categories, viz., normal, especific, nonspecific and other conditions. The specific group comprises the true presenile diseases of Alzheimer, Pick and Jakob-Creuzfeldt, in which the specific features of brain pathology are recognizable and in theory at least can be differentiated one from the other. The nonspecific group comprises those mixed conditions which defy clear-cut differentiation as well as the more rare and highly atypical conditions, such as those described in the Bronisch Monograph (1951). The third category contains those recognizable conditions which are not specific to the presenium and exist as identifiable diseases which already have a traditional place in medical nosology. They would include the cerebral arteriopathies, chronic meningoencephalitis, and so on. These categories are designated Groups I, II, III and V, respectively, in the tables.

Of the 32 patients remaining, after the "non-organic" patients had been excluded, 11 were classified by the pathologist as specific, 9 as nonspecific, and 12 as "other conditions." For the purpose of comparison, the records of the 9 deceased non-dementing patients were included in the analysis as control data, since it was hoped that some practical diagnostic value would attach itself to the process of psychometric differentiation of the four groups. Indeed, from the clinician's point of view, a valid discriminator between dementia and non-dementia is of more practical use than the differentiation of the subforms of presenile dementia, which in

Table I
Personality Factors in Presenile Dementia

Discriminant*	Group I	Group II	Group III	Group IV
Rorschach Color naming	0%	29%	19%	13%
Rorschach White Space Response	0%	28%	16%	0%
Rorschach expanded detail response	0%	48%	18%	0%
Piotrowski's organic signs	0%	59%	58%	29%
Dorken and Kral's organic signs	0%	100%	81%	59%

*Only discriminants at $P < 0.05$ or better are included in this table.

some cases may be no more than an interesting academic exercise. Even in the latter case, however, there may well be some important implications for management as Raskin and Ehrenberg (1956) have discussed.

In all but 3 of the many simple Rorschach Scores that were examined the variability of each group was too large to reveal any significance in the difference between means, although the means themselves showed interesting trends. Statistically significant differences were, however, found in 3 of the so-called pathognomonic signs which Rorschach related to intracranial organic pathology, viz., the color-naming response (Cn), the white space response (S), and the expanded detail response (DW). These were entirely absent from the records of patients in Group I and in some of those from Group IV, but were present in a significant number of the presenile dementia patients. Their absence in some patients from the latter two groups points to the relative frequency of the false negatives. While for this group the presence of any of these signs is an indication of brain damage, the absence of such signs has no differentiating power. Piotrowski's signs (1940) yield a better discriminant, and the organic signs of Dörken and Kral (1952) are even more efficient in differentiating between the non-organic, the specific presenile dementias, and the other brain-damaged. No statistically significant differences emerged from any of the other personality tests used. It is obvious that such tests are not appropriate as diagnostic instruments in the differentiation of types of brain damage, although when some pathological signs

Table II
Cognitive Factors in Presenile Dementia

Discriminant*	Group I	Group II	Group III	Group IV
Wechsler Bellevue Mean IQ	90.5	94.1	93.9	83.0
Wechsler Bellevue Conceptual Quotient**	87.4	62.7	67.3	74.5
Wechsler Memory Quotient	79	67	58	70
Tien Organic Integrity Score	85.2	22.9	29.7	47.1
Kahn Symbol Arrangement Score	89.3	15.7	23.6	58.8
**CQ = BD + Sim + 2 x Voc				

*Only discriminants at P < 0.05 or better are included in this table

appear, they do seem to indicate unequivocally the presence of organic brain pathology.

It will be seen from Table II that the cognitive measures proved to be better discriminators than the peronality ones. The Wechsler IQ's were separated mainly because of the low variability of Groups II and III, and the same applied to the Conceptual quotients. The lack of differentiation of the Memory Scale is explicable both in terms of the age range of the sample in each group, and also because of the lumping together of 3 disparate diseases in Group I. The dysmnesias of morbus Pick and morbus Alzheimer are different both in stage of onset and quality of impairment. Memory loss occurs relatively early in cases of Alzheimer's Disease, whereas patients suffering from morbus Pick tend to show a good preservation of memory functions until the atrophic cortical processes are relatively well advanced. Thus by merging these two disorders into one group, one of the essential differentiating characteristics has been submerged, and the group scores from tests of memory function cannot adequately reflect the discriminating power of these tests. Nevertheless, it will be remembered that these patients were investigated at the time when they first came for medical help and when diagnosis would be important, and from the practical point of view the lack of discrimination of memory function, using this particular test, is very relevant.

Group I, the pseudodementia depressives, and Group IV, the mixed organic cases (mainly cerebro-arteriosclerotic), both showed a wide variation of intellectual efficiency within the group, while

Table III
Stress Responses in Presenile Dementia

Discriminant*	Group I	Group II	Group III	Group IV
Psychomotor efficiency	21	91	94	77
Psychomotor stress response	9.3	31	27	24
Mean cardiac changes under stress	2%	8%	9%	5%
Mean respiratory changes under stress	7%	20%	17%	12%
Mean skin temperature changes under stress	1%	4%	4%	2%
Mean GSR changes under stress	11%	47%	39%	26%

*Only discriminants at $P < 0.05$ or better are included in this table.

Groups II and III, the specific and nonspecific presenile dementias, were much more homogenous. Both Tien's and Kahn's organic tests separated the groups at better than the 1% level of probability, mainly because they incorporated a measure of psychotic process in with this measurement of organicity. Both of these latter tests could be used confidently to separate Group I (non-organic) from Groups II, II and IV (organic) and could separate the presenile dementic patient from the other organic conditions with 91% accuracy. The relatively small size of the sample precludes the extrapolation of this level of predictive efficiency to other samples, but the author has found both tests to be particularly useful in differentiating the elderly pseudo-demented depressive patients from the true case of organic pathology. The psychomotor task possessed a discriminating power comparable to that of the organic tests of Tien and Kahn, and although appearing a little less efficient in separating the Group IV patients from the two presenile groups, actually was superior to any other measure because of the small variation in group scores. There were large differences between the mean scores of the 3 presenile dementias, but the small sample size precludes any meaningful discussion of such differences.

DISCUSSION

The depressive retardation of the pseudo-dementia group, which is not always clinically apparent, was clearly revealed in the test of psychomotor efficiency. It was this group of mainly elderly latent depressive patients that produced the strongly disbalanced sex ratio. Since psychomotor efficiency can be measured accurately and effectively in as little as 30 seconds (Adler and Walker 1974), there is clearly a good case to be made for the inclusion of this form of measurement in a diagnostic test battery. The Group I patients were also identifiable on the Rorschach Test in terms of personality constellations, even though individual scores were rarely significant. The depressive condition reveals itself in different ways according to the personality context in which it exists, and it would therefore be surprising to find any uniformity of psychological scores in this respect. The presenile dementias show the greater degree of anxiety, which was also present in the other organic group but absent from the depressives. It should be noted that while insight is retained in the incipient stages of dementia a certain degree of depressive overlay will frequently be found. Simple tests of depression are therefore not adequate by themselves as discriminating variables. The quality of the depression is of course different in the two cases, and the Rorschach, despite its poor showings in validation studies, nevertheless can be a useful instrument in expert hands for differential diagnosis.

Differentiation of various organic conditions is notoriously difficult even with cognitive tests, and although the Kahn and Tien tests are among the best for this particular purpose, they lose their discriminating power when functional psychotic states need to be differentiated from organic conditions. It is, of course, interesting that both of these tests rely on, *inter alia,* the scoring of chromophilic responses, and therefore share with the color naming response of the Rorschach the reliance upon the color responsivity of organic patients. Tien (1969) provides a plausible theoretical substrate for this finding, which need not be discussed here, but it is of psychometric importance insofar as the retarded depressive, who so often produces an "organic" score on tests of intellectual impairment, is nevertheless still form-dominant (if only because of his depressive aversion for bright color). Psychometric instruments which test this color responsivity therefore offer greater discriminating accuracy than those that examine only the intellectual efficiency.

Nevertheless, it is the stress tests which provide the easiest, quickest and most accurate differentiation between organic and non-organic patients, and between patients with various types of cerebral pathology. As one would expect, the pseudo-dementia depressives show relatively little sympathetic nervous response under stress. Moreover, their accuracy on complex psychomotor tasks reduces very considerably as soon as time pressures are imposed. If, however, their decrement in response is related to their basal level, these patients are found to be significantly less affected by the imposed stress than are the dementing patients. In the latter, imposed stress tends to have very profound effects. Goldstein's catastrophic reaction is a well-known concomitant of early dementia. At this stage insight is well preserved and the patient is only too well aware of his prematurely failing faculties; the precarious defenses built up to protect the ego from the conscious realization of personal disintegration can be all too readily swamped by a confrontation produced by a psychometric technique which lays bare and makes explicit to himself and to others the patient's real cognitive defects. Such a confrontation can have a devastating effect, and the decision to use psychological techniques of this sort require consideration of the same ethical and humanitarian factors as would be given to the decision to commit the patient to air ventriculography. Diagnostic ends may not always justify the means, but in cases of differential diagnosis related to the presenile dementics such risks have to be measured against the risk of failing to provide the appropriate treatment to patients for whom a prompt recovery with electroconvulsive therapy or anti-depressive medication would otherwise be predicted. Stress-inducing psychomotor tests, born in the psychological laboratory from a direct genetic strain which stems from Wundt in Leipzig and Titchener and Judd in America, are already proving their value as valid, efficient and practical discriminators in selecting astronauts, pilots, air traffic controllers, and the like. Their application to clinical psychology and to medical nosology has a history of less than two decades, and is still far from well known. Nevertheless, this study has demonstrated the particularly high level of discrimination obtainable in the sample examined. Further validation studies are, of course, necessary, but there is a reasonable expectancy that on the basis of the results obtained so far, this psychomotor task will join the Zero Input Tracking Analyzer and Synaptic Latency Meter as one of a group of new generation psycho-diagnostic aids.

ACKNOWLEDGMENT

The author wishes to acknowledge his immense debt of gratitude to the late Dr. S. Hurwiez, consultant pathologist, without whose painstaking investigations of autopsy materials this study could not have been undertaken. His untimely death severely reduced the duration of the study and prevented the inclusion of his autopsy data in this report.

REFERENCES

Adler, S.J., and Walker, N.K.: *Preliminary Tests on the use of ZITA/ADT in the Diagnosis and Treatment of Minimal Brain Dysfunction.* Bethesda, Maryland, Walker Associates, 1974.

Bini, L.: Le Demenze presenili. Rome, Ediz Italia, 1948.

Bronisch, S.W.: *Hirnatrophische Prozesse im mittleren Lebensalter.* Stuttgart, Thieme, 1951.

Dürken, H., and Kral, V.A.: The psychological differentiation of organic brain lesions and their localization by means of the Rorschach test. *Am. J. Psychiat.*, 108, 764, 1952.

Goldstein, K.: *The Organism.* New York, American Book Co., 1939.

Haward, L.R.C.: Effects of DPH and Pemoline upon concentration. In W.L. Smith (ed.), *Drugs and Cerebral Function.* Springfield, Ill., Thomas, 1971.

Kraepelin, E.: *Psychiatrie.* Leipzig, Barth, 1899.

Mansvelt, J. Van: Pick's Disease. Enschede, Loeff, 1954.

Mayer Gross et al.: *Clinical Psychiatry.* London. Cassell, 1954.

Moffie: Presenile Dementia. *Folia Psychiat. Neurol. Neurochir.* 56, 360–374, 1953.

Piotrowski, Z.: Positive and Negative Rorschach organic reactions. *Rorsch. Res. Ech.*, 4, 147, 1940.

Raskin, N., and Ehrenberg, R.: Senescence, Senility and Alzheimer's Disease. *Amer. J. Psychiat.*, 113, 133–136, 1956.

Schottky, J.: Über präsenile verblödung. *Ztschs. Neurol.*, 140, 33–341, 1932.

Sjögren, T., Sjögren, H., and Lindgren, A.G.H.: Morbus Alzheimer and Morbus Pick. *Acta Psychiat. Neurol. Scand.* Suppl. 82.

Tien, H.C.: Pattern Recognition and Mental Disorders, *Psychosomatics* 10, 29–34, 1969.

Valentine, M.: *An Introduction to Psychiatry.* Edinburgh, Livingstone, 1955.

8

Future Perspectives in Aging and Dementia

LESTON B. NAY

An enormous volume of literature is being contributed each year to medical journals throughout the world, as researchers attempt to understand better the aging process, with the implicit dream of forestalling, if not preventing, the ultimate disintegration of life. Interest has been concerned not only with longevity, but also with quality of life. The contrasts may be brought into sharp focus by considering, on the one hand, a remark attributed to Maurice Chevalier, who, when asked on his 80th birthday how it felt to be old, responded, "Great, when you consider the alternative," and, on the other hand, Shakespeare's description of the prospects of advancing age in *As You Like It*:

> Last scene of all,
> That ends this strange eventful history,
> Is second childishness and mere oblivion,
> Sans teeth, sans eyes, sans taste, sans everything.

203

We are all too conscious of this "second childishness and mere oblivion" and this must be one of the prime movers in the increasing examination of the aging brain.

Even a casual review of journal articles, as well as the chapters of this book, emphasizes the many directions explored in the quest for further understanding aging. This chapter is an effort to peer a bit into the future and contemplate at least a few areas that may occupy the interests of investigators as they pursue the will-o'-the-wisp fountain of youth.

The traditional approach to unraveling function is to first understand structure. Maturation of central nervous system function is clearly related to profound structural changes. Even gross observations bear this out: at birth the human brain weighs 350 grams, by six months weight has doubled to 700 grams, and nearly doubles again to a weight of 1,200 grams by four years. And since the number of neurons has generally been thought not to increase after birth—the ten billion cells are all considered to be post-mitotic—such increases in weight are due to a remarkable increase in complexity of these neurons, chiefly related to dendritic arborizations, allowing a manifold development of synapses, and therefore an unimaginable potential for inter-neuronal communication. With aging, we have all learned that there is a progressive decrease in brain weight, and a progressive loss of neurons—one estimate suggests that this amounts to 50,000 neurons a day. When one considers that there are probably only several million motor neurons, the ratio of association neurons to motor neurons of about 4,000:1 indicates that the vast bulk of the nervous system is concerned with integrative functions. It has always seemed reasonable to believe that each neuron, with its thousands of synapses, is *actively* involved in neural processes, and so cellular loss must play a major role in senescence. Recent studies have focused on dendritic changes with aging (Scheibel, 1975). It appears that a series of regressive or degenerative changes occur, with aging of neural elements, serving to effectively diminish the potential for complex interneuronal communication. It is an interesting observation that the progressive degenerative changes with aging retrace, in reverse, the sequence of developmental changes in dendritic envelopes during central nervous system maturation. The mechanisms of these degenerative changes are not known, but structural changes in tubular proteins (as neurotubules and neurofilaments) certainly play a role. It may be that those dendritic processes that are the last to develop phylogenetically and the latest to mature ontogenetically are the earliest to undergo aging-degenerative changes, and thus could correlate with the subtle impairments of integrative functions that are so characteristic of early aging changes.

The glial elements of the central nervous system have been viewed classically as a sort of scaffolding for the neural elements. Several lines of investigation have suggested that these cells may be less "passive" in neural events (Vernadakis, 1975). It has long been known that the "blood-brain barrier"—an interface between neurons and the vascular milieu, and in which the glial cells play a role—"develops" with brain maturation in the newborn. In a variety of ways, barrier function can be viewed as preserving the micro-environments of neurons, and neuropil generally, to ensure optimum functioning. Somewhat surprisingly, there are so far no systematic studies of blood-brain barrier mechanisms in the aging brain. I have already noted that neurons are post-mitotic. Glial cells, by contrast, continue to proliferate throughout life, and in senescence the ratio of neuron:glial cell has altered somewhat. What is the significance of this change? Again, viewed in the context of micro-environmental considerations, it is difficult to escape the probability that neuronal function is influenced, in ways yet to be explored, as a consequence of this aging change.

Current studies suggest that it may be necessary to challenge some generally held "facts" regarding structural changes with age. I have referred to the gradual loss of neurons with increasing age. An oft-quoted statistic is based, however, on material from three human cases, and involved study of only about 0.0005% of the total neuronal population of the cerebral cortex. A set of recent studies, involving counts of neurons in serial sections of the ventral cochlear nucleus of twenty-three human brains ranging in age from birth to 90 years, found no significant change with age (Konigsmark and Murphy, 1972). Another way of examining this question involves measure of the DNA content of neuron nuclei. When this was examined in mice and rat brains during maturation and aging (but not including senescent brains), the total cerebral DNA content was found to be relatively stable (Howard, 1973). Interpretation of this study is complicated by the fact that neuron DNA and glial DNA are not differentiated; it may, however, be concluded that for these species the total cerebral counts remain unchanged. If cell loss occurs, it must be balanced by new cell formation.

Weight of the human brain has been traditionally noted to decline with increasing age. But in an extensive study by Chernyshev, changes in brain weight could be more closely related to causes of death than to age (Blinkov and Glezer, 1968). Weights were greatest in cases of sudden traumatic death, and least following chronic illness lasting for months or years. Another study showed a less than 1% decrease in brain weight in women between ages 16 and 60, and a 3.5% decrease in men in the same age range. It seems quite evident that this ostensibly "simple" observation needs to be thoroughly reexamined. And in view of data accruing in instances of malnutrition, not only must there be explicit consideration of causes and acuteness of death, but also of nutritional status during infancy and early development, and perhaps maternal nutritional status as well.

DNA studies in subhuman primates have shown that limited neuron proliferation actually occurs in the early postnatal period, at least in the hippocampal area (Howard, 1973). These studies, which extend observations previously made in the mouse, have involved autoradiography of tritiated thymide in DNA, and emphasize that investigative procedures with increasing sophistication may very well lead to a reexamination of currently held structural "facts."

It seems quite clear, predominantly from subhuman studies, that *in utero* conditions and early postnatal environmental factors play a significant role in nervous-system development, not only regarding structural considerations, but also in relationship to function. How these factors relate to the development of aging changes in the central nervous system is only beginning to be examined.

This chapter will review problems related to dementia only sketchily because I believe that no substantial syntheses will be achieved until "normal" aging processes are better understood. But I should like to emphasize certain observations, already noted in this book, that do not reliably serve to distinguish dementia from aging, except perhaps in a quantitative sense. Central nervous system changes appearing with increasing frequency with advancing age include neurofibrillary degeneration, granulovacuolar degeneration, Lewy bodies, Hirano bodies, neutritic or senile plaques, lipofuscin accumulation, and corpora amylacea. These structural changes are not restricted to the human central nervous system: primates and other vertebrate species have shown similar changes in clinically healthy aged animals (Wisniewski and Terry, 1973). And some similar changes with aging have also been observed in invertebrate studies in Drosophila, the house fly, an interesting species for study because, with no vascular system, the aging nervous system changes cannot be attributed to arteriosclerosis (Herman, Miguel, and Johnson, 1971). But because these changes appear with increasing age, are they therefore the result of "normal" cell senescence?

One is back, in a sense, to square one.

For the moment I should like to leave primary considerations of structure and examine questions of function. There is no dearth of literature concerning *development* of function in the maturing nervous system. Examination of this aspect necessarily involves questions investigated by neurophysiologists, neurochemists, and investigators in the areas of behavior and ethology. If function, in its behavioral aspects, is somehow a summation of neurotransmitters (including synthesis and destruction), enzymes, and ultimately the availability of metabolic energy, then these "building blocks" must be examined in detail in the aging and senescent brain.

Changes in neurotransmitter substances in the maturing and aging central nervous system of the chicken have been studied by Vernadakis (Vernadakis, 1973). Activities of acetylcholine esterase (AChE) and choline acetyl-transferase (ChAT), the hydrolyzing and synthesizing enzymes of acetylcholine, have differing patterns during embryonic development and aging. During maturation, cerebral hemispheres contain high levels of both hydrolyzing and synthesizing enzymes, evidently reflecting the requirements of cholinergic neurons. But during aging AChE levels are high, and ChAT activity is low, and it is the latter that is an index of the presence of acetylcholine. With aging, then, either cholinergic neurons are at a low level of activity, or have decreased in number.

Monoaminergic neurotransmitters, however, show somewhat different patterns of change with aging. If norepinephrine activity (NE) may be taken as an index of noradrenergic neurons, and 5-hydroxy-tryptamine activity (5HT) an index of serotonergic neurons, then striking differences between these two systems emerge. During maturation, hemispheric norepinephrine activity either decreases or does not change, and 5HT activity increases. (In the cerebellum, opposite changes occur.) During aging, hemispheric activities of both NE and 5HT are at high levels. Thus neither noradrenergic neurons decrease during aging. These findings may lend further support to the view that whatever neuronal loss occurs with aging may be restricted to specific cell types (e.g., pyramidal cells of the cerebral cortex). But the presence of activity does not necessarily imply a continuation of *normal* activity. The accumulation of tritiated norepinephrine in cerebral hemisphere neurons is markedly impaired with aging (though it remains at high levels in the cerebellum), suggesting functional impairment of noradrenergic neurons in the cerebral hemisphere.

An important question, however, arises: Do the above studies really reflect neuronal activity, or is glial activity during aging also playing a role, in putative neurotransmitter activity?

Studies of changes with aging of free amino acids in the central nervous system have led to speculative efforts to make functional correlations (Timiras, Hudson and Oklund, 1973). Levels of aspartic acid decrease significantly with age in cerebral cortex, cerebellum and spinal cord, and a decrease in glutamic acid level also occurs in the spinal cord. Both these amino acids have been proposed as excitatory neurotransmitters, and thus the perhaps too vague suggestions that these changes reflect a decrease in "strength" of neuronal signals in the aging brain. Glycine, proposed as an inhibitory neurotransmitter shows relatively little change with age. Taurine, also suggested as an inhibitory neurotransmitter, decreases markedly with increasing age. Only very general conclusions can be drawn from these data: there are changes that seem to be age-related; these changes reflect, in complex ways, alterations in both structure and function; increasingly refined techniques, which permit examinations of more restricted neural regions, may permit more meaningful references to excitatory and inhibitory functions.

The materials so far discussed have considered aspects of aging in the central nervous system, almost as though "aging" were some sort of unitary process that runs down, like a pocket watch. Is it indeed "preprogrammed" to run down? And can the system be rewound, a little bit? Can the pace of winding down be modified?

It is clear that brain development and aging involve a number of genetic and environmental interactions. Environmental manipulations have already been alluded to briefly. Investigators have suggested (and others have argued) that "critical periods" exist in which only brain development postnatally is subject to considerable modification (Ordy and Schjeide, 1973). Environmental enrichment and deprivation schemata have been designed to examine structural and functional changes in rodent brain development, and significant changes have thereby been superimposed upon genetically determined patterns of growth. These changes involve both gross and ultra-structural phenomena—for instance, an alteration in synapse density—and neurochemical changes. How much structural and chemical plasticity is preserved in the central nervous system? Or rather, to what extent does a developmental potential persist during maturity and aging? Discounting, if possible, unitary concepts for terms like "aging," are such phases in nervous-system ontogeny really mutually exclusive?

In an attempt to approach these questions, certain points should be kept in mind. In general, in multicellular organisms, aging is a term applied to encompass a period of progressive decline after reproductive maturity, although in a sense development could be considered a form of aging, and aging a continuation of development. But the brain is different, with each neuron a post-mitotic structure, virtually as old as the individual, and therefore without distinct stages of development, maturity and senescence that characterize dividing cellular systems.

Life span is genetically determined. Tissue culture work, using human fibroblasts derived from embryo donors indicate a finite limit to the number of proliferations—the total number of doublings is 40 to 60. Fibroblasts obtained from adult donors, cultured under identical conditions, will double 10 to 30 times. The doubling sequences can be interrupted, for example by freezing, but when the process is resumed, the total number of doublings remains about 50 (Hayflick, 1975). This appeared inviolate until Goldstein and Lin, in 1972, fused senescent human fibroblasts with a permanent line of hamster kidney cells, achieving morphologically intermediate cells with twice the capacity for division as human embryo-derived fibroblasts (Goldstein and Lin, 1972). How is this achieved? It seems that, somehow, the genetic program is subject to manipulation. In general, however, ontogenic change seems to be a direct consequence of a genetically determined developmental program contained within DNA. This program "instructs" sequences for organization of the brain to create the potential for learning, response and, ultimately, dedifferentiation. But it has been suggested that if the developmental program were absolutely specific as to each dendritic branching and each synaptic contact, the number of genes necessary would at least equal the number of neurons. This does not seem to be the case, and requires that a degree of plasticity is indeed present, with many inter-neuronal connections determined by environmental considerations. Quite apart from environmental enrichment studies in rodents, learning as a phenomenon must be translatable to electro-chemical events, though we may not yet be able to define these. And this implies a degree of plasticity in neuronal function (? and structure). Exactly where this occurs remains a series of problems to be elucidated. Even taken in these terms, neural plasticity in man progressively decreases with maturation. The capacity to acquire a second language is a case in point. Nevertheless, the potential for modification is present, at least to presenescence, and more needs to be learned about the mechanisms involved.

Although aging has, so far, been described as a sort of built-in program, it may be that this, too, represents an occurrence by virtue of extrinsic or environmental factors. DNA damage, for instance, may occur because of mutations. Free radicals may produce both DNA damage and injury to other cellular structures. Errors of replication may gradually accumulate, or genetic material may actually be lost (Goldstein, 1971). Immunological defects also may contribute significantly to the aging process in the nervous system. An increase in autoantibodies has been demonstrated in aging mammals, though the role of antibodies in neuronal degeneration remains unclear. A gamma globulin binding fraction (probably antibody) against brain antigen has been found in the sera of aged but not young mice (Nandy, 1973).

The majority of the considerations thus far derive from the microcosm of the neuron and its immediate environs, and necessarily from nonhuman brains. How applicable are such studies to questions of aging in man? In some way, age equivalents must be utilized if extrapolations are to be made from, say, mouse to man. An investigation of age and regional differences in chemical composition of brains of mice, monkeys and humans led Samorajski and Rolsten to conclude that neurochemical changes in the brain of the rhesus monkey are similar to those occurring in man, but that neurochemical changes in the mouse brain were significantly dissimilar (Samorajski and Rolsten, 1973). This represents an important note of caution.

Further, if the ultimate point of aging research is to understand aging as a behavioral phenomen, and if behavior is a function of synaptic events, then measurements of neurotransmitters and other chemical substances from conglomerates of brain tissues are hardly likely to provide the sort of detailed information from which accurate models of aging can be constructed. More precise methods for separating and analyzing the component parts of brain specimens will be able to more clearly correlate structure, function and aging.

Moving from a microcosmic to a macrocosmic examination of aging, some new investigational techniques are becoming available that are applicable to human study, as well as to subhuman species.

Electroencephalography has, of course, been in clinical and investigational use for many years, and changes with aging have been well identified. A gradual slowing of background activity occurs in the 7th decade, and is more impressive in the 8th decade. Changes are more pronounced in temporal derivatives with increasing inter-lobar dyssynchrony. When, instead of this "static" examination of electrical activity, a more "dynamic" technique is utilized, changes evidently due to aging can be detected in the 5th decade. Evoked response studies, examining visual, auditory and somatosensory evoked responses and utilizing signal averaging techniques, indicate changes with a lag in "processing" these sensory stimuli, even though no significant delays occur in initial arrival of sensory stimuli at the cortical level. These data emphasize that our own visual processing (at any age) may not be sufficient to adequately analyze electroencephalographic information that has been available for many years. This readily available clinic investigative technique needs to be reevaluated utilizing modern electronic analyses. It seems quite probable that various pharmacologic agents that alter central nervous system function, applied in conjunction with computer-assisted electroencephalogaphic readouts, will enhance our understanding of "processing" in both the maturing and aging brain.

An entirely novel approach is also being gradually developed, with examination of magnetic activity in the central nervous system. Magnetoencephalography may ultimately offers some significant advantages over standard electroencephalographic methods. For instance, "electrodes" can be suspended in appropriate arrays about the head, rather than directly attached to the scalp. It is reasonable to predict that an analysis of the brain's fluctuating magnetic fields under both static and dynamic conditions utilizing varieties of display techniques will literally add a new dimension to the study of the aging brain.

Cerebrospinal fluid, and especially cerebrospinal fluid dynamics, have assumed a dramatically increased clinical significance with the definition of the low pressure, or occult, hydrocephalus syndrome. In this condition, progressive dementia may be reversed by shunting intraventricular cerebrospinal fluid to an extracerebral site (as the cardiac atrium) in order to circumvent an apparent aborption defect. That this therapeutic venture is not universally successful is evidence that multiple factors play roles in a variety of processes with somewhat similar clinical features that we somewhat naively term "a syndrome." In fact, it seems unlikely that such a complex and poorly defined problem as dementia can be explained, even in part by mechanical blockage of cerebrospinal fluid absorption. More likely, the cerebrospinal fluid contains a variety of substances, so far not defined, that play roles in central nervous system processing and integration. Concentration gradients between cerebrospinal fluid and neuropil, and factors related to both passive and active absorption, inasmuch as they affect the micro-environment of the central nervous system, must become areas for increasing research activities in the understanding of both aging and dementia.

Perhaps the most exciting development in the clinical neurosciences in many decades began in 1917 with the Austrian mathematician J. Radon, who proved that two-dimensional or three-dimensional objects could be reconstructed uniquely from the infinite set of their projections. Commercially available image reconstruction developed largely from the work of G.N. Hounsfield at the Central Research Laboratories of EMI Ltd. in England, and EMI scanners have absolutely revolutionized the examination of central nervous system structure especially as it relates to intracranial disease (Brown, 1975; Herman and Johnson, 1975; Robinson, 1975). Here one is literally at the threshold of experiences with devices of barely imaginable potentials, including image reconstruction utilizing radionuclides and magnetic fields. Using positron sources, such as carbon-11, nitrogen-13, and oxygen-15, it will become possible to label metabolically active compounds without altering their chemical or physiological behavior and then, by image reconstruction, examine their interactions in the central nervous system. As resolving capabilities are increased, truly dynamic events will be reconstructed in studies of maturing and aging brains, particularly in primates and other large animal species, and perhaps also in man.

Finally, the developing field of ethology, at one time the domain of behavioral scientists examining animal species, and now being applied to human development, nicely lends itself to examinations of aspects of aging and its interactional environmental, and genetic, and behavioral facets (Barnett, 1973). Earlier the point was made that aging becomes an issue ultimately because of its behavioral features, and thus interpretations from animal studies must perforce be suspect. Margaret Meade (1971) pointed out:

> At present, we are bombarded by ... extrapolations from animal experiments. It seems that we can pick and choose from the entire living world to find the creature whose characteristics reflect the moral wanted at the moment.

Those isolated areas of the world where exceptional longevity is achieved—Vilcabama, Ecuador, Hunza, West Pakistan, and the highlands of Georgia in the Soviet Caucasus—would seem to be obvious areas for studies by cultural ethologists (Leaf, 1973). Other populations, with some degrees of isolation and cohesiveness, that should lend themselves to such "free-field" studies would include primitive tribes in areas like New Guinea and the Amazon River basin, and the highly sophisticated Israeli kibbutzim. Studies, properly designed, and using complex multivariate statistical treatments, should enable a clearer weighting of the numerous factors involved in aging as a behavioral phenomenon. Pope, in the eighteenth century wrote: "The proper study of mankind is man."

Aging, the universal progression of life, is emerging as a complex mélange of genetic, environmental and behavioral factors. It may be, as we are admonished by cybernetics, that we can never absolutely understand our own complexity. But the vested interest that we all share ensures an increasing exploration of these many facets. The potential for modification spurs investigation, with the goal of improvement in the quality of life, so that one can say

> Grow old along with me!
> The best is yet to be,
> The last of life, for which the first was made.
> —Robert Browning

REFERENCES

Barnett, S.A. (ed.): Ethology and medical development. Spastics International Medical Publications. London, William Heinemann Medical Books, Ltd., 1973.

Blinkov, S.M., and Glezer, I.D. (1968) *The Human Brain in Figures and Fables.* A quantitative handbook. New York, Basic Books, Inc., Plenum Press, 1968.

Brown, J.W.: Image reconstruction (1). *Science* 190, 542, 1975.

Goldstein, S.: The biology of aging. *New Eng. J. Med.* 285, 1120–1129, 1971.

Goldstein, S., and Lin, C.: Rescue of senescent human fibroblasts hybridization with hampster cells in vitro. *Exp. Cell Res.* 70, 436–439, 1972.

Hayflick, L.: The limited in vitro lifetime of human diploid cell strains. *Exp. Cell Res.* 37, 614–636, 1965.

Herman, G.T., and Johnson, S.A.: (1975) Image reconstruction from projections. *Scientific American*, 233, 56–68.

Herman, M., Miguel, J., and Johnson, M.: Insect brain as a model for the study of aging. *Acta neuropath* (Berlin) 19, 167, 183, 1971.

Howard, E.: DNA content of rodent brains during maturation and aging, and autoradiography of postnatal DNA synthesis in monkey brain. *Prog. Brain Res.* 40, 91–114, 1973.

Himwich, W.A.: Problems in interpreting neurochemical changes occurring in developing and aging animals. *Prog Brain Res.* 40, 13–24, 1973.

Konigsmark, B., and Murphy, E.: *J. Neuropath. Exp. Neurol.* 31, 304, 1972.

Leaf, A.: Getting old. *Scientific American* 229, 44–52, 1973.

Nandy, K.: Brain-reactive antibodies in serum of aged mice. *Prog. Brain Res.* 40, 437–454, 1973.

Ordy, J.M., and Schjeide, O.A.: Univariate and multivariate models for evaluating long-term changes in neurobiological development, maturity and aging. *Prog. Brain Res.* 40, 25–52, 1973.

Robinson, A.L.: (1975) Image reconstruction (11). Science 190, 647.

Samorajski, T., and Rolsten, C.: Age and regional differences in the chemical composition of brains of mice, monkeys and humans. *Prog. Brain. Res.* 40, 253–266, 1973.

Scheibel, H.: Progressive dendritic changes in aging human cortex. *Exper. Neurol.* 47, 392–403, 1975.

Timiras, P.S., Hudson, D.B., and Oklund, S.: Changes in central nervous system free amino acids with development and aging. *Prog. Brain Res.* 40, 267–276, 1973.

Vernadakis, A.: Comparative studies of neurotransmitter substances in the maturing and aging central nervous system of the chicken. *Prog. Brain Res.* 40, 231–244, 1973.

Vernadakis, A.: Neuronal-glial interactions during development and aging. *Fed. Proc.* 34, 89–95, 1975.

Wisniewski, H.M., and Terry, R.D.: Morphology of the aging brain, human and animal. *Prog. Brain Res.* 40, 167–186, 1973.

9

Cognitive Decline with Advancing Age: An Interpretation

MARCEL KINSBOURNE

A progressive decrease in the capability for adaptive behavior, and the correlated decline in level of performance on certain psychometric instruments, are prevalent among elderly people. These behavioral changes may be investigated in pursuit of either or both of two quite distinct goals. One may wish to determine, in the universal sense, what the relationship is between advancing age and the pattern of cognitive abilities. Or one may wish to determine at what intersect of relevant parameters old people remain most capable of performing particular socially relevant tasks. The methodological challenge and the information that may result are quite different with respect to these two objectives of research, the former of which is the subject of this discussion.

In order to identify some universal behavioral correlates of aging, one chooses a representative sample of the age group in question. One then determines how the experimental group differs from some reference group with respect to the parameters under scrutiny. The situation is complicated if the experimental group shows vastly greater variability in relevant respects than does the control group. Under these circumstances, which particularly obtain for elderly populations, investigators either deliberately reduce the variability of their experimental population by excluding subgroups on a basis of specified criteria, or implicitly reduce that variability by a variety of sampling and matching devices. The desired outcome of a relatively homogeneous experimental group is achieved but at the cost of making the group unrepresentative of the elderly population as a whole. The findings, then, have a very restricted generality, and the effort to extract universals fails.

ELDERLY SAMPLES AND "NORMAL AGING"

Among old people, diseases that generate behavioral symptomatology are rife. Strokes, brain tumors, a variety of toxic reactions, as well as the more insidiously progressive cerebral arterial disease and primary cerebral degeneration affect large subsets of the elderly population and do so with great variability of severity of impact and pattern of behavioral outcome. If one were to wish to derive some probabilistic impression of what might happen to people as they grow older, then, of course, the study must encompass all of these important groups. If, however, one wishes to study the behavioral consequences of "normal aging" uncontaminated by current disease, then "diseased" individuals must be excluded from the sample.

In effect, such exclusion is very generally practiced but in an uncontrolled and probably uncontrollable fashion. Severely sick persons are not available and people with a variety of behavioral symptoms refuse to volunteer for study. People with available hospital records of disease, and people with obvious manifestations, such as paralysis, are excluded at the screening stage of subject enlistment. A more meticulous approach will in addition exclude less overt disabilities such as hypertension and diabetes. This leaves one with a practical problem and also a problem in principle.

The practical problem is that the harder one looks for disease the more likely it is that one will find it. On the other hand, the more subtle manifestations of disease are increasingly dubious in their relevance to the behavioral variables under scrutiny, and such exclusions further encroach upon the sample size and the representative status of the sample. This is because the definition of a normally aging sample is purely a process of exclusion and illustrates the general fact that it is not possible to prove the negative. In practice, one is left with a sample of rather robust and ostensibly healthy old people, who serve excellently to illustrate the point that even being alive for very many years is not necessarily accompanied by significant behavioral deficit—a point which unfortunately applies only to a small minority of people who are old. There is, in addition, a troublesome problem in principle. This is with regard to the supposition that the physical changes that characterize "aging" are in some sense categorically distinct from the effects of the range of diseases that afflict the brain with increasing frequency and severity as the individual gets older. Psychologically speaking, the cause for "normal aging" would be made if it could be shown that the mere passage of time and its experiential correlates induce cognitive change, holding brain anatomy and physiology constant. Attempts to demonstrate such an effect have invariably failed (e.g., Ruch, 1934; Korchin and Basowitz, 1957). Certainly, mere passage of time affects attitudes of and toward the elderly person, and in these changing times tends to harm him in a practical sense by outdating his repertoire of educational and technical skills. But the cognitive decline sustained by many old people goes far beyond anything that could be explained as situationally determined. Correlated with this is the regular finding of neuronal changes of a nature suggestive of disordered function in the brains of old people without obvious intercurrent disease (see Tomlinson's chapter in this book). In other words, the fact has to be faced that both behaviorally and neurohistologically the changes in extreme old age are very similar to the changes in certain forms of dementia regardless of age. Thus, the behavioral and brain changes of old age, when they are uncomplicated by other disease, can with some validity be regarded as representing yet another disease, of the nature of a dementia with predilection for old people. If one studies that subset of dementing old people which shows no evidence of intercurrent disease, one may in no important sense be studying aging as such, but merely focusing on a particular subset of old people, namely those subject to one particular dementia rather than some other. The findings, then, would neither be representative of old people in general, nor of any age-related developmental phase. The contrast may be clarified by contrasting the situation with that in child development. As children grow older, and if they are unaffected by disease, they evolve through a series of cognitive developmental changes which is orderly in sequence though variable in time-base. Now, there is great variability with respect to the point in cognitive development which any given child reaches at a given age, and to the plateau of intellectual skill that the individual will ultimately attain. But there is considerable communality with respect to the sequence of developmental change. With respect to old people, no such regularities obtain. Rather, different old people suffer handicaps with respect to different aspects of intellect at different rates and to different extents. It may be possible to delineate the characteristic progression of deepening severity of loss with respect to a particular cognitive skill, but only in a very narrow sense, and one in no way reminiscent of a rolling back of the intellect as it develops in childhood.

How then are we to conceive of the cognitive profile of the behaviorally impaired older person?

An intense research effort has focused on the objective of defining particular areas of relative weakness and by implication, therefore, of residual areas of relative strength in old people in general. The investigators have attempted to define parameters along which aging shifts an individual, and thereby establish environmental adjustments which will reinstate the individual's ability to function with what was his customary efficiency when young. Indeed, many studies have purported to demonstrate that old people suffer disproportionately in some respects as compared to others (Botwinick, 1967). The effort to identify these effects continues, but we will raise the question whether there is any continuing need for this effort. It may be that the rules that govern the profile of age-related cognitive decline are already apparent from the results to date.

The characteristics of age-related cognitive deficit can be explored by psychometric and by experimental (information-processing) studies.

Psychometric findings have tended to show that certain skills, as tested by certain intelligence scale subtests, are more vulnerable to age-related decline than others. For instance, in the Wechsler Adult Intelligence Scale, the verbal subscale scores are more resistant to age-related decline than the performance subscale scores (Wechsler, 1958). This might suggest that left hemispheric verbal skills are relatively invulnerable to the adverse influence that accompanies advancing age, whereas right hemispheric performance skills are more sensitive. However, the tests that "hold" with aging and those that do not "hold" differ in other respects as well as in the mode of thinking (verbal versus spatial) that they call for. They differ in the extent to which performance is paced (time-restricted) and to the extent to which it calls for new and creative thinking, as opposed to the utilization of information that people put into store many years earlier. The Vocabulary and Comprehension subtests rely largely upon the cumulatively stored fund of information, whereas performance subtests confront the subject with a novel challenge, the answer to which he has to work out on the spot. It is well established that whereas it requires efficient mental processes to accumulate a substantial fund of information, this fund then remains available to the individual long after he has become incapable, by virtue of disease, of the kind of processing which he had to deploy to amass it in the first instance. Thus, a score on a vocabulary test does not guarantee a particular level of verbal intelligence in the individual at the time of testing. Rather, it makes a statement of an approximate nature about the plateau of efficiency which the person achieved with regards to relevant aspects of verbal skill at some time in his life cycle. These are tests of, to use Cattell's term, "crystallized" intelligence—in contradistinction to the "fluid" intelligence that goes into the solution of novel problems and unexpected predicaments (Cattell, 1957). The greater the loading of a test on fluid intelligence the more apt it seems to present difficulties to people of advanced age. As various psychometric measures are very unevenly loaded on these two aspects of intelligence, a correspondingly uneven profile of psychometric decline is to be expected, and is obtained. It would follow that if the extent to which a test is loaded on fluid intelligence is factored out, then age-related decline on all tests should essentially be abolished. One way of achieving this type of outcome is to include in a test battery a measure which is virtually exclusively one of fluid intelligence and then partial out scores on this measure when calculating the relative degree of decline on other ones. Kinsbourne (1974) did this using the Raven's Progressive Matrices test as his measure of exclusively fluid intellect, and found, indeed, that another measure on which old people showed substantial decline as compared to young ones (identification of cue-depleted sketches) was rendered completely undiscriminating between young and old when matrices scores were partialed out. On the other hand, a verbal test, which one would expect to have measured crystallized intelligence, was not affected by the partialing-out computation.

We are left with the simple and unexciting generalization that the harder the test the greater the relative decrement it reveals in old as compared to younger subjects as a group ("hard" being defined by the extent to which on the spot problem-solving is required). It seems advisable that any further psychometric studies that are undertaken with respect to age effects should follow some procedure which enables the relative contributions of fluid and crystallized intelligence components to age-related differences to be separately appraised. If the situation is as simple as is here proposed, then it might soon be possible to do without further such studies, as they would only confirm what is already known.

In the final analysis, the situation with respect to experimental studies of age effects on cognition is not dissimilar. Admittedly, numerous investigators have pointed to differential deficits on various types of material under various display and response conditions, and have proposed generalizations such as, for instance, that pacing disproportionately handicaps the aged. These studies are hard to interpret for a number of methodological reasons. First of all, the aged sample is customarily matched with a normal sample of younger people on the basis of a psychometric measure, usually a vocabulary test. To some extent this tends to select above averagely intelligent old people for the experiments (except in the relatively few situations where care is taken to make dull normal young subjects available as controls for testing). More seriously, the various experimental conditions that are used are not necessarily equally discriminating between subjects. The more discriminating a test is, the more likely it is to reveal intergroup differences (Chapman and Chapman, 1973). Finding a significant difference between old and young on one test but only a nonsignificant trend on another may merely reflect the less discriminating nature of the second test, not necessarily saying anything about differential loss of aptitude with advancing age. It would be necessary to inspect the frequency distribution of various scores on the measures concerned to ensure that this artifact does not obtrude.

Another factor that is often left grossly uncontrolled is overt task difficulty. Those circumstances under which old people are reported as suffering disproportionately in their performance are typically circumstances in which the task, per se, is made more difficult. For instance, when investigators look at the effect of differently paced presentations on the learning of young and old people (Canestrari, 1963; Arenberg, 1965, 1967; Eisdorfer, 1963), they fail to hold total learning time constant, and thus, with the more quickly paced material, present subjects with an overall shorter time to assimilate the material and so, effectively, a much harder task. Under these circumstances the amount learned by the old people has been found to be disproportionately little. This may be no more funamentally interesting than is the challenge effect. This is the tendency of normal people who tend to rise to the challenge of an ostensibly difficult task and produce extra mental capacity so as to do disproportionately well. In old people, who have become accustomed to failure and personal shortcomings, such a challenge effect might not obtain and the person faced with an exceedingly difficult task might either refuse to perform or perform mindlessly in a chance fashion. Pursuing the matter of pacing, with respect to paired associate learning, Kinsbourne and Berryhill (1972) were able to show that if total learning time was held constant, there was in fact no effect, within the range studied, of pacing of presentations. In other words, it was equally effective to present the subjects with longer inspection periods and fewer recurrences of the material and to present them with shorter inspection periods and more recurrences of the material, provided that the total exposure time of the set was the same in each of the two conditions. Thus, the "total time hypothesis" holds for old people as it does for young (Bugelski, 1962), and pacing does not disproportionately embarrass the older people. Eisner and Kinsbourne (1975) replicated this finding and further found a linear increase in gain of information with increase in total learning time for young and old groups, though of more gradual slope for the older group.

The experimental method makes it possible to deconfound a situation previously alluded to. This is co-variation of difference in mode of thought (verbal versus spatial) and degree of familiarity of the material (crystallized versus fluid). Using experimental paradigms, it is possible to construct closely analogous verbal and nonverbal tasks which are equally unfamiliar and, in fact, identical in all respects except for the nature of the code used. In such an experiment, Elias and Kinsbourne (1974) found that there was no overall advantage to the old people of using verbal or spatial code per se, although embedded in the data were intriguing sex differences deserving further investigation.

Yet another source of spurious disproportionalities in age-related cognitive decline arises from the nature of the statistical computation used. If untransformed scores are fed into an analysis of variance design, then the existence of a significant interaction between condition and age group may depend upon something as trivial as the particular metric used, be it, for instance, number of responses per unit time as compared to time per unit response. This is because young and old groups do not share any common base state in performance and therefore arithmetic differences between the performance of the young and the old at various points along a continuum are hard to interpret. More properly, the proportion of change should be the factor taken into consideration, by, for instance, the use of a logarithmic transformation. What one really wants to know is not so much how young and old people differ with respect to their performance at a given intersect of conditions, but whether young and old people are proportionately equivalently affected by changes along particular parameters. If the question is asked in the latter way, it would appear from a scrutiny of existing literature that the answer tends to be affirmative. In other words, the difference between the performance of young and old people seems to be quantitative rather than qualitative;

changes along dimensions that make for greater task difficulty for the young also do for the old and vice versa. Illustrative is a study by Kinsbourne (1973a) in which young, old, and aphasic subjects were tested on their ability to repeat letter sequences varying in the degree of transitional probability (from zero approximation to fourth order approximation to the language). The young control subjects, as one might expect, were progressively better able to reproduce the material as it became more wordlike (i.e., more closely approximated letter groupings to be found in conventionally spelled English). Aphasic subjects differed qualitatively in that they showed no such relationship. That is, their letter span did not increase as approximation to the language was increased. But the old subjects differed only quantitatively. At all points their performance was significantly lower than that of the young, but the same relationship between approximation to the language and performance held for them as it did for the young subjects.

In another study (Kinsbourne, 1972) the focus of interest was on the relative degree of age-related decline in two types of visual performance: rapid enumeration ("subitizing") and discrimination. Subjects were presented with brief displays of filled, unfilled and partially filled circles. In one condition ("whole report") they were asked to enumerate all stimuli regardless of degree of filling. In the other condition ("part report") they only enumerated the filled circles. In part report the task of enumerating was therefore simplified, as there were fewer stimuli to count. But instead, subjects had to expend mental capacity on discriminating the filled from the unfilled circles before adding the former to their count. This made it possible, for each age, to compare time taken to add one item to the count and time taken to exclude one item from the count. Briefly, old people took longer than young to process information in both of these ways, but not disproportionately in either. Thus a model of uniform decline in processing ability is again supported. This experiment is unusually significant in that an effort was made to compare two different processes under identical conditions, which is the only way in which a valid test of the hypothesis can be achieved.

An overview of the experimental literature suggests a trivially simple proposition. The performance of old subjects, as a group, is subject to exactly the same determinants as the performance of younger controls. Apparent findings to the contrary are due to the choice of inappropriate tests, artifacts of sampling and artifacts of statistical analysis. To use a computer analogy, the elderly subject computes according to the same principles as a young subject but his is a depleted computer that transmits less information per unit of time. The extent to which it is less efficient naturally depends upon the age sample chosen, not only with respect to the mean age but to the various factors that determine intellectual outcome during aging such as sex, social class and medical history.

What does this insight tell us about the effect of aging on the brain basis of behavior? An economical interpretation would be that in aging there occurs a homogeneous impairment in cerebral function, perhaps due to diffuse and steadily progressive neuronal fallout, and behavioral capability co-varies with this along all its dimensions. However, such an interpretation fails to take account of the variability between subjects. Actually, only a few experimental studies use samples of old people to show greater within group variability than do the younger controls. However, sampling procedures, as has already been discussed, are heavily biased to mitigate any such tendency. It is likely that were one to take really large samples of subjects one would find a far greater variability among the old than the young not only in severity of impairment along a given behavioral dimension, but in the particular pattern of the profile of skills across such dimensions. In other words, we are suggesting that the impression of a homogeneous loss of intelligence may be a group artifact. That is, if one has many subjects each showing a different pattern of cognitive loss of fluid type distributed differentially across the various modes of problem-solving (and corresponding to different patterns of cerebral insult underlying this), then summing it all together one might find overall an approximately equal loss in all modes (but a far greater intersubject variability). The study that would show this conclusively has not been done. It would have to be unusually large in scale and deviate from the customary sampling patterns to give a more candid view of the cognitive situation among human beings of a given age. But until this hypothesis has been tested, it cannot be assumed that because a group behavioral decline is uniform across tasks, the various members in a group contribute equally to that pattern of decline.

What kind of brain changes would underlie such variability? the simplest assumption is that the various parts of the cerebral cortex are all vulnerable to a variety of different insults, some more vulnerable to one, some to another. Thus, for instance, given that the vascular supply to the cerebral cortex is of "end artery" type, arterial blockage would tend to punch out areas of brain in the center of the territory perfused by a given artery. On the other hand, precipitous drop in blood pressure would tend to destroy the complementary watershed areas between foci of arterial blood supply. If these two types of catastrophe were roughly equal in incidence, then an impression of overall homogeneous decline within the total group might eventuate.

In neuropsychology we study the effect of focal cerebral lesions on behavior. This study has revealed the highly differentiated nature of cerebral localization of function. Different functions are localized in the brain in remarkably fine grain (Kinsbourne, 1971). In old people not suffering from very focal damage, one might imagine lesions to be more patchy but still irregular in their distribution. If one were to arrive at a summation of all possible neuropsychological deficits, would one not end up with an across-the-board dementia which would be identical with the end point also of senile changes in the aging brain?

At this point there are two alternative possibilities. One is that generalized dementia and the overall cognitive decline in large groups of old people is a simple arithmetic sum of loss of the various faculties represented by various parts of the cerebral cortex. There is, however, a possible alternative to this mosaic theory. This is that there are certain aspects of behavior not subserved by particular cerebral localities but, rather, dependent on the integrity of wider overlapping areas of brain. A diffuse loss of neurons might handicap the victim in such general mental skills as flexible problem-solving, the ability to change set and entertain improbable outcomes as possibilities, as well as to focus, maintain and then adaptively detach attention in a task (Kinsbourne, 1974).

It is simply not known whether behavioral capabilities such as those just listed are diffusely represented or not. Certainly, no one location is known which if damaged causes an overwhelming defect of this type. However, one might argue that these attributes are selectively applicable to the various modes of intellectual functioning, so that damage in any one mode would embarrass processing in the mode in some or all of the ways mentioned. This would be an elaboration of the mosaic theory, which remains a viable alternative to the notion of a multitiered model of cerebral function in which certain parts of the brain are specialized in tightly knit exclusive fashion, while other parts function in a more diffuse (for instance, holographic) manner.

Particularly ill-studied are those aspects of behavior that are better described as "selection" rather than "processing." Normal behavior involves processing information, but antecedent to this is the selection of the processor to use (adopting task-appropriate mental set). That selection itself is vulnerable to brain damage with respect to its efficiency and appropriateness, and a variety of defects in attention and task orientation themselves can be indications of brain involvement by disease (Kinsbourne, 1976b). Inefficient selection might make it hard to adopt an intensive mental set to solve a difficult problem even if the cerebral processors were themselves still in good functional condition. In appropriate focusing could restrict the area within which old people can deploy their intellectual capabilities. Do old people overfocus their attention and keep it rigidly on a very restricted subset of environment input? Or do they, on the contrary, underfocus, and impulsively react in a relatively indiscriminate fashion? In fact, both types of behavior occur but perhaps not in the same individuals. This can be readily understood once the distribution of attention is recognized as resulting from moment-to-moment changes in the tolerance within an opponent mechanism in the brain. There exists between a fine and a coarse focus of attention a dynamic balance, as, for instance, between looking to the right and looking to the left (Kinsbourne, 1974). The intact individual is able to behave adaptively by modifying that balance in the called-for direction at any time. However, if one of the opponent mechanisms is disproportionately damaged by disease, then the other will assume excessive control and the subject will be locked into one attending mode to the exclusion of the other. That attending mode will be adaptive only in a limited set of circumstances in which the opposite mode would be called for. Now diffuse disease, apt to impinge unequally on the aging brain, could easily, in one instance, selectively handicap the opponent process making for intense focus and in another individual do the exact opposite. In this way, both types of attentional difficulty will be prevalent (though mutually exclusive) among old people and be described as possible concomitants of aging. Here is an area that demands investigation, particularly as it is known that stimulant medications can sharpen underfocused attention and sedative medications open up attention that is overfocused (Wender, 1971; Kinsbourne, 1976a). It is essential to discover whether old people can be helped to live more adaptively by some such expedient.

Whereas some strategic deviations in aging can properly be regarded as suggestive of damage to the brain substructure of the strategy in question, others are more reasonably viewed as compensatory for loss of cerebral computing power. The subject appraises the cost/benefit equation in a given situation and determines at what level of efficiency (speed, error rate) it would be expedient to perform. He then trades off one against the other. If he wishes to hold down his error rate he will work more slowly (as an aging and slow-reacting driver will hold down his accident rate by driving at a lower speed than the younger more rapidly reacting individual). In another situation the same individual might choose to hold pace constant and permit his error rate to rise. Thus, when old people are described as cautious (Botwinick, 1966), rigid or conservative, this should not necessarily suggest some maladaptive personality trait or product of adverse experience which it would be advisable to correct by encouragement, exhortation or material incentive. Rather, that conservatism might be based on a perfectly realistic appraisal of the efficiency of personal performance and serve to limit the individual's rate of failure to a level that falls short of being destructive both to his social position and his self-respect. Such adaptations are not to be tampered with. If an old person cognizant at either the explicit or the implicit level of his latterly limited capabilities correspondingly restricts the arena of his functioning, this is to be regarded as appropriate compensation.

These considerations highlight the dangers inherent in the attempt by some sociologists to write off the phenomenon of age-related intellectual decline as the self-fulfilling consequence of labeling or adverse, even possibly hostile perception of the old person by younger people. One need not make the mistake of denying the possibility of such prejudice if one cautions against any wholesale attempt to write off the very real and troublesome cognitive changes that attend aging as spurious. The danger is that if one does not believe in the existence of these declines, one can do nothing to help the victims of such decline. They will then have to trade personal effectiveness and even happiness for the satisfaction of a more optimistic label. As in the area of sex and socioeconomic class differences in various achievements, the thing to do is not to deny that they exist but to recognize that they do, and do something about it.

These considerations are not meant to obstruct the search for maladaptive strategies assumed by particular old people or to discourage attempts to correct them (Labouvie-Vief and Gonda, 1976). Rather, they are meant to caution against assuming that any deviation of strategy adopted by the old, as compared to the young, is necessarily maladaptive and that to reassume the usual strategy would generate a more useful performance.

At the level of neural modeling, it is not difficult to describe the effect of more limited computing capacity on the problem-solving behavior of the older people. Let us suppose that the appearance of a cognitive challenge triggers a brainstem-based activating system which selectively activates the relevant cerebrally located processors. Let us further suppose that that activation will continue, and that therefore processing will continue until there is sufficient closure with respect to a solution of the problem, to satisfy some internally set criterion. In other words, the activation and therefore selective processing continues until uncertainty has been reduced to an extent that meets a criterion determined by the individual's personality and experience (Kinsbourne, 1976a). To present the individual with further problems before that criterion is reached overloads his activation system, causing psychological discomfort and rejection of that second task (or abandoning the first uncompleted in its favor). The more limited computer takes longer to arrive at a sufficiently close solution to permit the focus of activation to shift. For this reason the subject is slower to make his decisions, and at times seems pedantic, because what for a more effectively computing person are trivial residual details may for him be other than trivial and constitute substantial failure to meet his internal criteria. Therefore, his processing may continue in what may seem to be a compulsive manner. Further intellectual challenge in this period of time may so grossly overload the system that it will cause anxiety, various displacement activities (nervous or compulsive behavior) (Kinsbourne, 1976a), and even refusal to undertake the task.

This model suggests a type of experimentation that is not usually applied in this particular area of research. This is the scrutiny of old people's ability to time-share between concurrent performances. Given a fixed total mental capacity, a subject is able either to devote his all to a particular task or to share it between two or more concurrent tasks. It has been found that when in circumstances of dual concurrent performance subjects time-share between two tasks, a proportion of the mental capacity is allocated to some clerical function hitherto conceived as regulating the flow of information into the two orthogonal channels. Our recent work suggests to us that some, if not all, of this mental capacity is used for what we call an insulating function (Kinsbourne and Hicks, 1976): to insulate two concurrently active brain centers from each other so that the activity of one does not overflow and contaminate the activity of the other. One might conceive of such insulation as consisting of a neuronally inhibitory surround (though there is no objective evidence of this at this time). Now, the brain is in any case a very highly linked system, such that between any one neuron and any other only a few synapses are interposed. This is what makes it necessary to throw inhibitory surrounds around active brain locations. In the depleted brain, such insulation might be particularly hard to achieve and it might indeed be found that old people are embarrassed by the demands of dual-task performance to quite a disproportionate degree. In other words, the amount of mental capacity allocated to insulating function would be disproportionate. Alternatively, that insulation just would not appear and the concurrent performance would instead be flawed by the cross-talk that would otherwise have been averted. Certainly, impressionistically old people are often observed to behave in such ways as to reduce the probability of having to do two things at the same time unless one be totally automatic, and therefore not demanding of mental capacity.

While it would be incorrect to regard aging as merely a rolling back of the development of the intellect, it is profitable in some respects to compare old people with young children. Young children are under the spell of the salience of immediate experience (Kinsbourne, 1975). They attend to the here and now and fail to qualify it by reference to previous contradictory events (for instance, in the famous conservation paradigm). With respect to immediate appearances their attention is unduly compelled and held by salient perceptual attributes such as shape or color and precluded from traveling down the perceptual hierarchy to such other attributes as orientation and sequential arrangement in space. When one's perceptual systems are in this kind of state, then he is able to discriminate and identify objects only if identity is multiply specified so that there is a redundancy to buffer the limited unsystematic and redundant search through attributes. Therefore, young children learn to recognize real-life objects well before they can distinguish and selectively identify such minimally differing items as graphic characters. In old people, too, though not with respect to over-learned skills like reading and writing, there is a predominance of the salient here and now and the need for redundancy (i.e., extreme familiarity) of most of the setting that they are in. As already specified in our neural model, thrusting the old person into a novel environment will so overburden his cerebral system of activators and processors that he will become overaroused and disoriented or withdrawn. It is well recognized that to take an old person out of his familiar home setting, say, into a strange location, such as a hospital or institution, may completely disorient him and render his behavior senseless (Lieberman, 1974). It is this sudden and simultaneous overload which has that effect. Once this is recognized, provision can be made to phase in novelty in a graduated fashion and thereby avoid such cognitive decompensation.

At this point, we can return to our distinction between the two quite different goals that one might aim at in research on cognitive decline in aging. One was to establish the universals that characterize the manner in which behavior is affected by advancing age, or at any rate in people as they grow older. To define samples for such an enterprise, one matches on a task of crystallized intelligence what one is, in a cross-sectional fashion, comparing people at different ages who can be presumed (admittedly with severe provisos) to stimulate the kind of changes that one would have found had one been able to follow a given individual longitudinally a long enough number of years. We have seen that insofar as universals can be arrived at they simply state that as a group effective total mental processing power is lost with advancing age uniformly across all modes of cognitive functioning. However, this is the group outcome of quite different deleterious processes in different individuals with quite distinct, but ultimately complementary, cognitive consequences. We have suggested that there is little need for further such investigation both because in the long run they are likely to continue to justify the above generalization, rather than in any way extend or further illuminate it, and also because the group findings are likely to be applicable only to small subsets of the elderly population and lack the generality that one looks for in this form of research.

Another type of paradigm, which in many ways is much more interesting seems rarely to be used. This is to equate people of different ages on the basis of mental capacity (by matching them on a test of fluid intelligence) and then comparing the adaptation of these mentally equally agile individuals to a variety of circumstances (with, of course, special reference to the passage of historical time). Obviously, in order to do this, one would be using either mentally very superior very old people or mentally dull young ones and one will keep this distinction in mind when drawing conclusions. But this form of sampling would bring one closer to determining what is indeed the effect on one's behavior of being old as opposed to being mentally dull.

However, I suggest that the most important type of research to be done with respect to cognition in old people falls into neither of these categories. Rather, it should take the form of research in individual differences. After all, aging is prototypically the arena for vast individual differences, and bureaucratic attempts to come up with formulations that suit all or most people should not be encouraged by comparable research but, rather, should be discouraged because it will inevitably be oppressive to some. In studying old people it is much more reasonable to proceed in the way one proceeds in studying children with learning disability (Kinsbourne, 1973b). That is, not so much to arrive at generalization about the group, but to try to specify the particular cognitive profile that characterizes each individual. Only by doing so will it become possible to determine what is the optimum intersect of environmental circumstances that will permit the old person the greatest possible personal freedom and self-realization. We therefore suggest that behavioral research into aging be discontinued and research into characteristics of old people be substituted.

REFERENCES

Arenberg, D.: Anticipation interval and age differences in verbal learning. *Journal of Abnormal Psychology,* 70, 419–435, 1965.

Arenberg, D.: Age differences in retroaction. *Journal of Gerontology,* 22, 88–91, 1967.

Botwinick, J.: Cautiousness in advanced age. *Journal of Gerontology,* 21, 347–353, 1966.

Botwinick, J.: *Cognitive Processes in Maturity and Old Age.* New York: Springer, 1967.

Bugelski, B.R.: Presentation time, total time and mediation in paired-associates learning. *Journal of Experimental Psychology,* 63, 409–412, 1962.

Canestrari, R.E., Jr.: Paced and self-paced learning in young and elderly adults. *Journal of Gerontology,* 18, 165–168, 1963.

Cattell, R.G.: *Personality and Motivation Structure and Measurement.* New York: World Book, 1957.

Chapman, L.J., and Chapman, J.P.: Problems in the measurement of cognitive deficit. *Psychological Bulletin,* 79, 380–385, 1973.

Eisdorfer, C., Axelrod, S., and Wilkie, F.L.: Stimulus exposure time as a factor in serial learning in an aged sample. *Journal of Abnormal and Social Psychology,* 67, 594–600, 1963.

Eisner, H.C., and Kinsbourne, M.: Age and presentation time effects on free recall. Paper presented to Gerontological Society, Louisville, Kentucky, 1975.

Elias, M.F., and Kinsbourne, M.: Age and sex differences in the processing of verbal and non-vebal stimuli. *Journal of Gerontology,* 29, 162–171, 1974.

Kinsbourne, M.: Cognitive deficit: Experimental analysis. In J. McGaugh (ed.), *Psychobiology*. New York: Academic Press, 1971.

Kinsbourne, M.: Age-related changes in counting and discounting. Paper presented to the American Psychological Association, Honolulu, Hawaii, 1972.

Kinsbourne, M.: Age effects on letter span related to rate and sequential dependency. *Journal of Gerontology*, 28, 317–319, 1973a.

Kinsbourne, M.: School problems: *Pediatrics*, 52, 697–710, 1973b.

Kinsbourne, M.: Cognitive deficit and the aging brain: A behavioral analysis. *International Journal of Aging and Human Development*, 5, 41–49, 1974.

Kinsbourne, M.: Looking and listening strategies and beginning reading. In J. Guthrie (ed.), *Aspects of Reading Acquisition*. Delaware: International Reading Association, 1975.

Kinsbourne, M.: The mechanism of hyperactivity. In *Topics in Child Neurology*. New York: Spectrum Publications, 1976a. In press.

Kinsbourne, M.: The neuropsychological analysis of cognitive deficit. In Grenell, R.G., and Gabay, S., (eds.) *Biological Foundations of Psychiatry*. New York: Raven Press, 1976b.

Kinsbourne, M., and Berryhill, J.: The nature of the interaction between pacing and the age decrement in learning. *Journal of Gerontology*, 27, 471–477, 1972.

Kinsbourne, M., and Hicks, R.E.: Mapping functional cerebral space: Competition and collaboration in human performance. In M. Kinsbourne (ed.), *The Asymmetrical Function of the Brain*. New York: Cambridge University Press. In Press.

Korchin, S.J., and Basowitz, H.: Age differences in verbal learning. *Journal of Abnormal Social Psychology*, 54, 64–69, 1957.

Labouvie-Vief, G., and Gonda, J.N.: Cognitive strategy training and intellectual performance in the elderly. *Journal of Gerontology*, 31, 327–332, 1976.

Lieberman, M.A.: Why nursing homes do what they do. *Gerontologist*, 14, 494–501, 1974.

Ruch, F.L.: The differentiative effects of age upon human learning. *Journal of General Psychology*, 11, 261–285, 1934.

Wechsler, D.: *The Measurement and Appraisal of Adult Intelligence*. Baltimore: Williams & Wilkins, 1958.

Wender, P.M.: *Minimal Brain Dysfunction in Children*. New York: Interscience, 1971.

Subject Index